CRIMSON FLOWER™

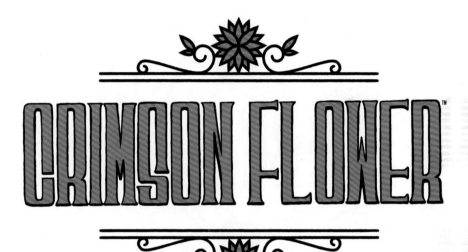

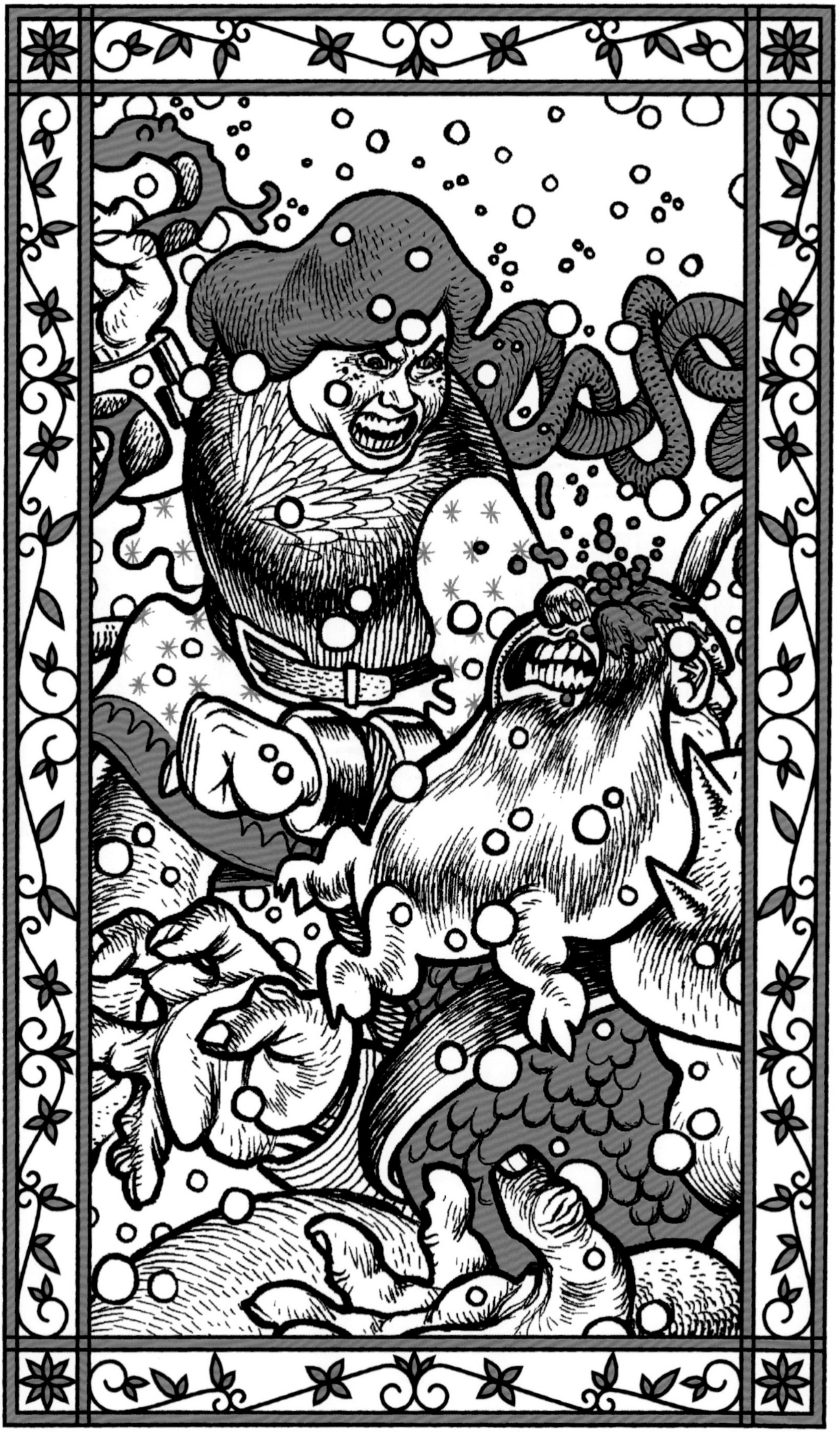

CRIMSON FLOWER™

Writer
MATT KINDT

Art and Letters
MATT LESNIEWSKI

Colors
BILL CRABTREE

Standard Cover Artist
MATT LESNIEWSKI with BILL CRABTREE

Crimson Flower created by
Matt Kindt and Matthew Lesniewski

DARK HORSE BOOKS

President & Publisher
MIKE RICHARDSON

Editor
DANIEL CHABON

Assistant Editors
CHUCK HOWITT and KONNER KNUDSEN

Designer
ETHAN KIMBERLING

Digital Art Technician
ADAM PRUETT

Neil Hankerson, Executive Vice President • Tom Weddle, Chief Financial Officer • Randy Stradley, Vice President of Publishing • Nick McWhorter, Chief Business Development Officer • Dale LaFountain, Chief Information Officer • Matt Parkinson, Vice President of Marketing • Vanessa Todd-Holmes, Vice President of Production and Scheduling • Mark Bernardi, Vice President of Book Trade and Digital Sales • Ken Lizzi, General Counsel • Dave Marshall, Editor in Chief • Davey Estrada, Editorial Director • Chris Warner, Senior Books Editor • Cary Grazzini, Director of Specialty Projects • Lia Ribacchi, Art Director • Matt Dryer, Director of Digital Art and Prepress • Michael Gombos, Senior Director of Licensed Publications Kari Yadro, Director of Custom Programs • Kari Torson, Director of International Licensing Sean Brice, Director of Trade Sales

CRIMSON FLOWER

Collects *Crimson Flower* #1–#4.

Published by
Dark Horse Books
A division of Dark Horse Comics LLC
10956 SE Main Street
Milwaukie, OR 97222

DarkHorse.com

To find a comics shop in your area,
visit comicshoplocator.com

First edition: August 2021
Ebook ISBN 978-1-50672-198-9
Trade paperback ISBN 978-1-50672-197-2

1 3 5 7 9 10 8 6 4 2
Printed in China

Library of Congress Cataloging-in-Publication Data

Names: Kindt, Matt, writer. | Lesniewski, Matt, artist, letterer. | Crabtree, Bill (Comic book colorist), colourist.
Title: Crimson flower / writer, Matt Kindt ; art and letters, Matt Lesniewski ; colors, Bill Crabtree.
Description: First edition. | Milwaukie, OR : Dark Horse Books, 2021. | "Collects Crimson Flower #1-#4, including all covers and bonus material." | Summary: "After losing her family in a violent home invasion, a woman uses folk tales to cope. In a blood-soaked journey toward revenge, she tracks down the man responsible for her family's deaths, only to discover a startling government plot-to weaponize folk tales and use them to raise children into super assassins"– Provided by publisher.
Identifiers: LCCN 2021009694 (print) | LCCN 2021009695 (ebook) | ISBN 9781506721972 (trade paperback) | ISBN 9781506721989 (ebook)
Subjects: LCSH: Comic books, strips, etc.
Classification: LCC PN6728.C6976 K56 2021 (print) | LCC PN6728.C6976 (ebook) | DDC 741.5/973–dc23
LC record available at https://lccn.loc.gov/2021009694
LC ebook record available at https://lccn.loc.gov/2021009695

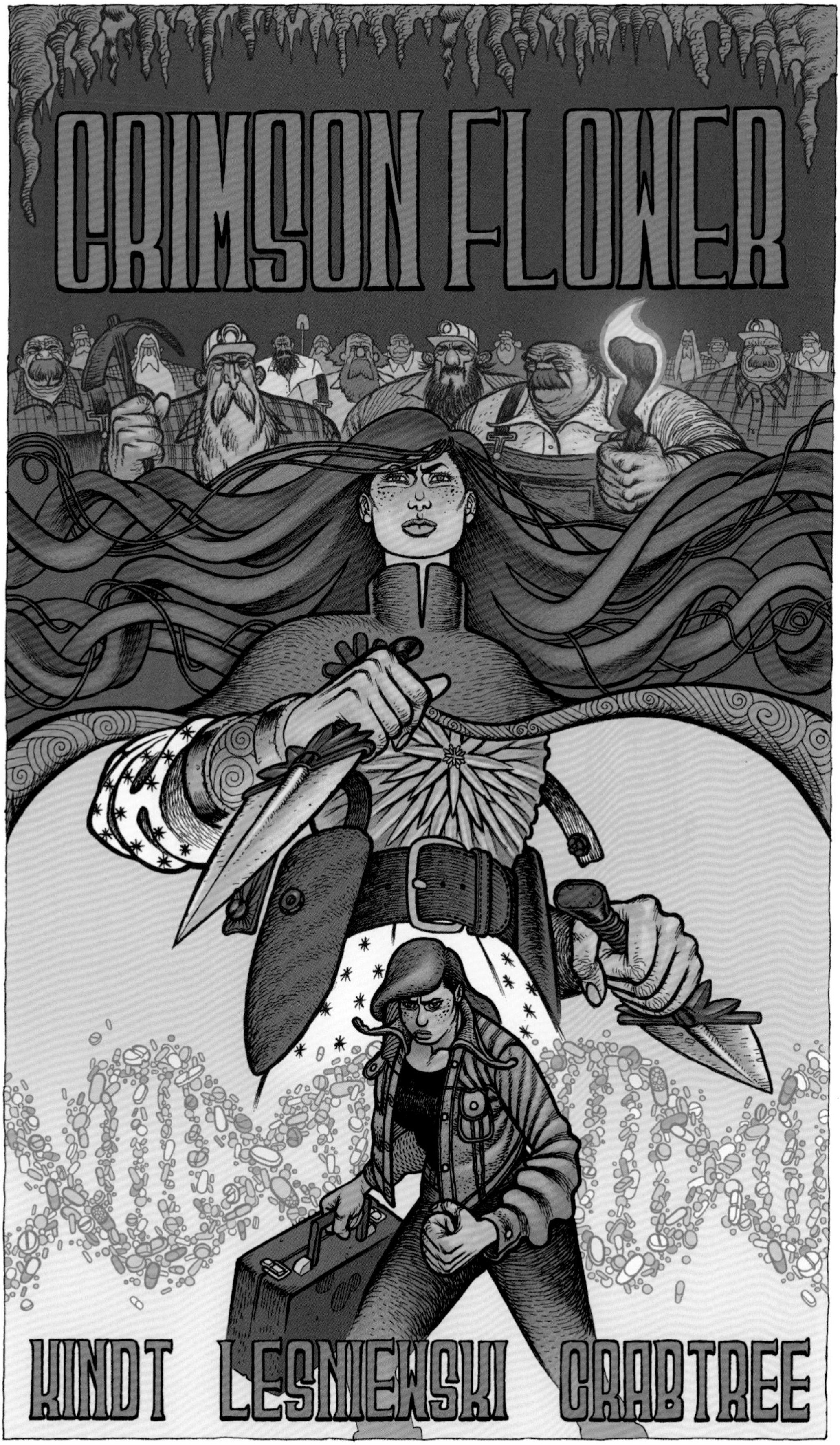
CRIMSON FLOWER
KINDT LESNIEWSKI CRABTREE

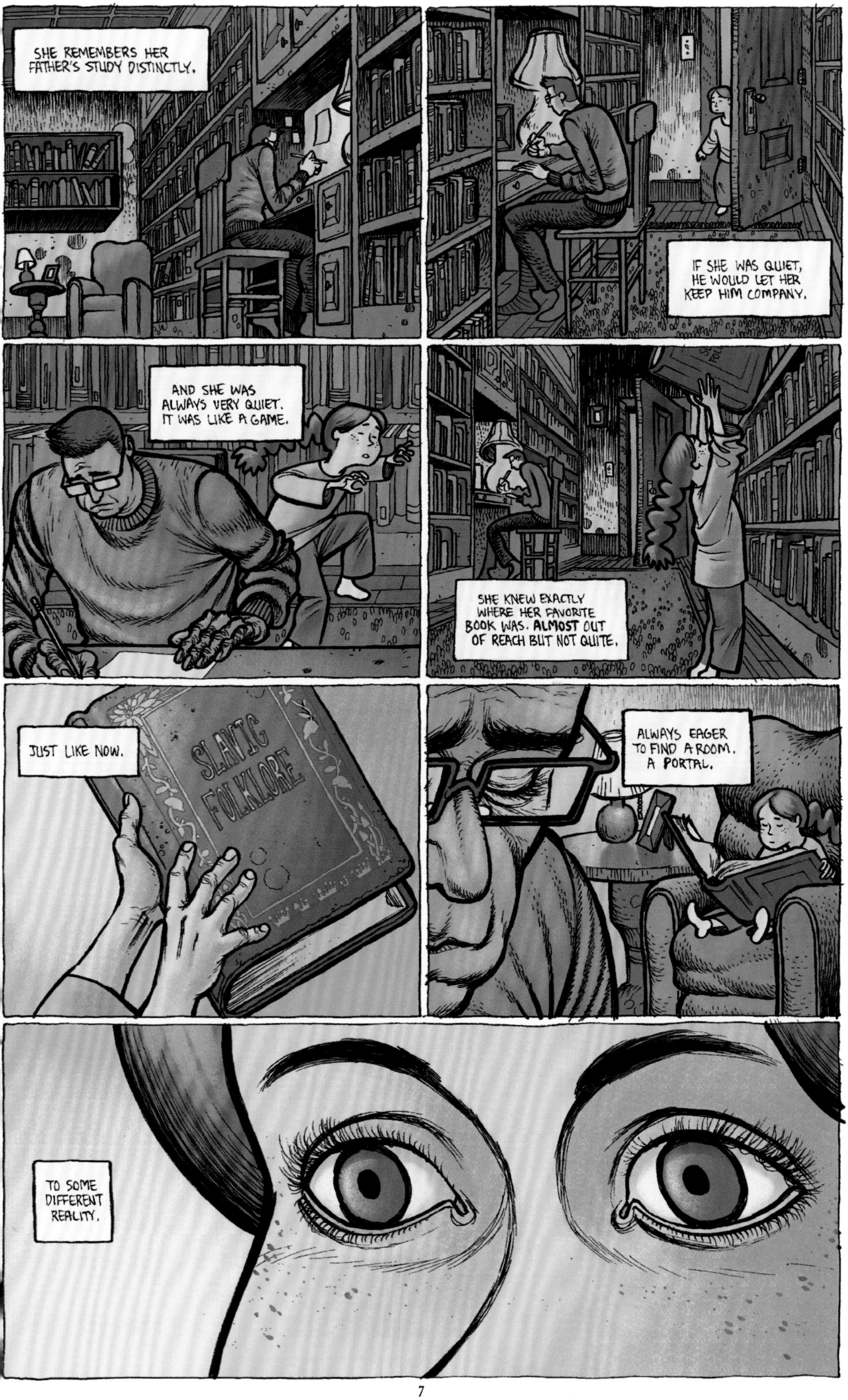
SHE REMEMBERS HER FATHER'S STUDY DISTINCTLY.
IF SHE WAS QUIET, HE WOULD LET HER KEEP HIM COMPANY.
AND SHE WAS ALWAYS VERY QUIET. IT WAS LIKE A GAME.
SHE KNEW EXACTLY WHERE HER FAVORITE BOOK WAS. **ALMOST** OUT OF REACH BUT NOT QUITE.
JUST LIKE NOW.
SLAVIC FOLKLORE
ALWAYS EAGER TO FIND A ROOM. A **PORTAL**.
TO SOME DIFFERENT REALITY.

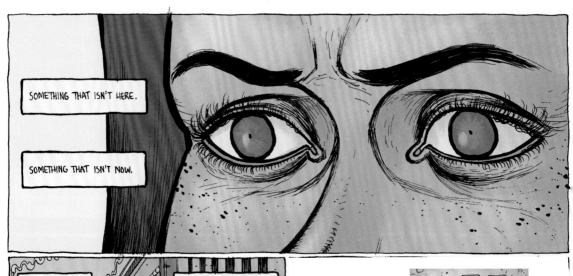

SOMETHING THAT ISN'T HERE.

SOMETHING THAT ISN'T NOW.

SHE ROAMS THE CITY STREETS OF ST. PETERSBURG WITH PURPOSE.

THE CITY, THE STREETS, REMIND HER OF HER CHILDHOOD AND, AT THE SAME TIME, BECOME THE REALITY OF HER ADULT SELF.

BUT SHE KNOWS THAT SHE IS UNIQUE.

THE PRESCRIPTION THEY SUPPLY HELPS A LITTLE. THE LABELS NOT AT ALL.

SHE HAS A HANDLE ON IT. SHE DOESN'T HAVE A PROBLEM. THIS IS WHY **CARDINAL PERENNIAL PHARMACEUTICALS** TRUSTS HER.

ALWAYS ON THE MOVE IN HER SALES ZONE. EVERY TOWN BETWEEN ST. PETERSBURG AND MOSCOW.

HER PITCH IS WELL HONED. SMOOTH, INFORMATIVE. BUT SHE UNDERSTANDS WHY SHE IS SUCCESSFUL.

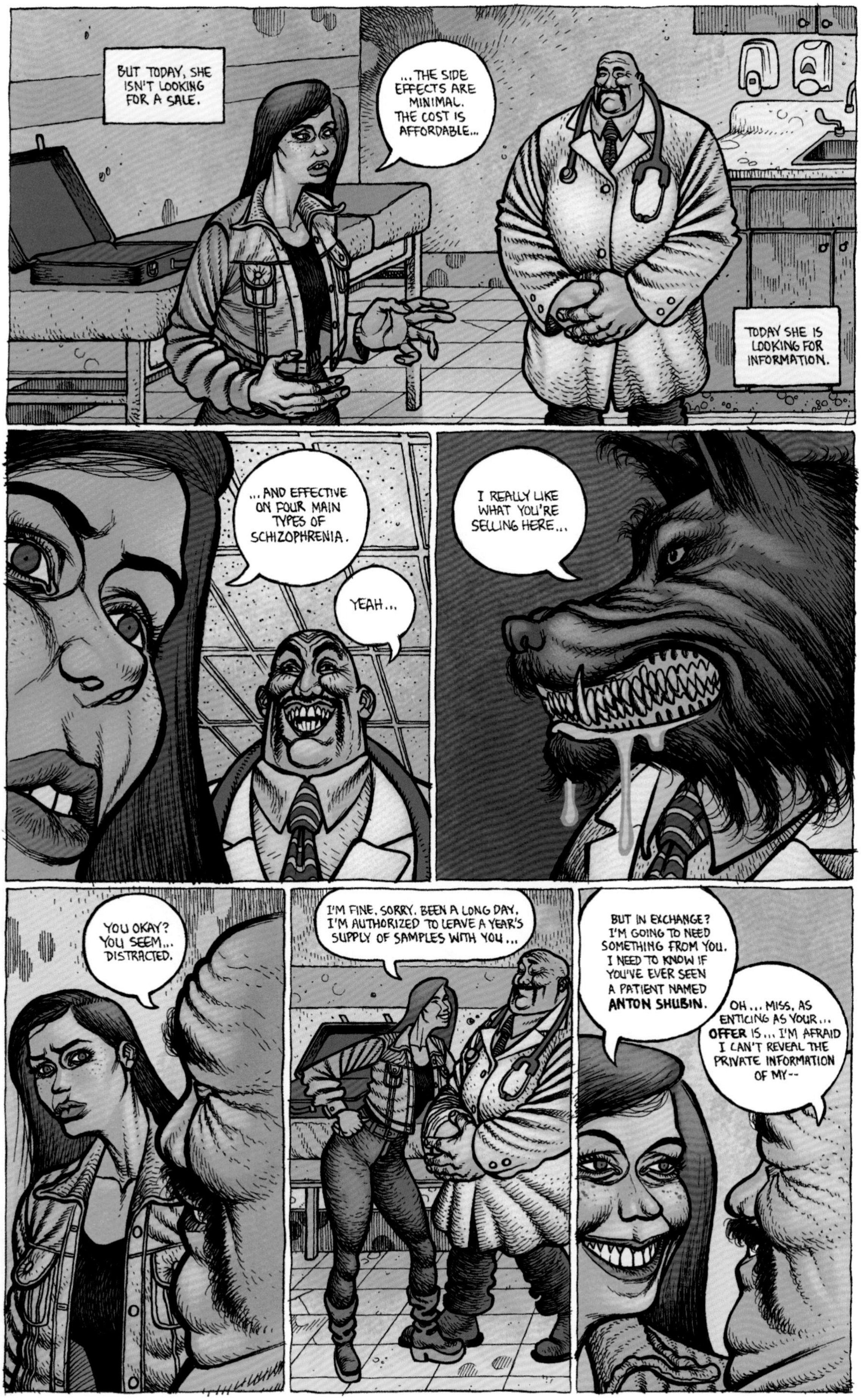

BUT TODAY, SHE ISN'T LOOKING FOR A SALE.
...THE SIDE EFFECTS ARE MINIMAL. THE COST IS AFFORDABLE...
TODAY SHE IS LOOKING FOR INFORMATION.
...AND EFFECTIVE ON FOUR MAIN TYPES OF SCHIZOPHRENIA.
YEAH...
I REALLY LIKE WHAT YOU'RE SELLING HERE...
YOU OKAY? YOU SEEM... DISTRACTED.
I'M FINE. SORRY. BEEN A LONG DAY. I'M AUTHORIZED TO LEAVE A YEAR'S SUPPLY OF SAMPLES WITH YOU...
BUT IN EXCHANGE? I'M GOING TO NEED SOMETHING FROM YOU. I NEED TO KNOW IF YOU'VE EVER SEEN A PATIENT NAMED **ANTON SHUBIN**.
OH... MISS. AS ENTICING AS YOUR... **OFFER** IS... I'M AFRAID I CAN'T REVEAL THE PRIVATE INFORMATION OF MY--

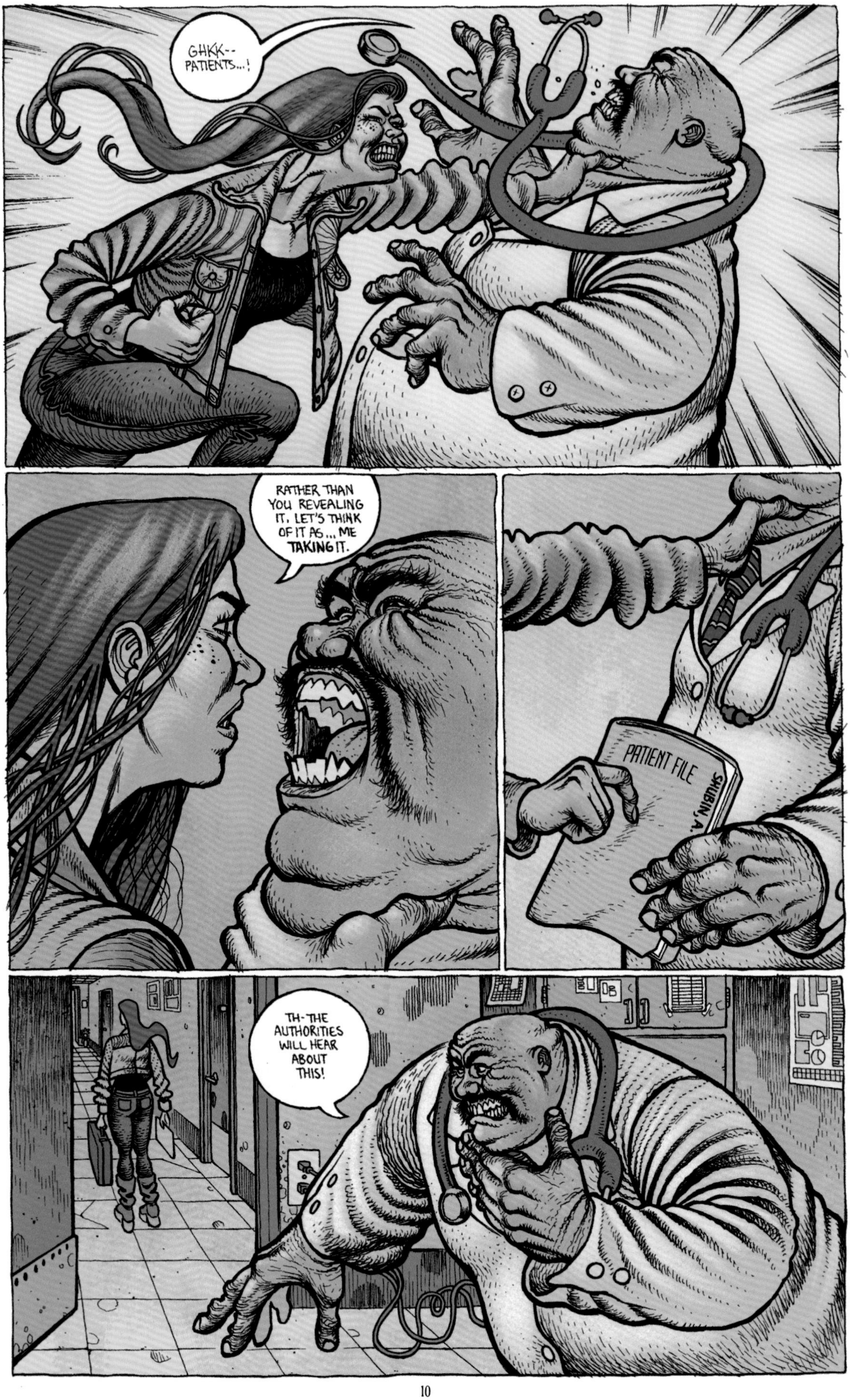
GHKK-- PATIENTS...!
RATHER THAN YOU REVEALING IT, LET'S THINK OF IT AS... ME **TAKING** IT.
PATIENT FILE
SHUBIN, A.
TH-THE AUTHORITIES WILL HEAR ABOUT THIS!

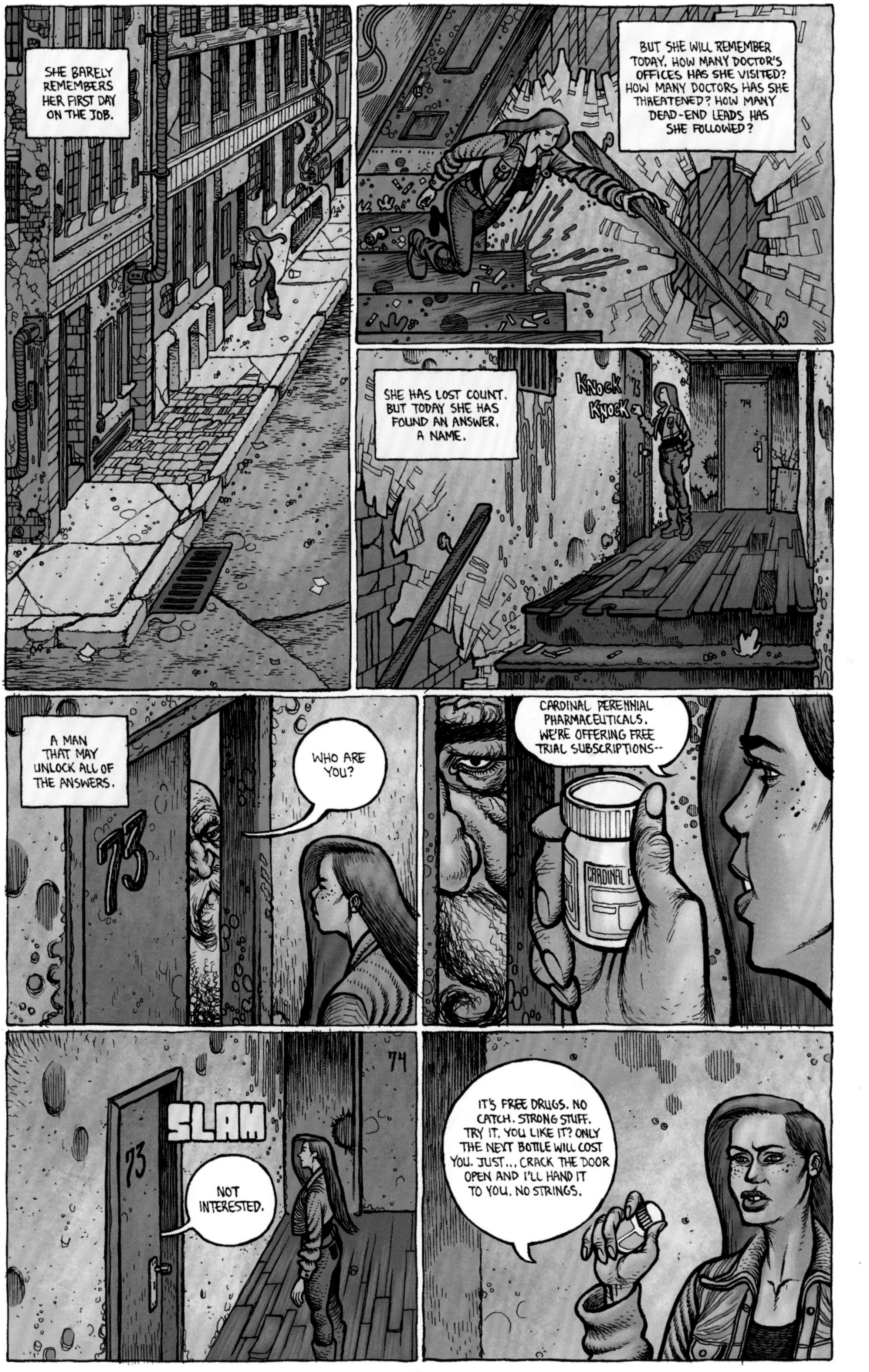
SHE BARELY REMEMBERS HER FIRST DAY ON THE JOB.
BUT SHE WILL REMEMBER TODAY. HOW MANY DOCTOR'S OFFICES HAS SHE VISITED? HOW MANY DOCTORS HAS SHE THREATENED? HOW MANY DEAD-END LEADS HAS SHE FOLLOWED?
SHE HAS LOST COUNT. BUT TODAY SHE HAS FOUND AN ANSWER. A NAME.
KNOCK KNOCK
73
74
A MAN THAT MAY UNLOCK ALL OF THE ANSWERS.
73
WHO ARE YOU?
CARDINAL PERENNIAL PHARMACEUTICALS. WE'RE OFFERING FREE TRIAL SUBSCRIPTIONS--
74
SLAM
73
NOT INTERESTED.
IT'S FREE DRUGS. NO CATCH. STRONG STUFF. TRY IT. YOU LIKE IT? ONLY THE NEXT BOTTLE WILL COST YOU. JUST... CRACK THE DOOR OPEN AND I'LL HAND IT TO YOU. NO STRINGS.

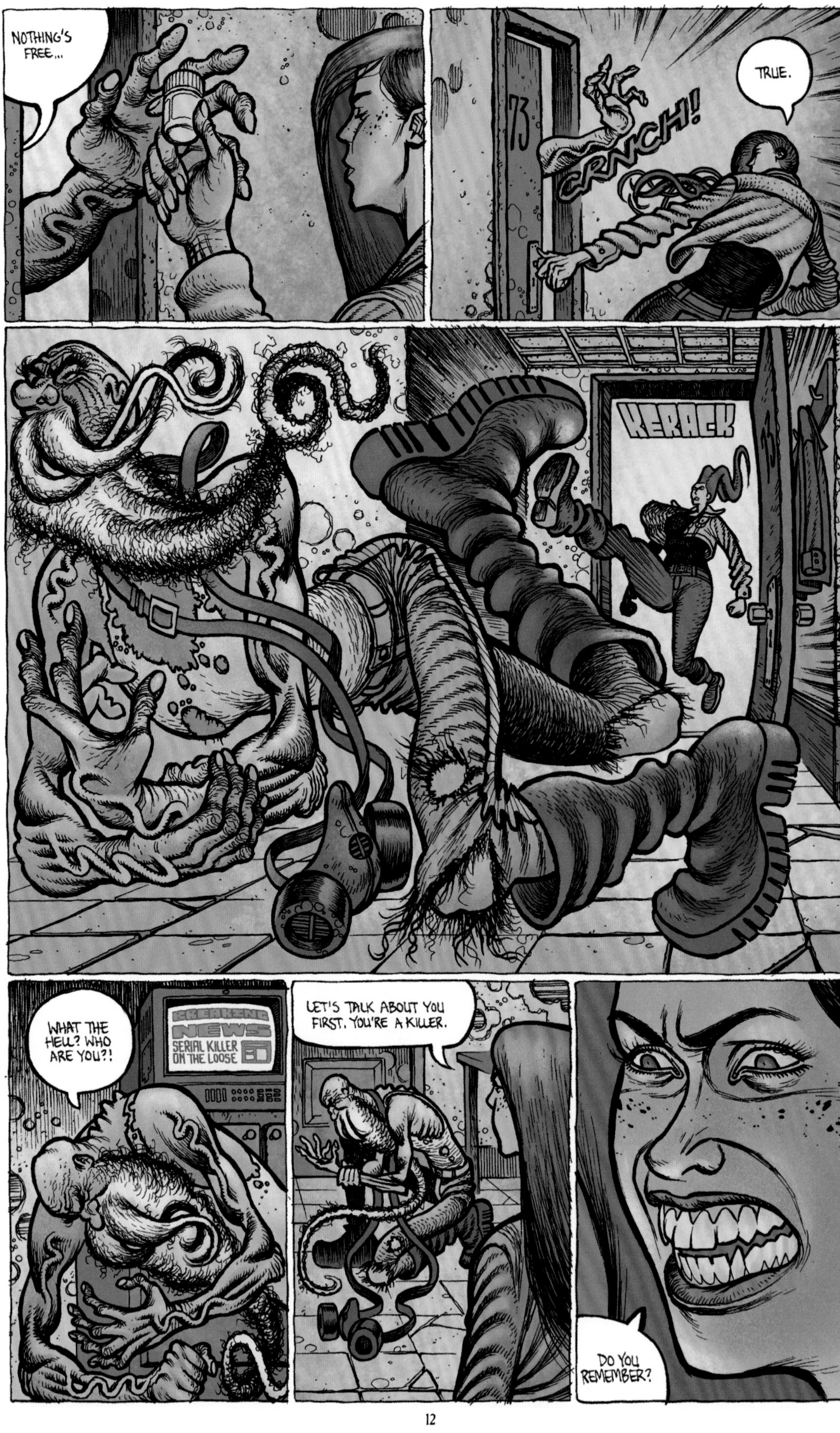
NOTHING'S FREE...
CRNCH!
TRUE.
KERACK
WHAT THE HELL? WHO ARE YOU?!
NEWS
SERIAL KILLER ON THE LOOSE
LET'S TALK ABOUT YOU FIRST. YOU'RE A KILLER.
DO YOU REMEMBER?

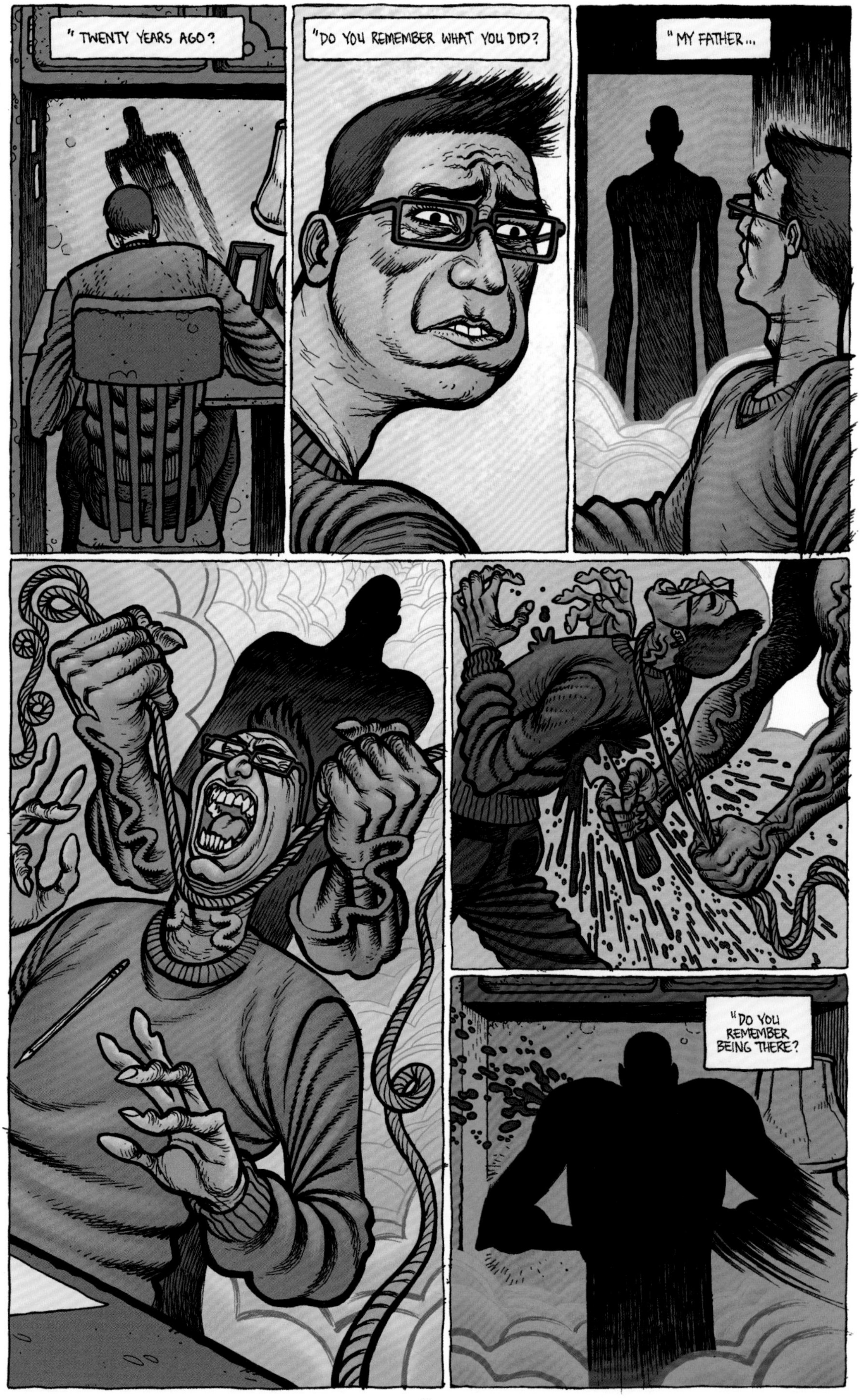
"TWENTY YEARS AGO?
"DO YOU REMEMBER WHAT YOU DID?
"MY FATHER...
"DO YOU REMEMBER BEING THERE?

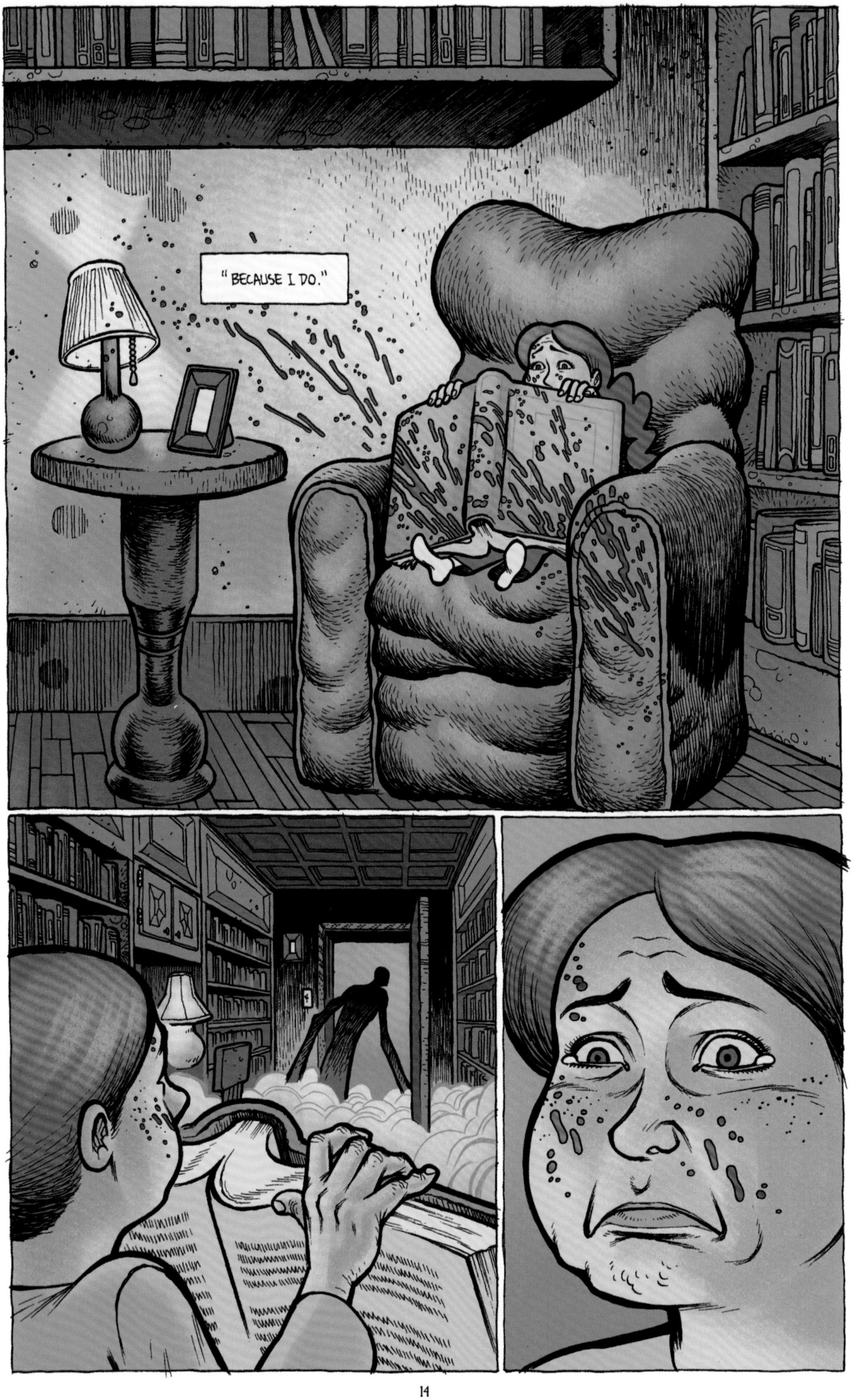
"BECAUSE I DO."

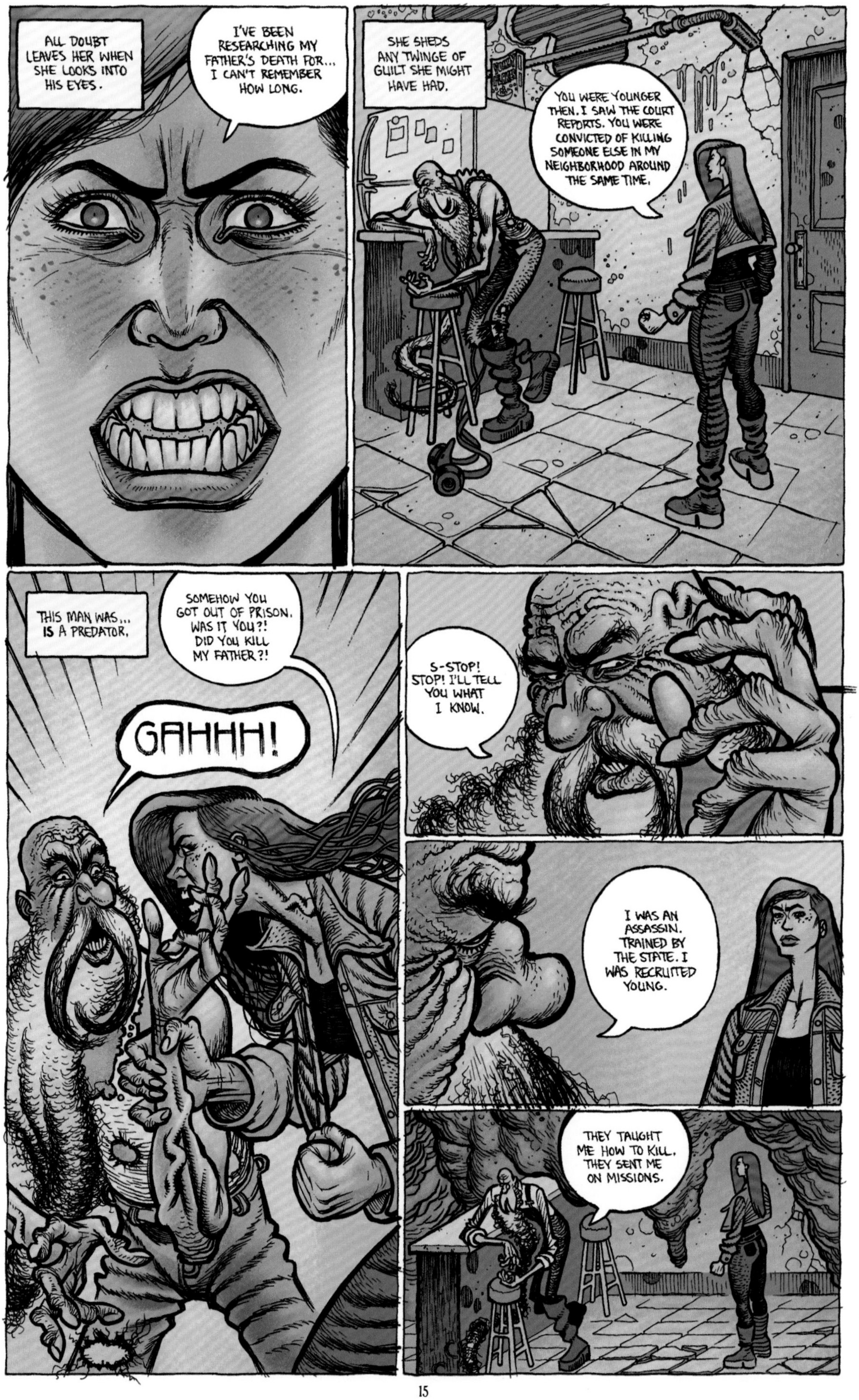

ALL DOUBT LEAVES HER WHEN SHE LOOKS INTO HIS EYES.
I'VE BEEN RESEARCHING MY FATHER'S DEATH FOR... I CAN'T REMEMBER HOW LONG.
SHE SHEDS ANY TWINGE OF GUILT SHE MIGHT HAVE HAD.
YOU WERE YOUNGER THEN. I SAW THE COURT REPORTS. YOU WERE CONVICTED OF KILLING SOMEONE ELSE IN MY NEIGHBORHOOD AROUND THE SAME TIME.
THIS MAN WAS... **IS** A PREDATOR.
SOMEHOW YOU GOT OUT OF PRISON. WAS IT YOU?! DID YOU KILL MY FATHER?!
GAHHH!
S-STOP! STOP! I'LL TELL YOU WHAT I KNOW.
I WAS AN ASSASSIN. TRAINED BY THE STATE. I WAS RECRUITED YOUNG.
THEY TAUGHT ME HOW TO KILL. THEY SENT ME ON MISSIONS.

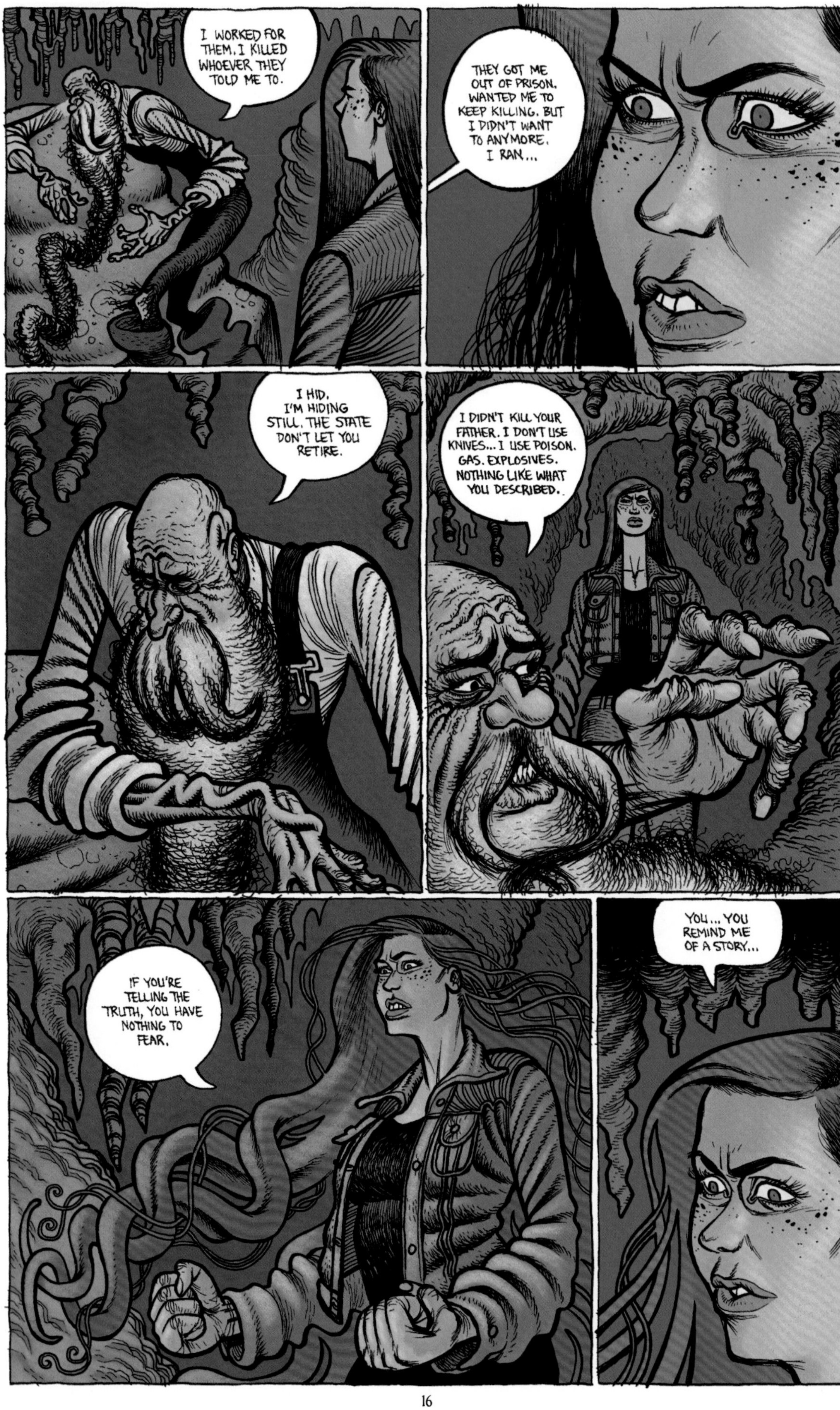
I WORKED FOR THEM. I KILLED WHOEVER THEY TOLD ME TO.
THEY GOT ME OUT OF PRISON. WANTED ME TO KEEP KILLING. BUT I DIDN'T WANT TO ANYMORE. I RAN...
I HID. I'M HIDING STILL. THE STATE DON'T LET YOU RETIRE.
I DIDN'T KILL YOUR FATHER. I DON'T USE KNIVES... I USE POISON. GAS. EXPLOSIVES. NOTHING LIKE WHAT YOU DESCRIBED.
IF YOU'RE TELLING THE TRUTH, YOU HAVE NOTHING TO FEAR.
YOU... YOU REMIND ME OF A STORY...

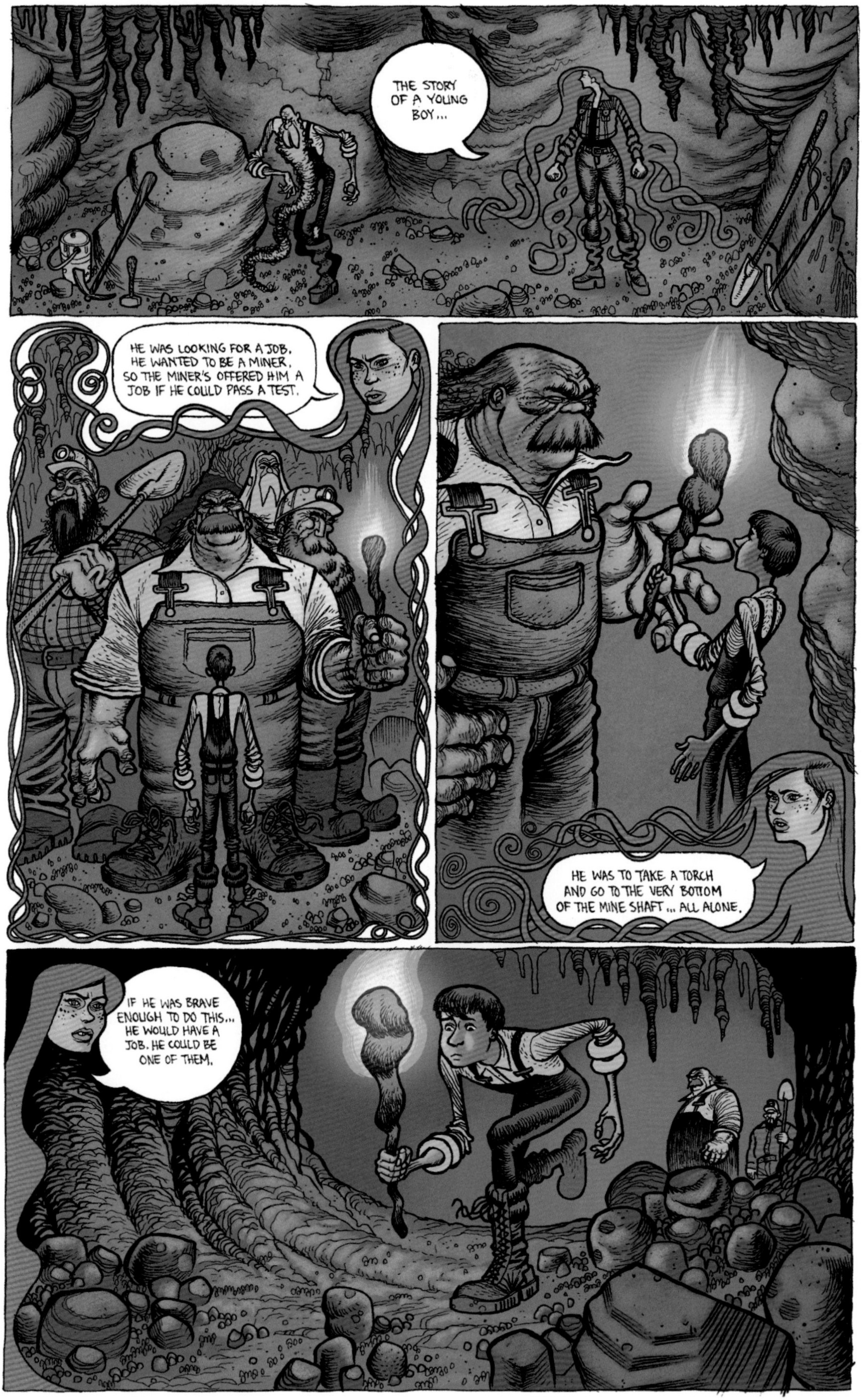

THE STORY OF A YOUNG BOY...
HE WAS LOOKING FOR A JOB. HE WANTED TO BE A MINER, SO THE MINER'S OFFERED HIM A JOB IF HE COULD PASS A TEST.
HE WAS TO TAKE A TORCH AND GO TO THE VERY BOTTOM OF THE MINE SHAFT... ALL ALONE.
IF HE WAS BRAVE ENOUGH TO DO THIS... HE WOULD HAVE A JOB. HE COULD BE ONE OF THEM.

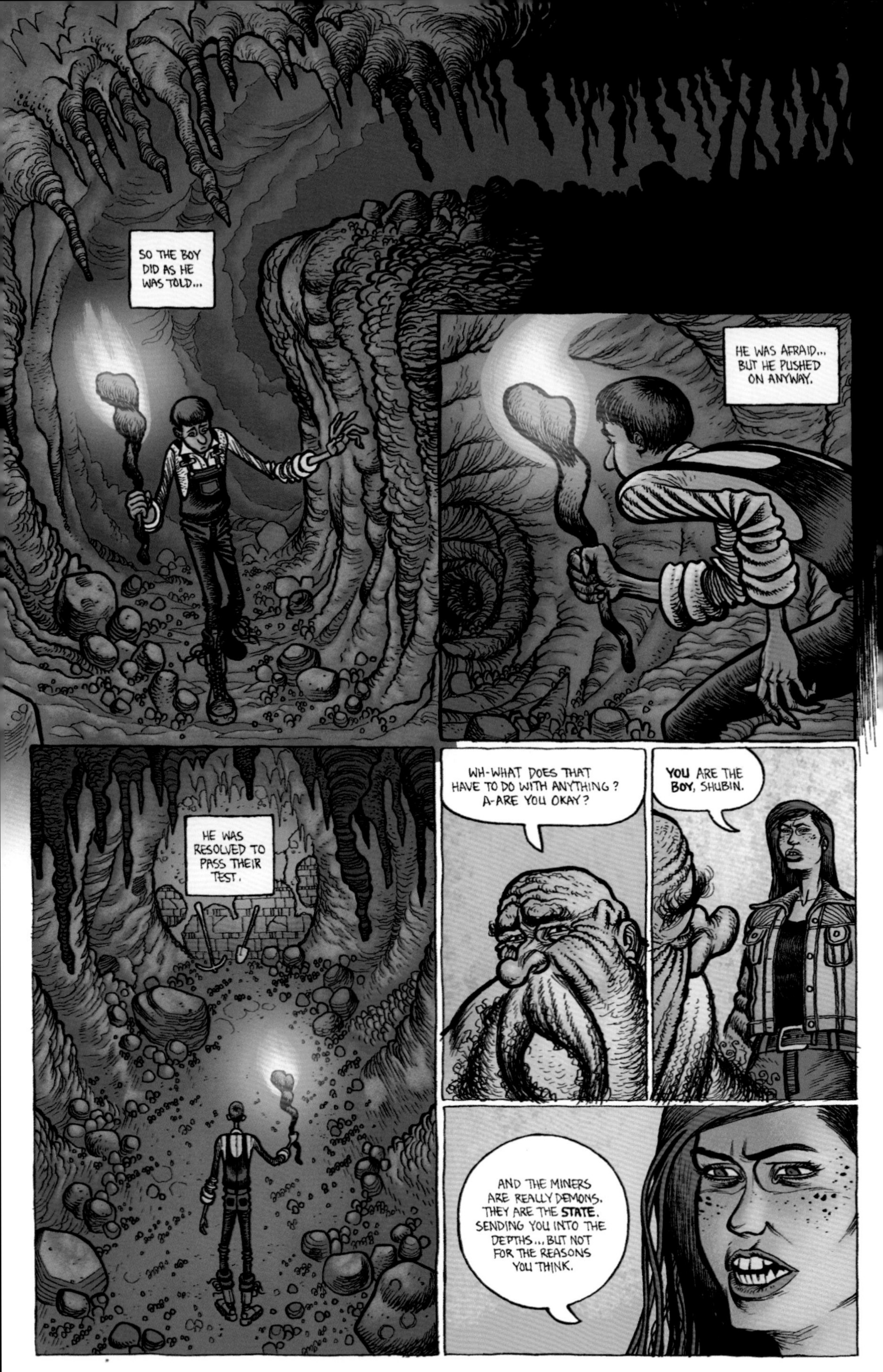

SO THE BOY DID AS HE WAS TOLD...
HE WAS AFRAID... BUT HE PUSHED ON ANYWAY.
HE WAS RESOLVED TO PASS THEIR TEST.
WH-WHAT DOES THAT HAVE TO DO WITH ANYTHING? A-ARE YOU OKAY?
YOU ARE THE **BOY**, SHUBIN.
AND THE MINERS ARE REALLY DEMONS. THEY ARE THE **STATE**, SENDING YOU INTO THE DEPTHS... BUT NOT FOR THE REASONS YOU THINK.

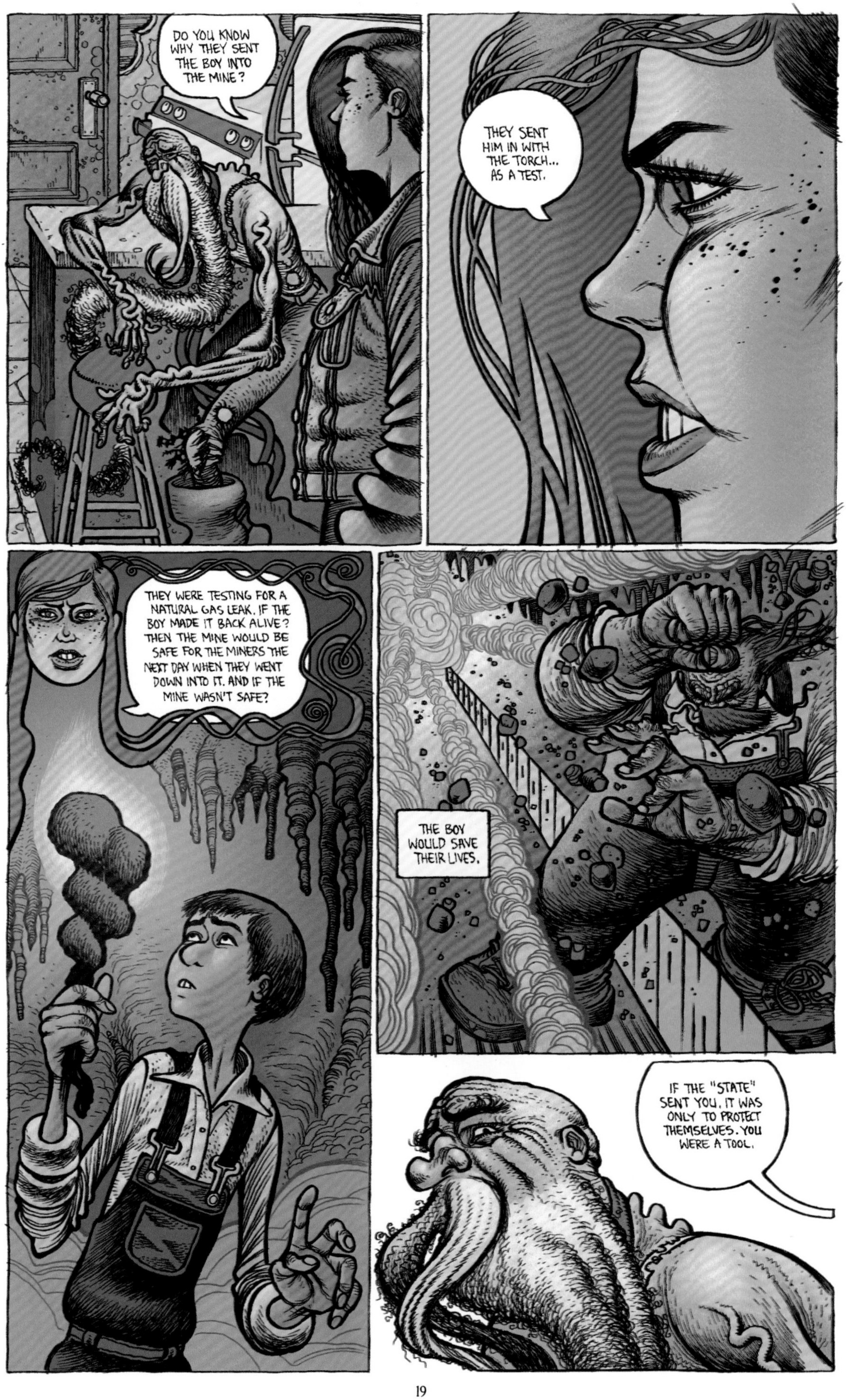
DO YOU KNOW WHY THEY SENT THE BOY INTO THE MINE?
THEY SENT HIM IN WITH THE TORCH... AS A TEST.
THEY WERE TESTING FOR A NATURAL GAS LEAK. IF THE BOY MADE IT BACK ALIVE? THEN THE MINE WOULD BE SAFE FOR THE MINERS THE NEXT DAY WHEN THEY WENT DOWN INTO IT. AND IF THE MINE WASN'T SAFE?
THE BOY WOULD SAVE THEIR LIVES.
IF THE "STATE" SENT YOU, IT WAS ONLY TO PROTECT THEMSELVES. YOU WERE A TOOL.

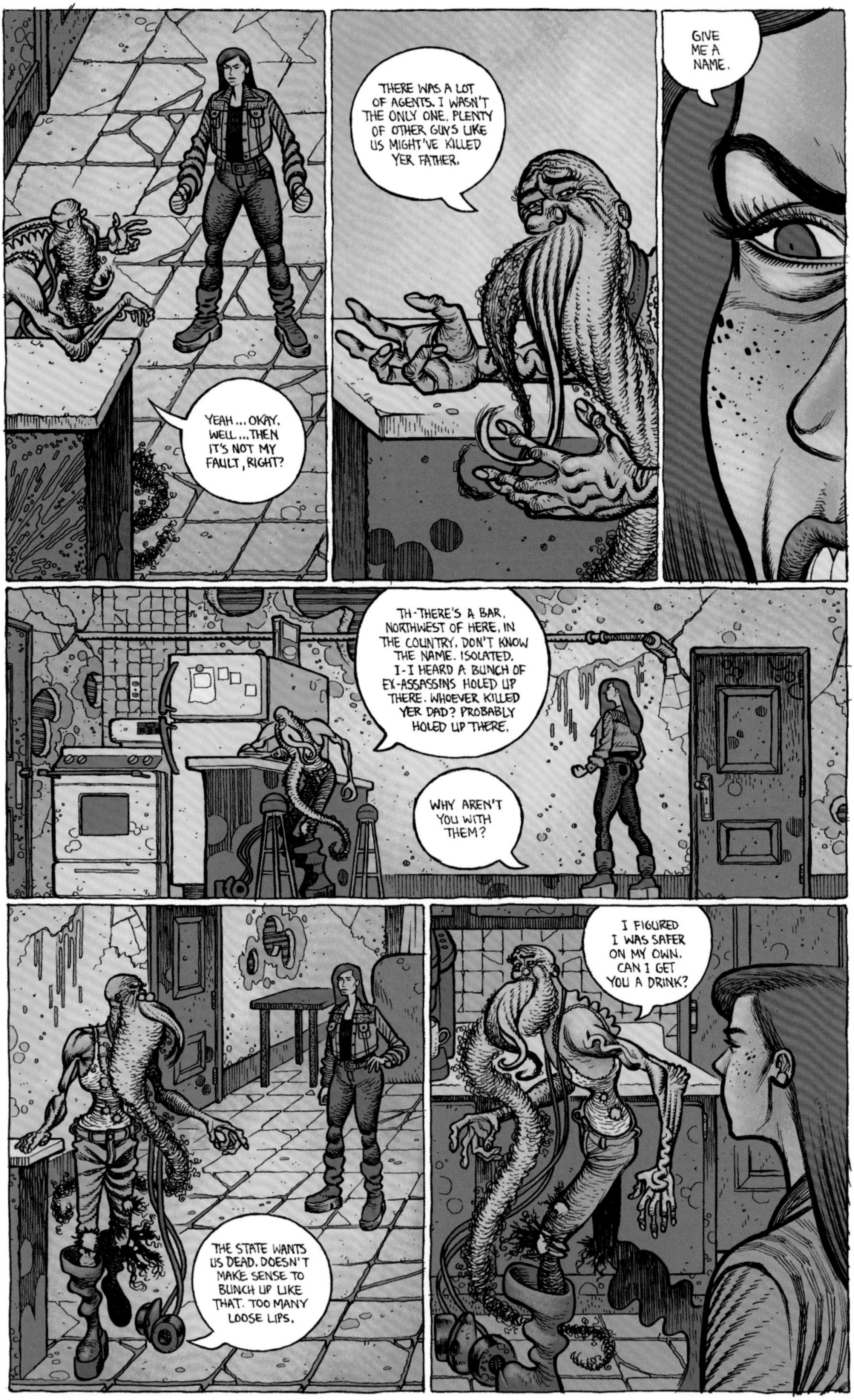
YEAH ... OKAY. WELL ... THEN IT'S NOT MY FAULT, RIGHT?
THERE WAS A LOT OF AGENTS. I WASN'T THE ONLY ONE. PLENTY OF OTHER GUYS LIKE US MIGHT'VE KILLED YER FATHER.
GIVE ME A NAME.
TH-THERE'S A BAR, NORTHWEST OF HERE, IN THE COUNTRY. DON'T KNOW THE NAME. ISOLATED. I-I HEARD A BUNCH OF EX-ASSASSINS HOLED UP THERE. WHOEVER KILLED YER DAD? PROBABLY HOLED UP THERE.
WHY AREN'T YOU WITH THEM?
THE STATE WANTS US DEAD. DOESN'T MAKE SENSE TO BUNCH UP LIKE THAT. TOO MANY LOOSE LIPS.
I FIGURED I WAS SAFER ON MY OWN. CAN I GET YOU A DRINK?

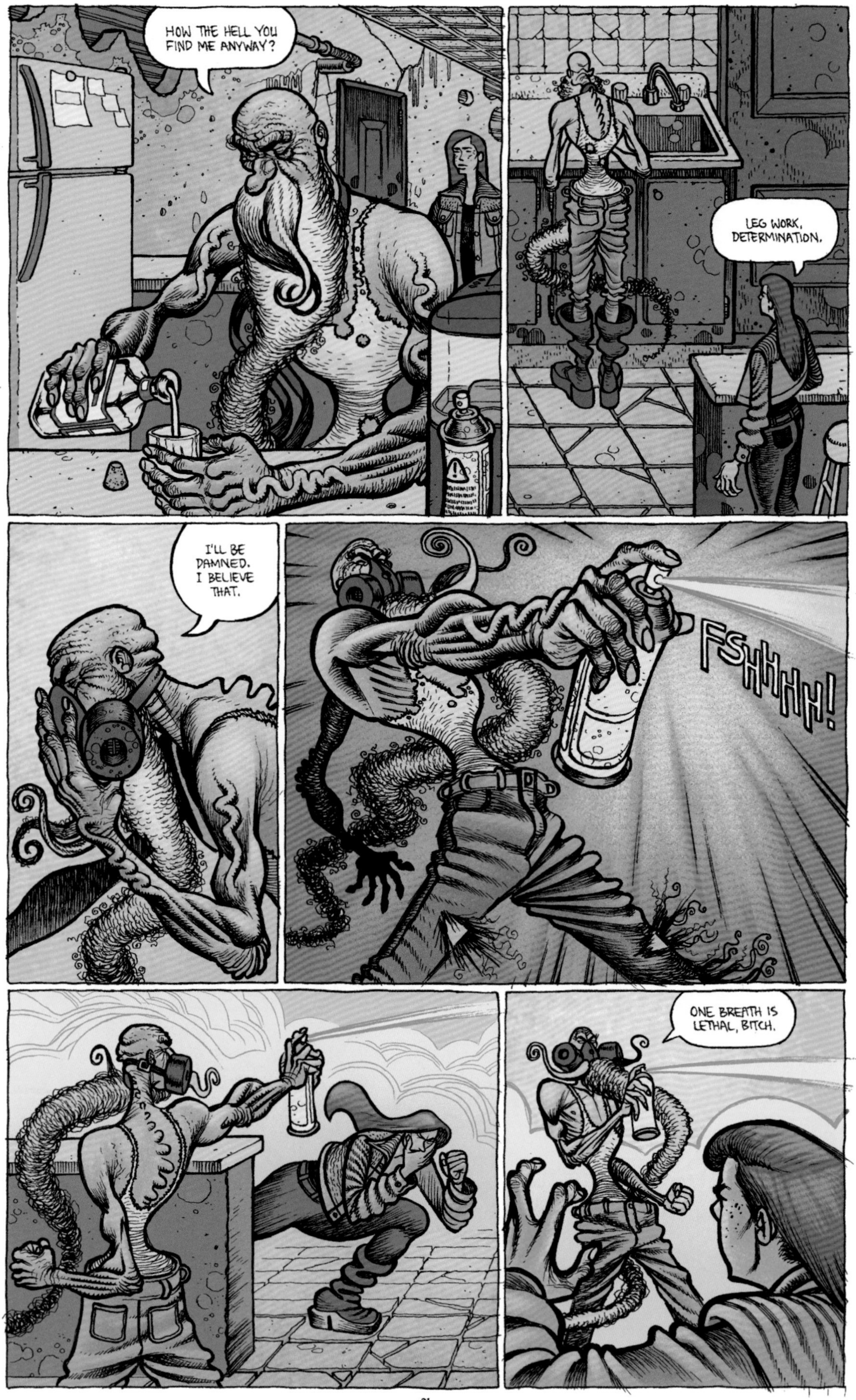
HOW THE HELL YOU FIND ME ANYWAY?
LEG WORK, DETERMINATION.
I'LL BE DAMNED. I BELIEVE THAT.
FSHHHHH!
ONE BREATH IS LETHAL, BITCH.

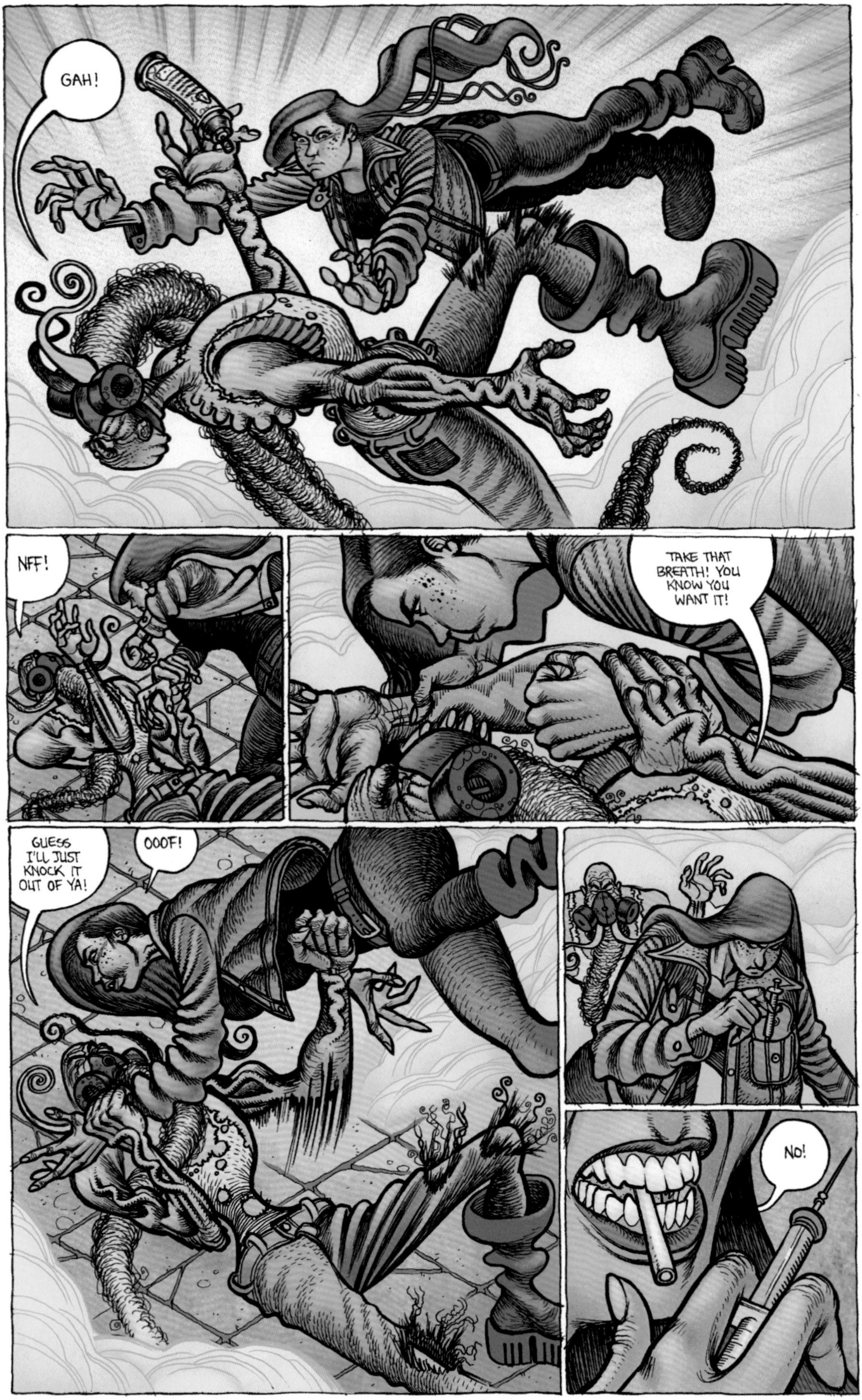
GAH!
NFF!
TAKE THAT BREATH! YOU KNOW YOU WANT IT!
GUESS I'LL JUST KNOCK IT OUT OF YA!
OOOF!
NO!

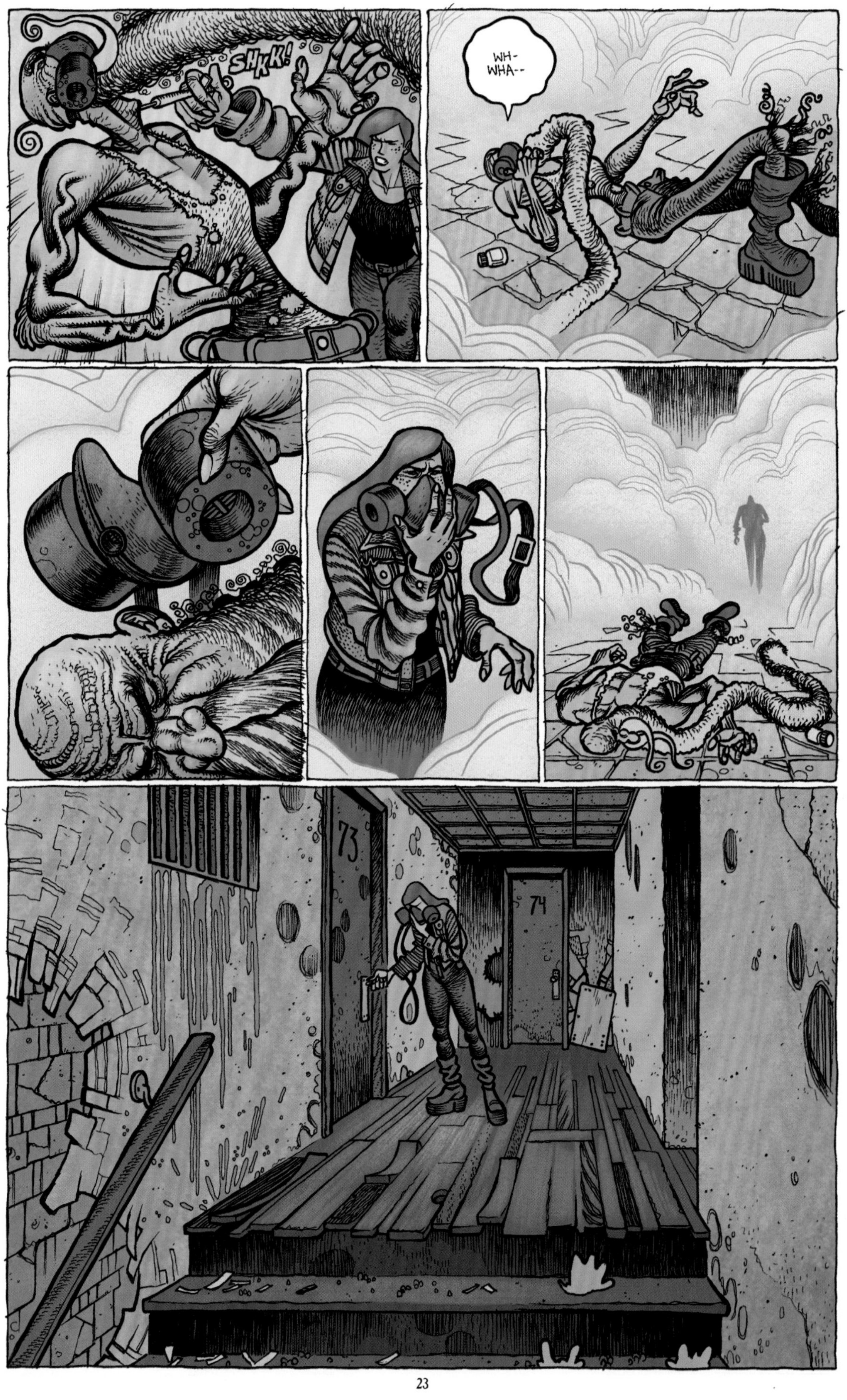
SHKK!
WH-
WHA--
73
74

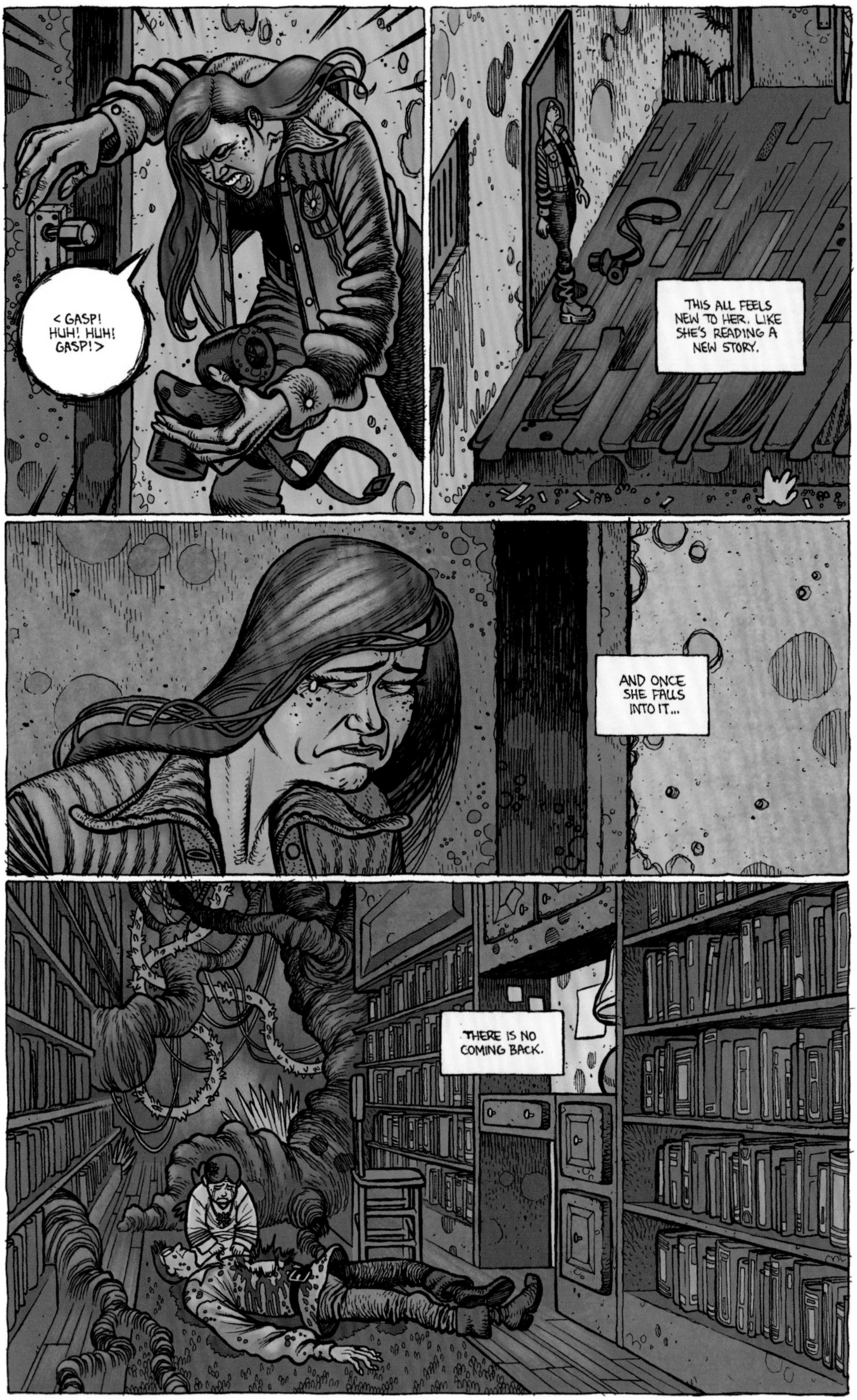
< GASP! HUH! HUH! GASP! >
THIS ALL FEELS NEW TO HER. LIKE SHE'S READING A NEW STORY.
AND ONCE SHE FALLS INTO IT...
THERE IS NO COMING BACK.

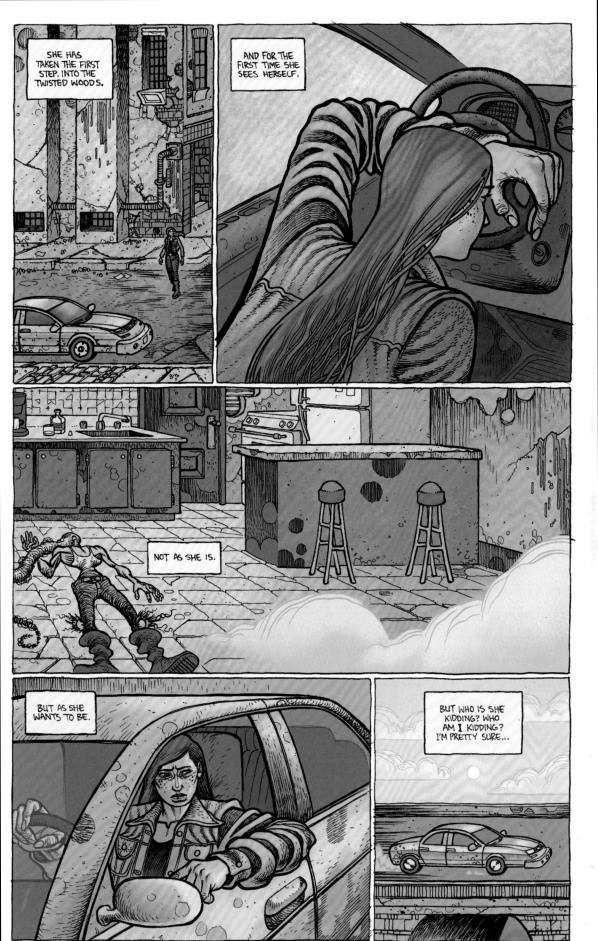

SHE HAS TAKEN THE FIRST STEP. INTO THE TWISTED WOODS.

AND FOR THE FIRST TIME SHE SEES HERSELF.

NOT AS SHE IS.

BUT AS SHE WANTS TO BE.

BUT WHO IS SHE KIDDING? WHO AM I KIDDING? I'M PRETTY SURE...

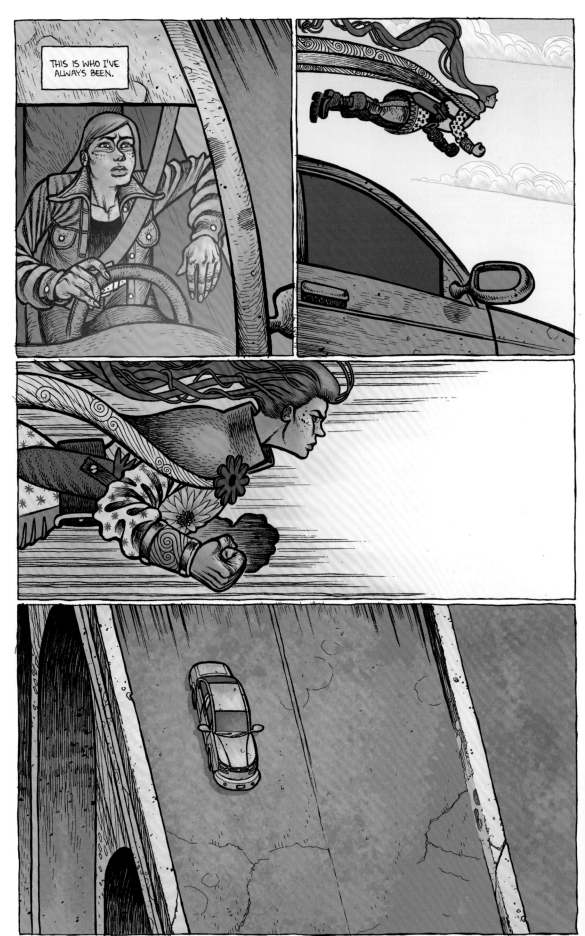

THIS IS WHO I'VE ALWAYS BEEN.

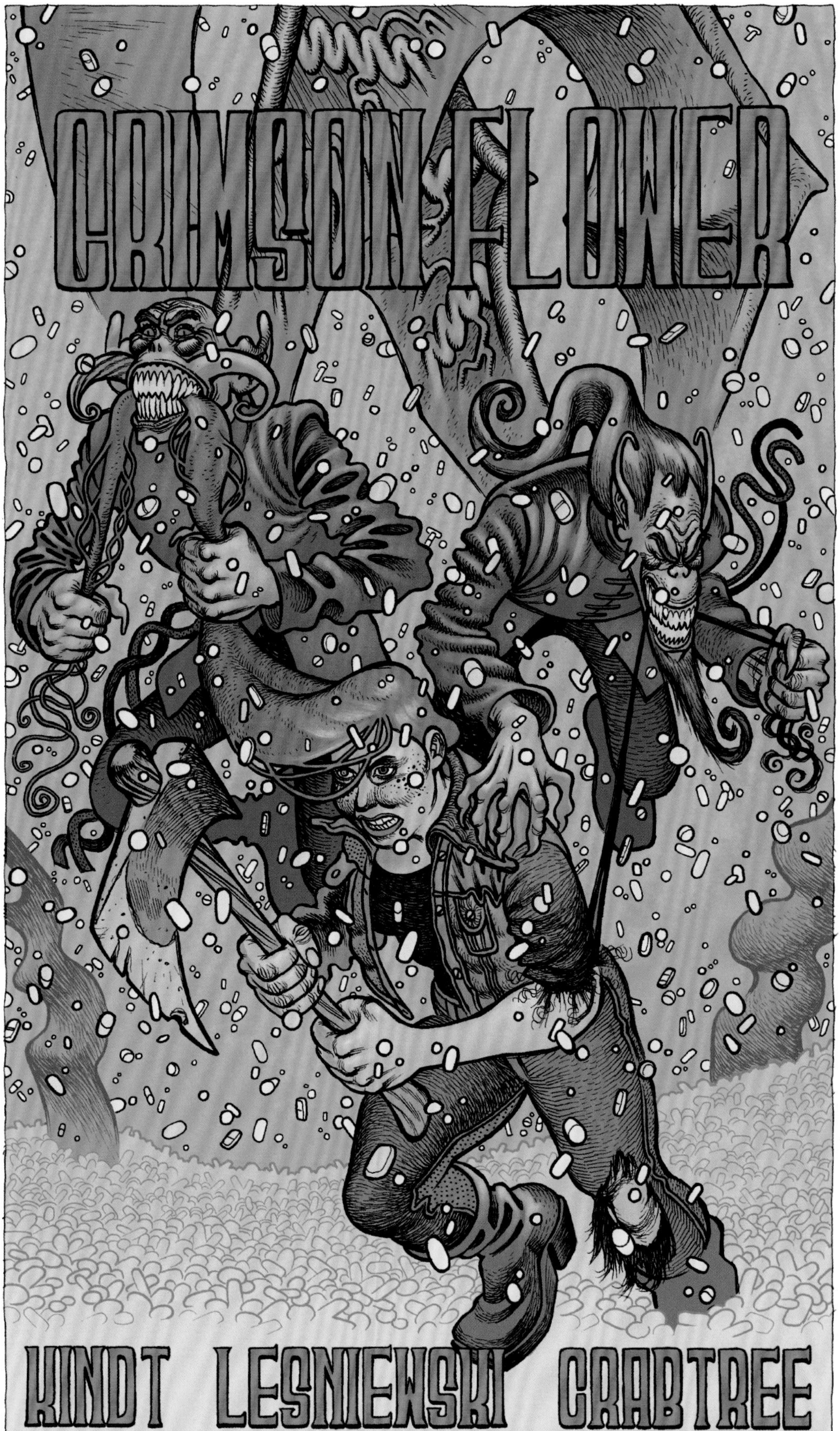
CRIMSON FLOWER
KINDT LESNIEWSKI CRABTREE

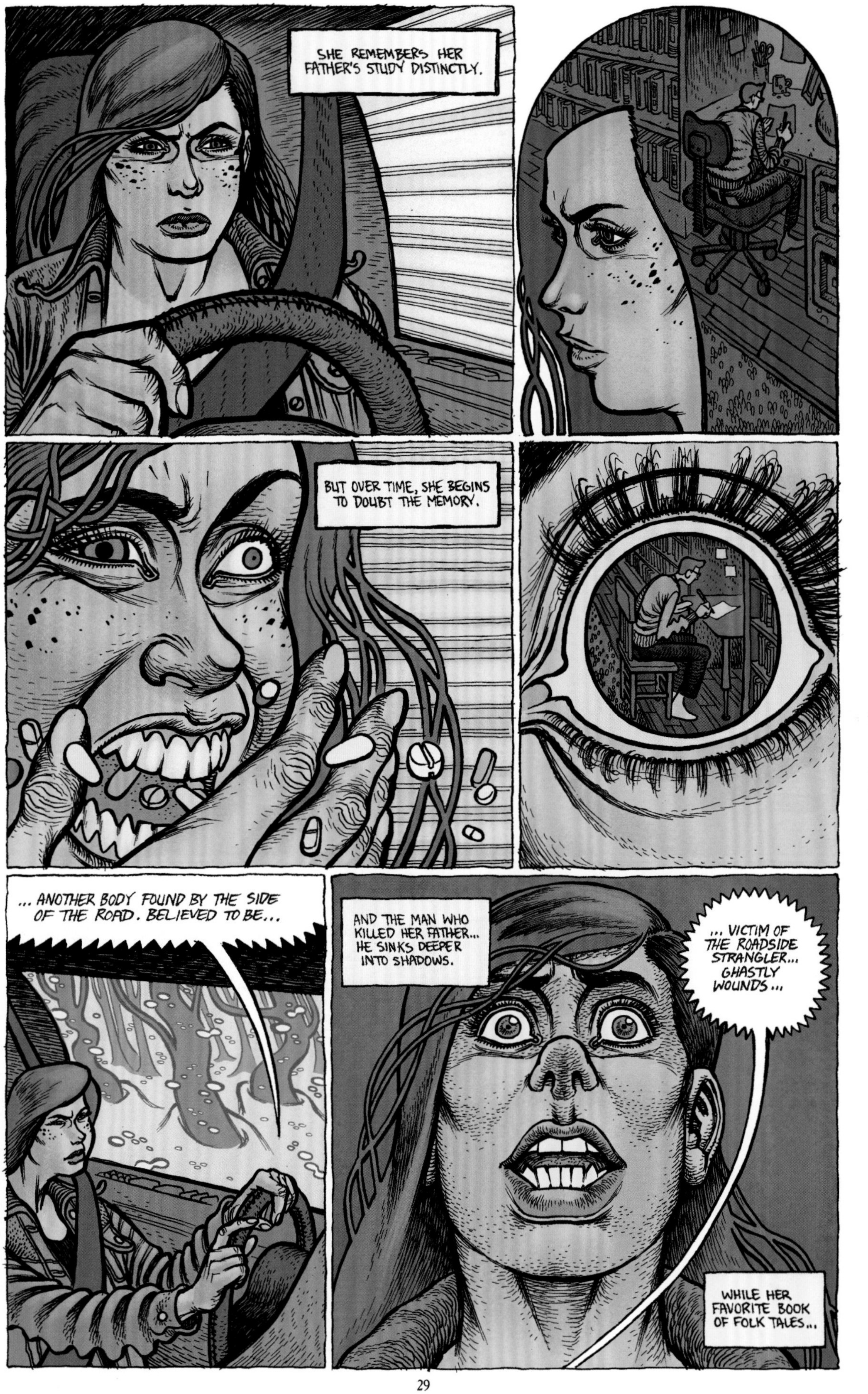
SHE REMEMBERS HER FATHER'S STUDY DISTINCTLY.
BUT OVER TIME, SHE BEGINS TO DOUBT THE MEMORY.
... ANOTHER BODY FOUND BY THE SIDE OF THE ROAD. BELIEVED TO BE...
AND THE MAN WHO KILLED HER FATHER... HE SINKS DEEPER INTO SHADOWS.
... VICTIM OF THE ROADSIDE STRANGLER... GHASTLY WOUNDS...
WHILE HER FAVORITE BOOK OF FOLK TALES...

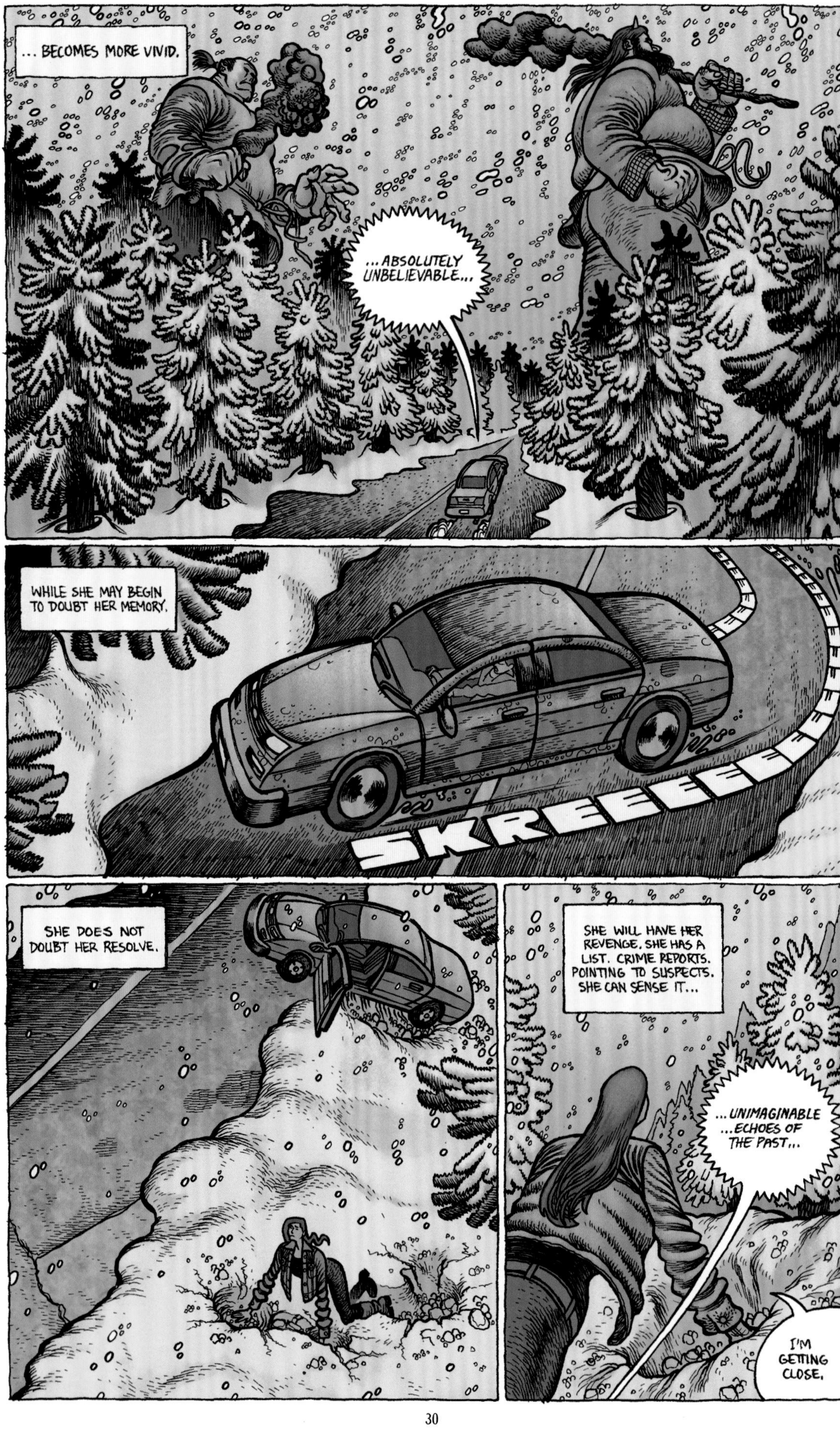
... BECOMES MORE VIVID.
...ABSOLUTELY UNBELIEVABLE...
WHILE SHE MAY BEGIN TO DOUBT HER MEMORY,
SKREEEEEE
SHE DOES NOT DOUBT HER RESOLVE.
SHE WILL HAVE HER REVENGE. SHE HAS A LIST. CRIME REPORTS. POINTING TO SUSPECTS. SHE CAN SENSE IT...
...UNIMAGINABLE ...ECHOES OF THE PAST...
I'M GETTING CLOSE.

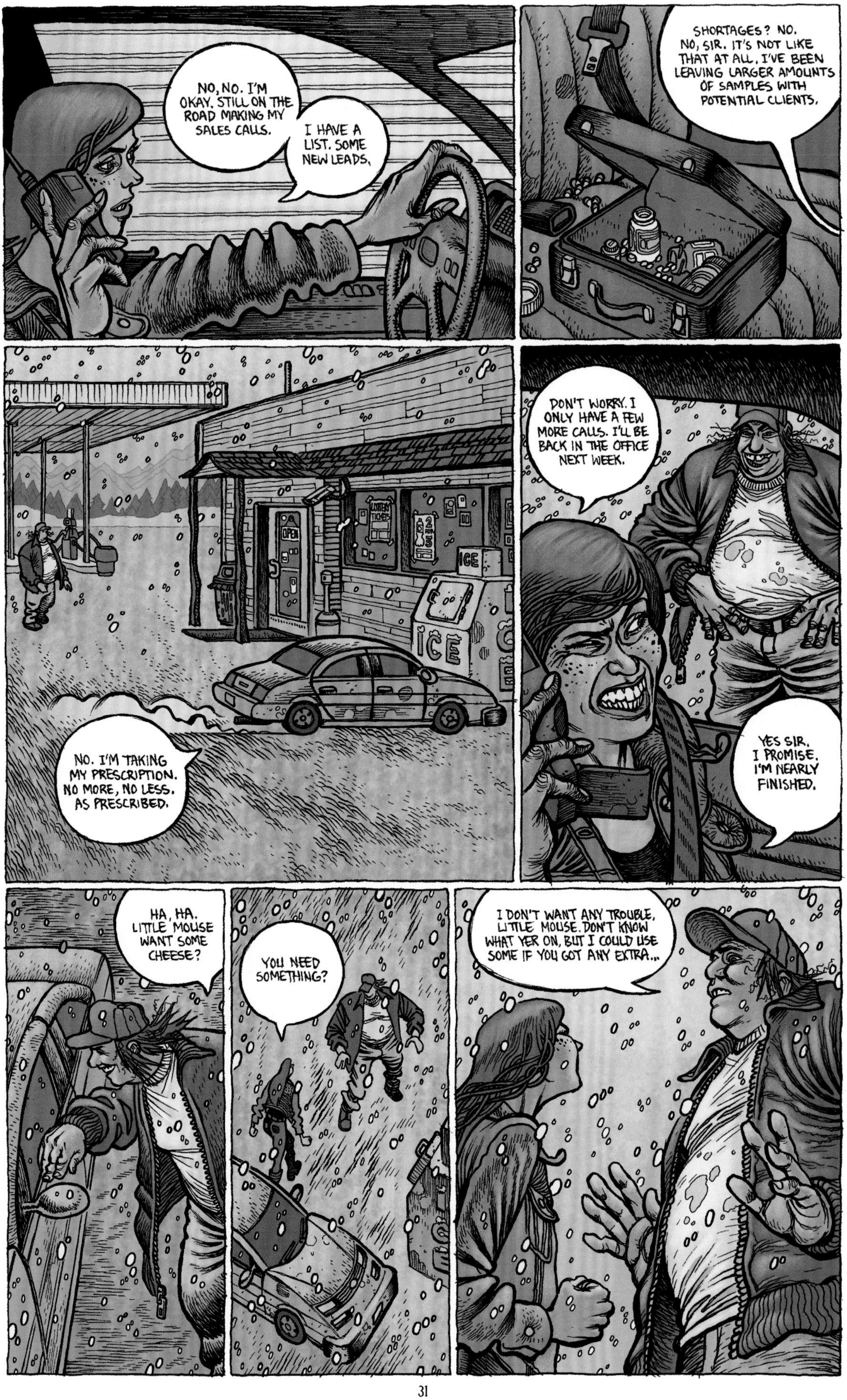
NO, NO. I'M OKAY. STILL ON THE ROAD MAKING MY SALES CALLS.
I HAVE A LIST. SOME NEW LEADS.
SHORTAGES? NO. NO, SIR. IT'S NOT LIKE THAT AT ALL. I'VE BEEN LEAVING LARGER AMOUNTS OF SAMPLES WITH POTENTIAL CLIENTS.
OPEN
LOTTERY TICKETS
ICE
ICE
NO. I'M TAKING MY PRESCRIPTION. NO MORE, NO LESS. AS PRESCRIBED.
DON'T WORRY. I ONLY HAVE A FEW MORE CALLS. I'LL BE BACK IN THE OFFICE NEXT WEEK.
YES SIR. I PROMISE. I'M NEARLY FINISHED.
HA, HA. LITTLE MOUSE WANT SOME CHEESE?
YOU NEED SOMETHING?
I DON'T WANT ANY TROUBLE, LITTLE MOUSE. DON'T KNOW WHAT YER ON, BUT I COULD USE SOME IF YOU GOT ANY EXTRA...

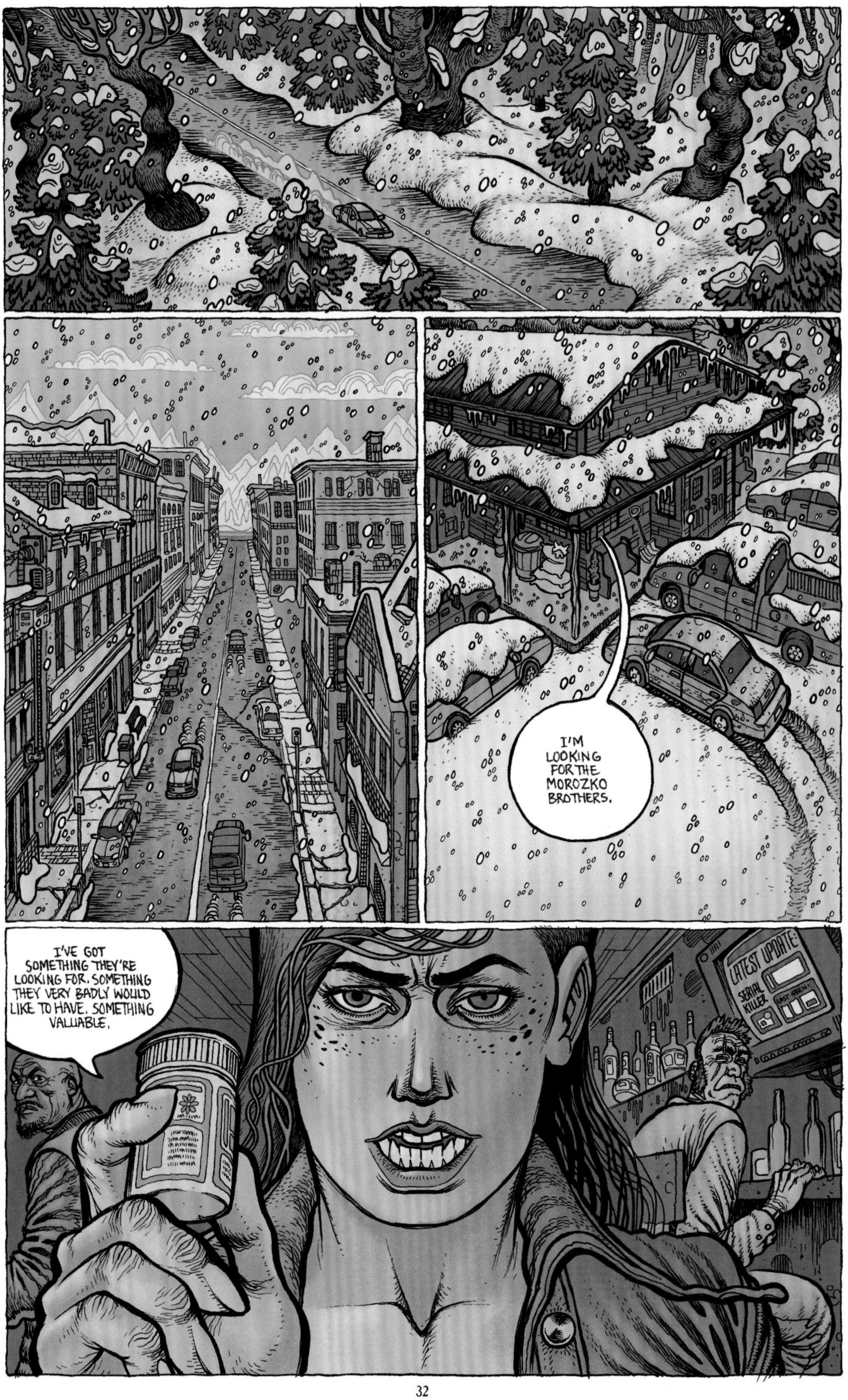
I'M LOOKING FOR THE MOROZKO BROTHERS.
I'VE GOT SOMETHING THEY'RE LOOKING FOR. SOMETHING THEY VERY BADLY WOULD LIKE TO HAVE. SOMETHING VALUABLE.
LATEST UPDATE:
SERIAL KILLER

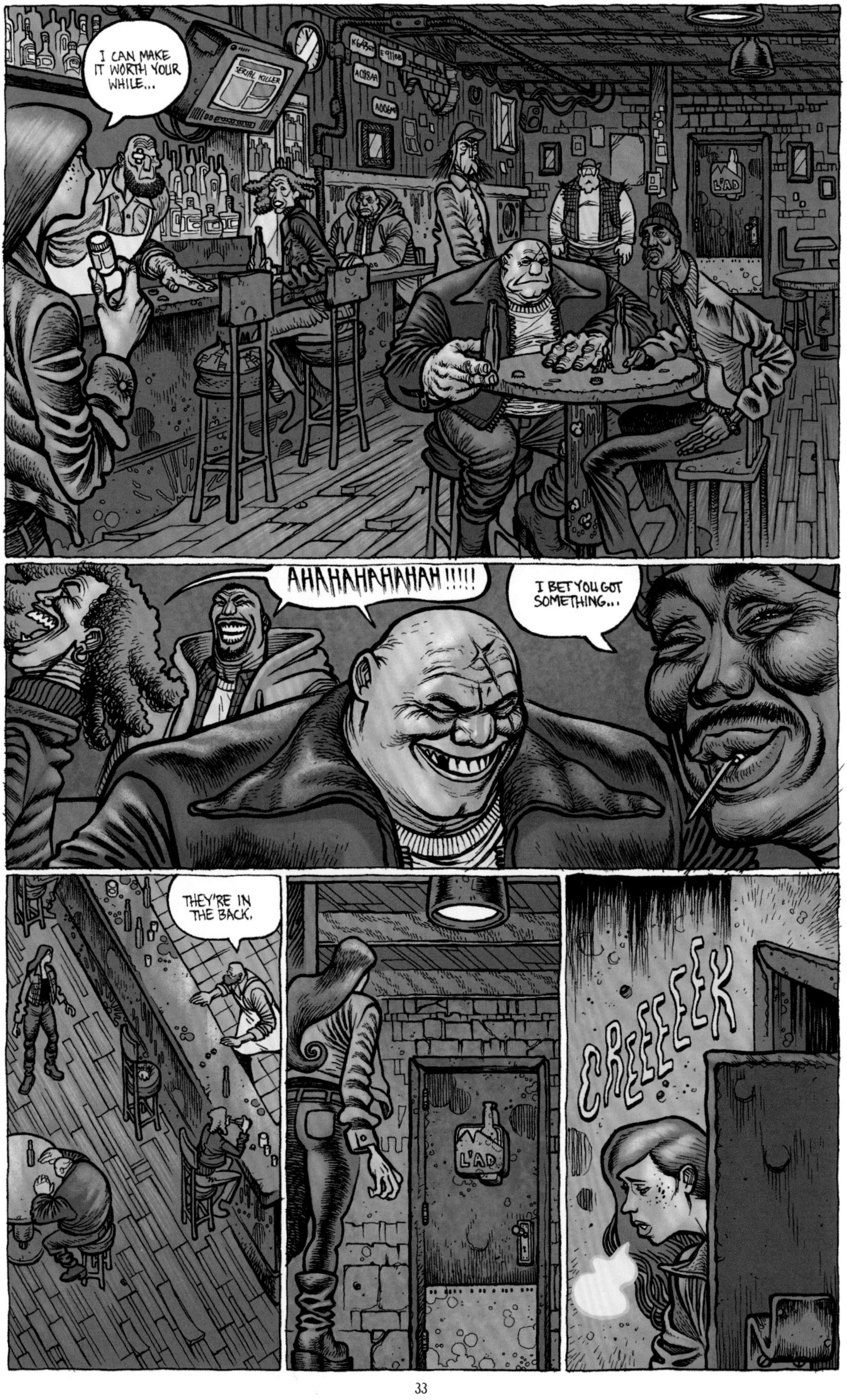
I CAN MAKE IT WORTH YOUR WHILE...
SERIAL KILLER
L'AD
AHAHAHAHAHAH!!!!!
I BET YOU GOT SOMETHING...
THEY'RE IN THE BACK.
L'AD
CREEEEK

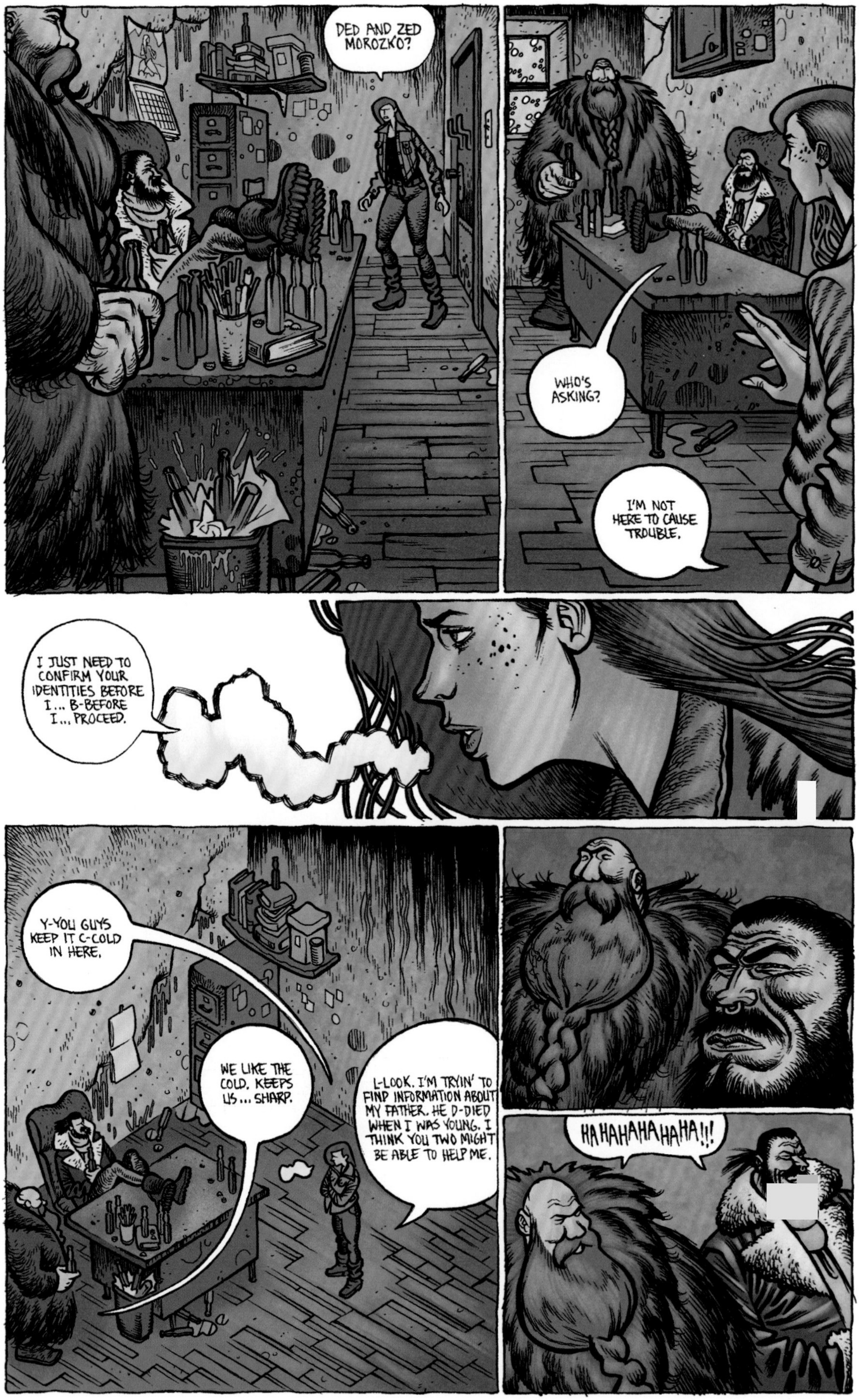
DED AND ZED MOROZKO?
WHO'S ASKING?
I'M NOT HERE TO CAUSE TROUBLE.
I JUST NEED TO CONFIRM YOUR IDENTITIES BEFORE I... B-BEFORE I... PROCEED.
Y-YOU GUYS KEEP IT C-COLD IN HERE.
WE LIKE THE COLD. KEEPS US... SHARP.
L-LOOK. I'M TRYIN' TO FIND INFORMATION ABOUT MY FATHER. HE D-DIED WHEN I WAS YOUNG. I THINK YOU TWO MIGHT BE ABLE TO HELP ME.
HAHAHAHAHAHA!!!

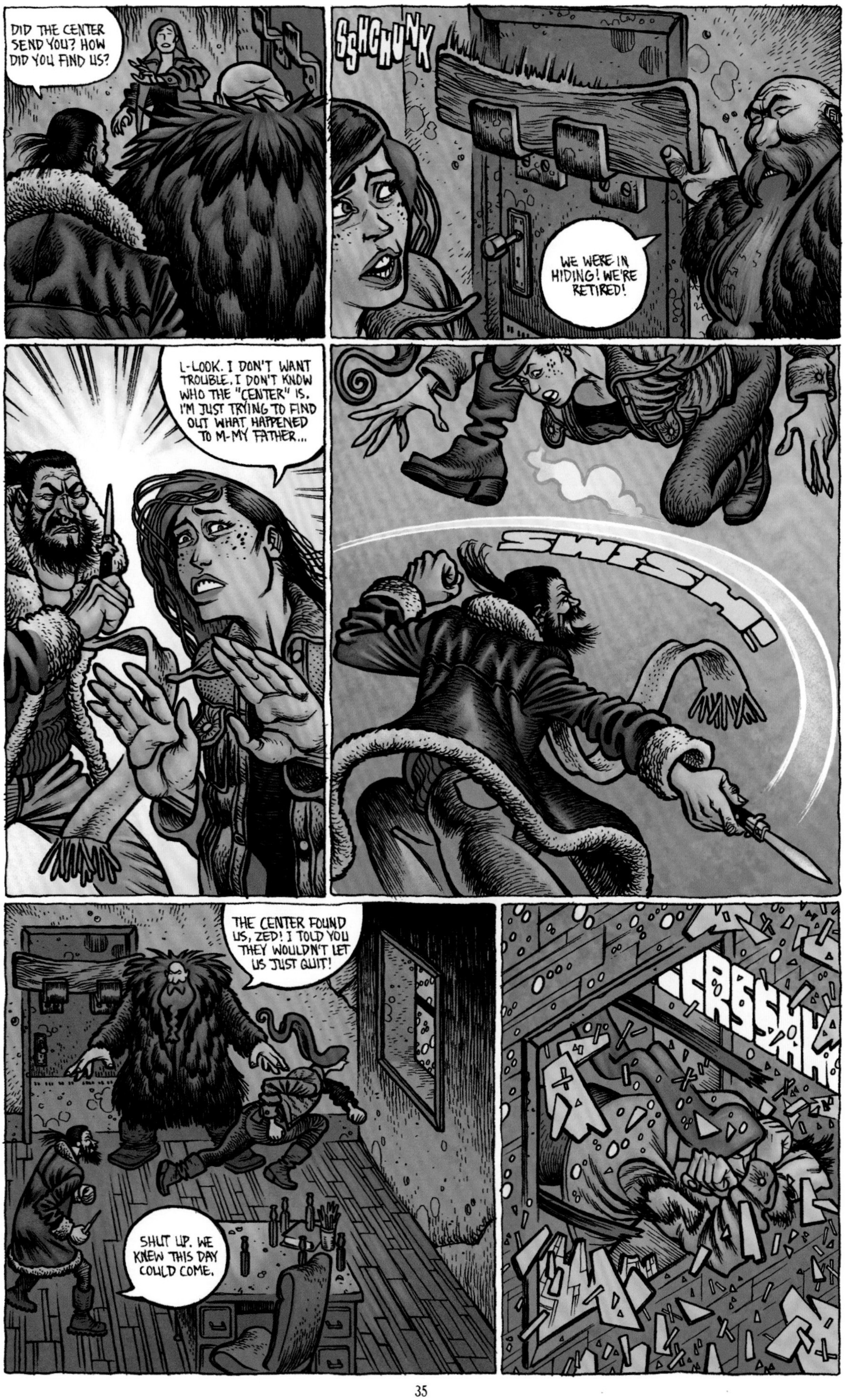
DID THE CENTER SEND YOU? HOW DID YOU FIND US?
SSHCHUNK
WE WERE IN HIDING! WE'RE RETIRED!
L-LOOK. I DON'T WANT TROUBLE. I DON'T KNOW WHO THE "CENTER" IS. I'M JUST TRYING TO FIND OUT WHAT HAPPENED TO M-MY FATHER...
SWISH
THE CENTER FOUND US, ZED! I TOLD YOU THEY WOULDN'T LET US JUST QUIT!
SHUT UP. WE KNEW THIS DAY COULD COME.
CRSCHK

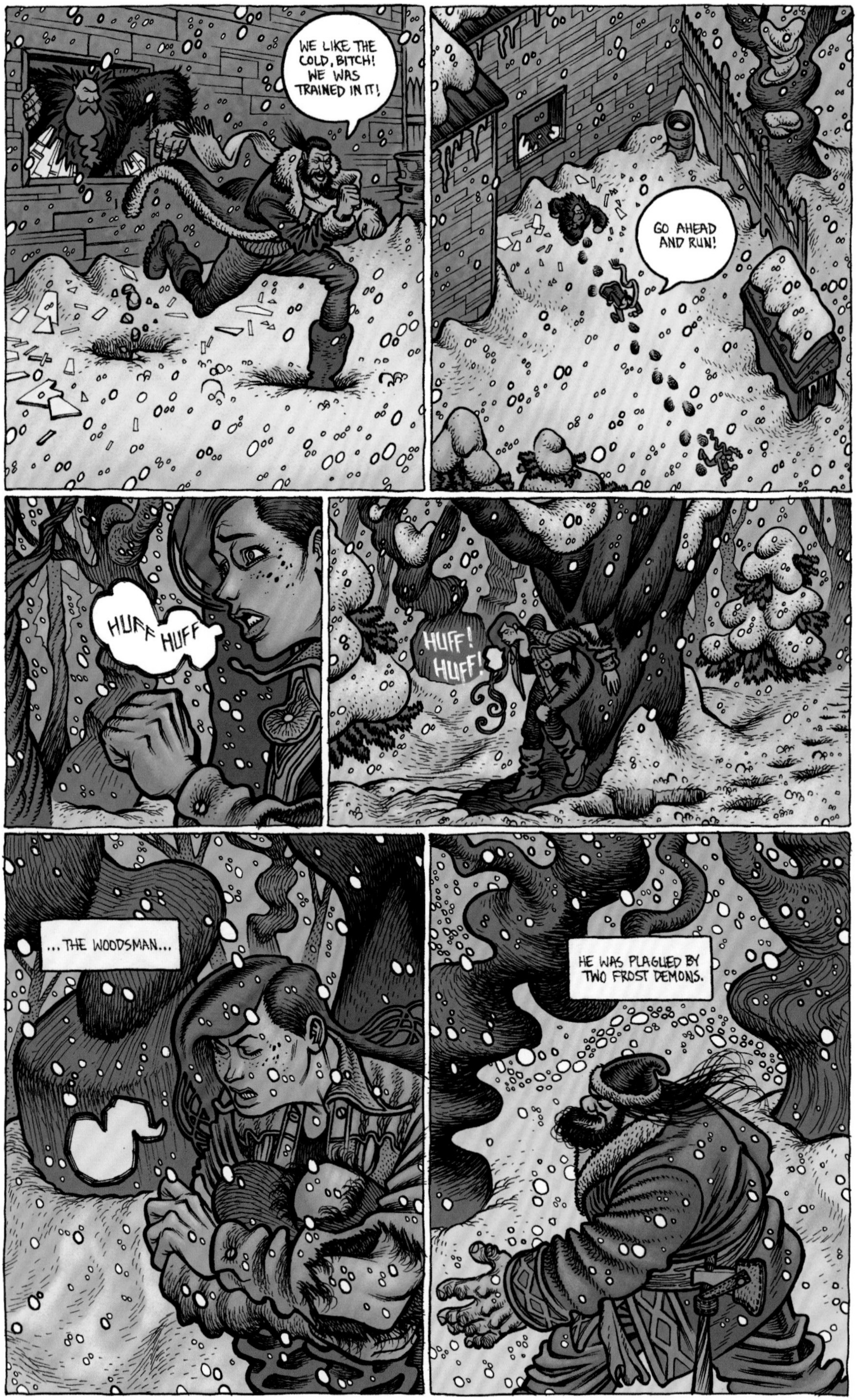
WE LIKE THE COLD, BITCH! WE WAS TRAINED IN IT!
GO AHEAD AND RUN!
HUFF HUFF
HUFF! HUFF!
...THE WOODSMAN...
HE WAS PLAGUED BY TWO FROST DEMONS.

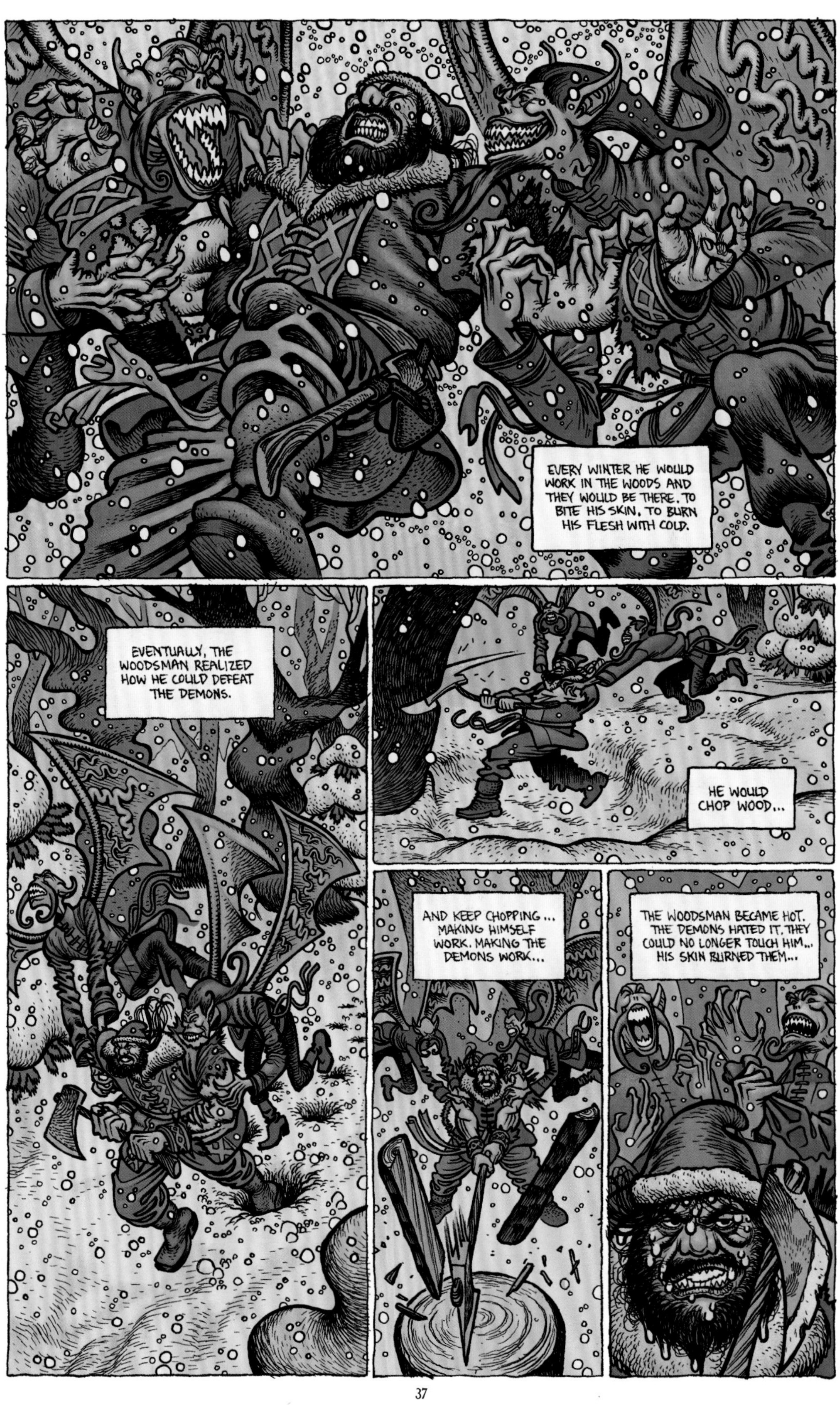
EVERY WINTER HE WOULD WORK IN THE WOODS AND THEY WOULD BE THERE. TO BITE HIS SKIN, TO BURN HIS FLESH WITH COLD.
EVENTUALLY, THE WOODSMAN REALIZED HOW HE COULD DEFEAT THE DEMONS.
HE WOULD CHOP WOOD...
AND KEEP CHOPPING... MAKING HIMSELF WORK. MAKING THE DEMONS WORK...
THE WOODSMAN BECAME HOT. THE DEMONS HATED IT. THEY COULD NO LONGER TOUCH HIM... HIS SKIN BURNED THEM...

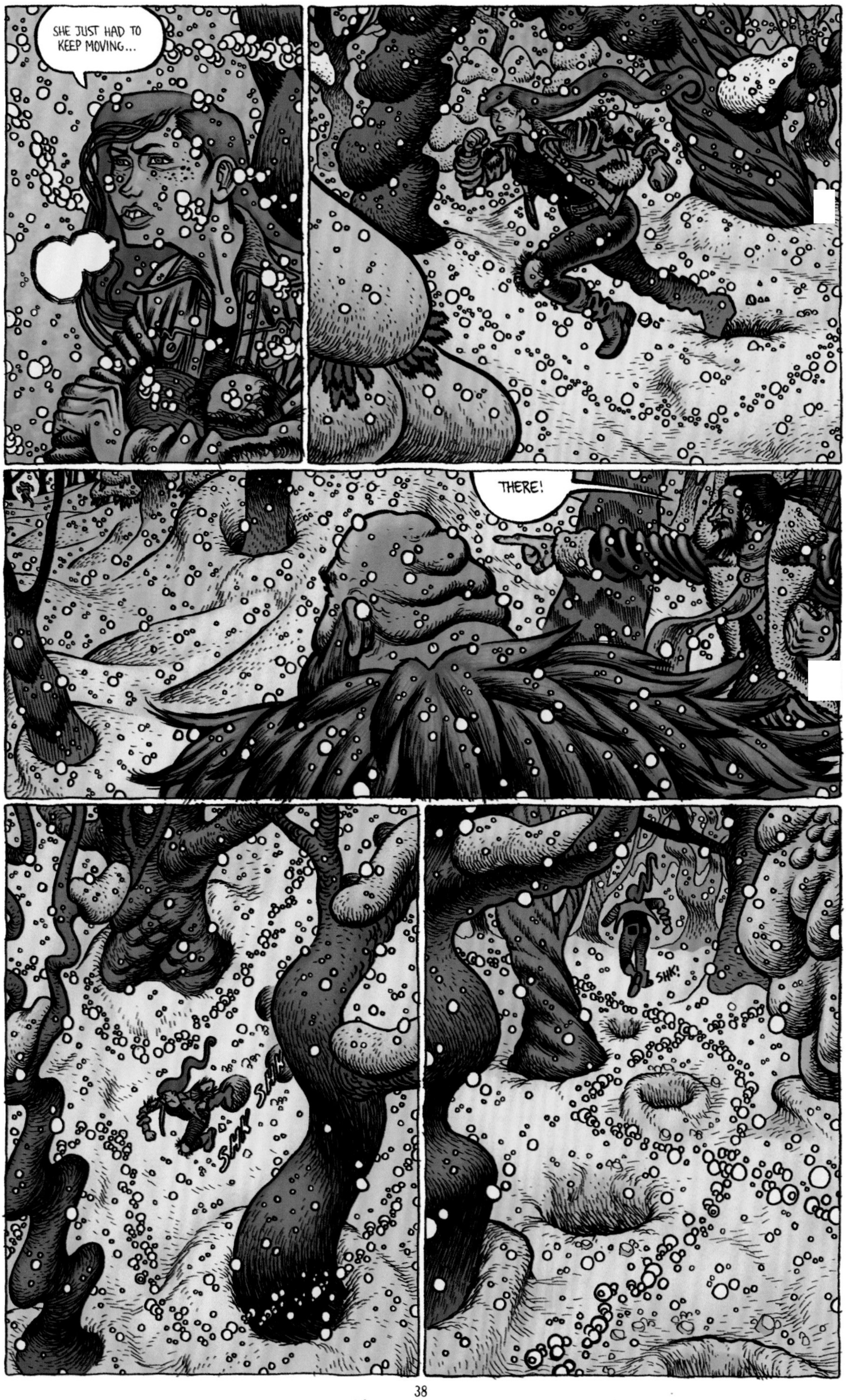
SHE JUST HAD TO KEEP MOVING...
THERE!
SHK!

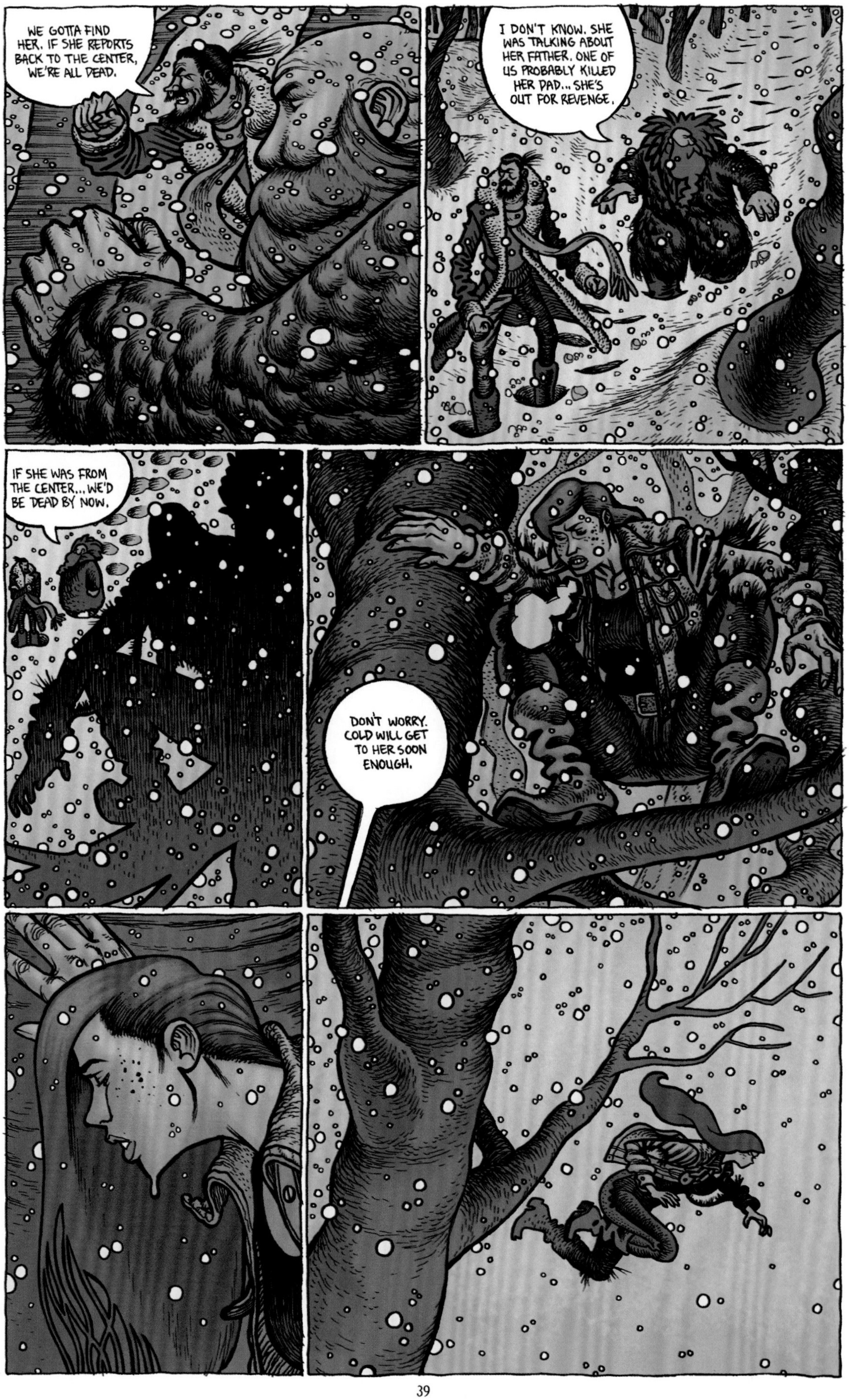
WE GOTTA FIND HER. IF SHE REPORTS BACK TO THE CENTER, WE'RE ALL DEAD.
I DON'T KNOW. SHE WAS TALKING ABOUT HER FATHER. ONE OF US PROBABLY KILLED HER DAD... SHE'S OUT FOR REVENGE.
IF SHE WAS FROM THE CENTER... WE'D BE DEAD BY NOW.
DON'T WORRY. COLD WILL GET TO HER SOON ENOUGH.

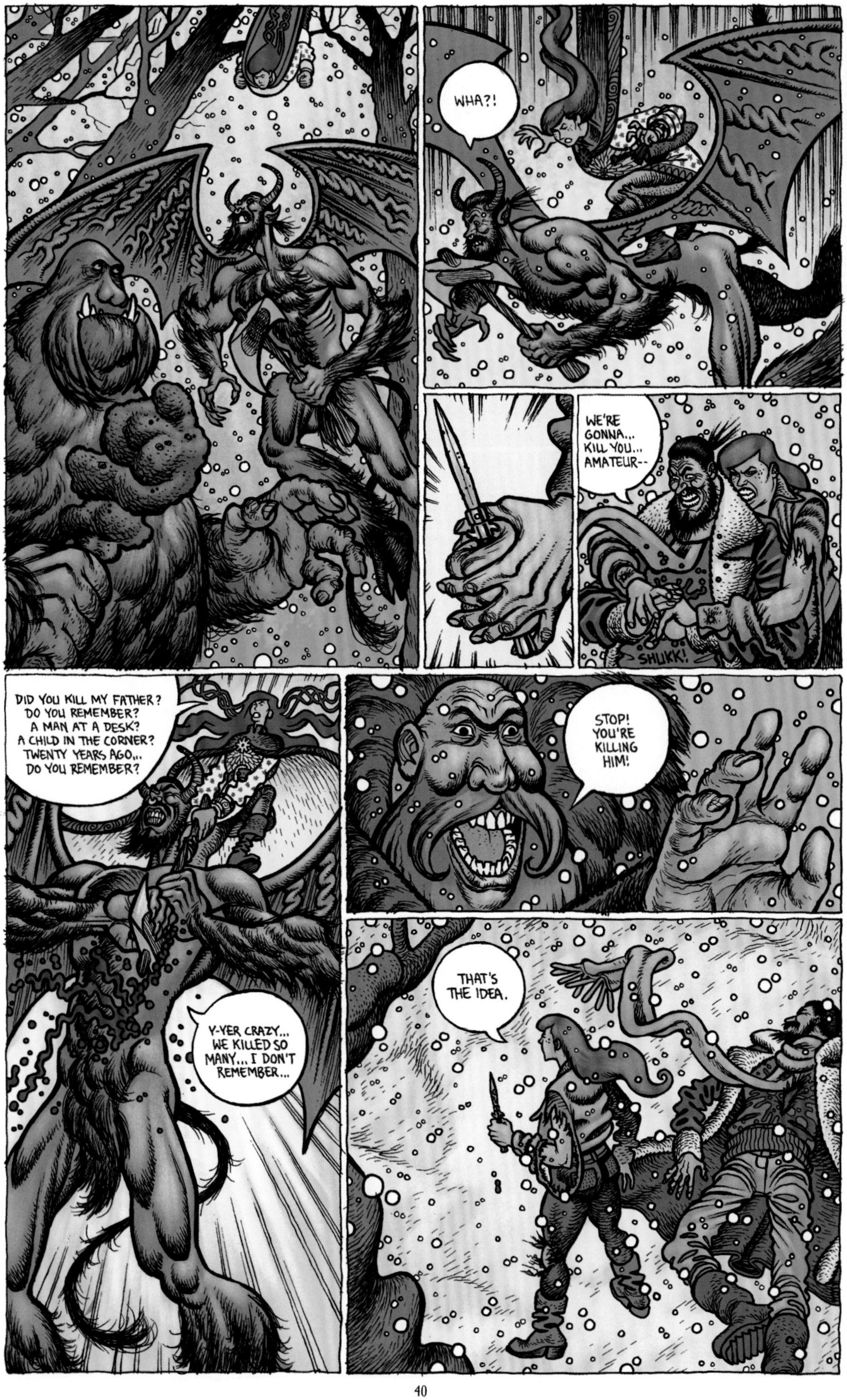
WHA?!
WE'RE GONNA... KILL YOU... AMATEUR--
SHUKK!
DID YOU KILL MY FATHER? DO YOU REMEMBER? A MAN AT A DESK? A CHILD IN THE CORNER? TWENTY YEARS AGO... DO YOU REMEMBER?
Y-YER CRAZY... WE KILLED SO MANY... I DON'T REMEMBER...
STOP! YOU'RE KILLING HIM!
THAT'S THE IDEA.

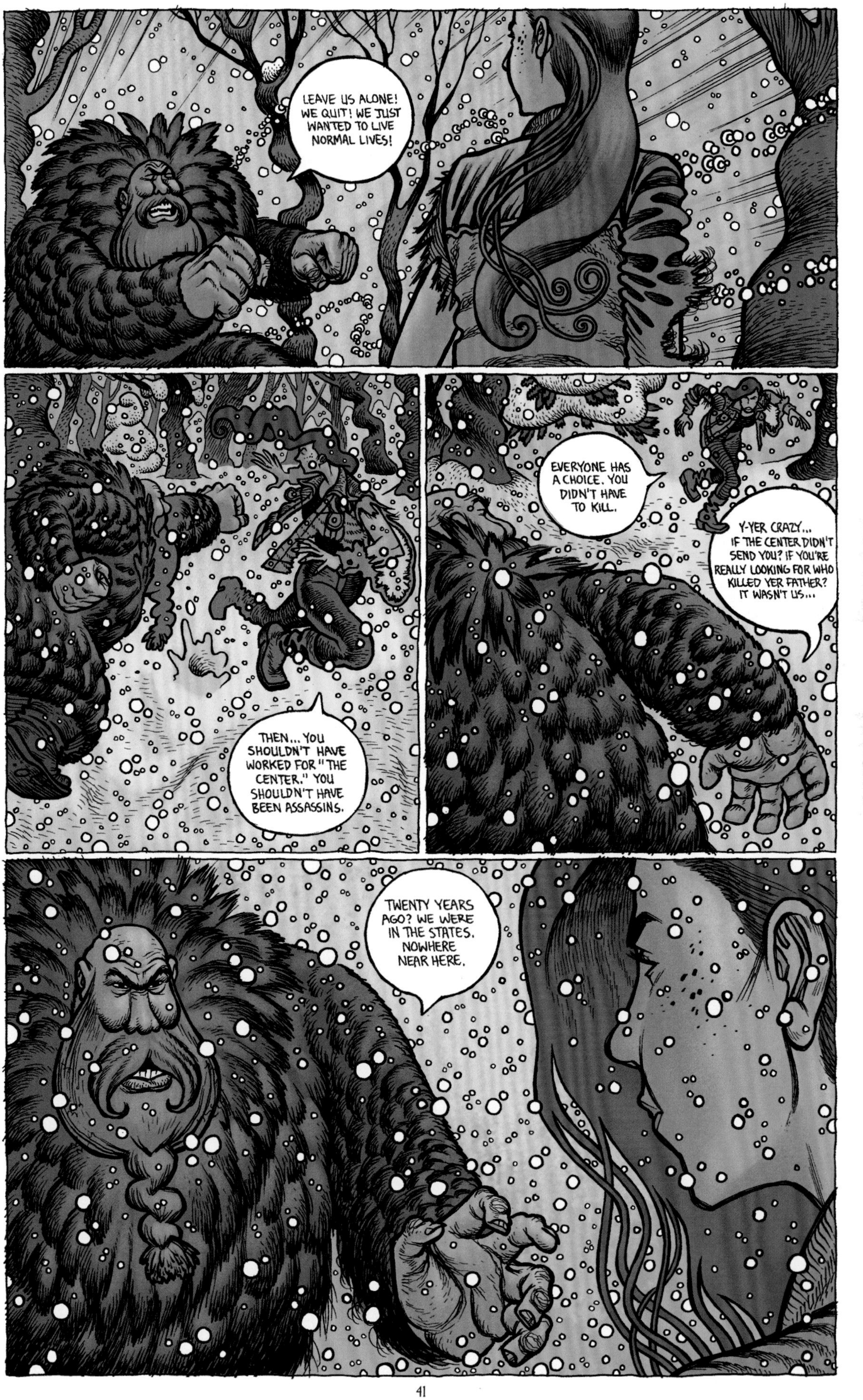
LEAVE US ALONE! WE QUIT! WE JUST WANTED TO LIVE NORMAL LIVES!
THEN... YOU SHOULDN'T HAVE WORKED FOR "THE CENTER." YOU SHOULDN'T HAVE BEEN ASSASSINS.
EVERYONE HAS A CHOICE. YOU DIDN'T HAVE TO KILL.
Y-YER CRAZY... IF THE CENTER DIDN'T SEND YOU? IF YOU'RE REALLY LOOKING FOR WHO KILLED YER FATHER? IT WASN'T US...
TWENTY YEARS AGO? WE WERE IN THE STATES. NOWHERE NEAR HERE.

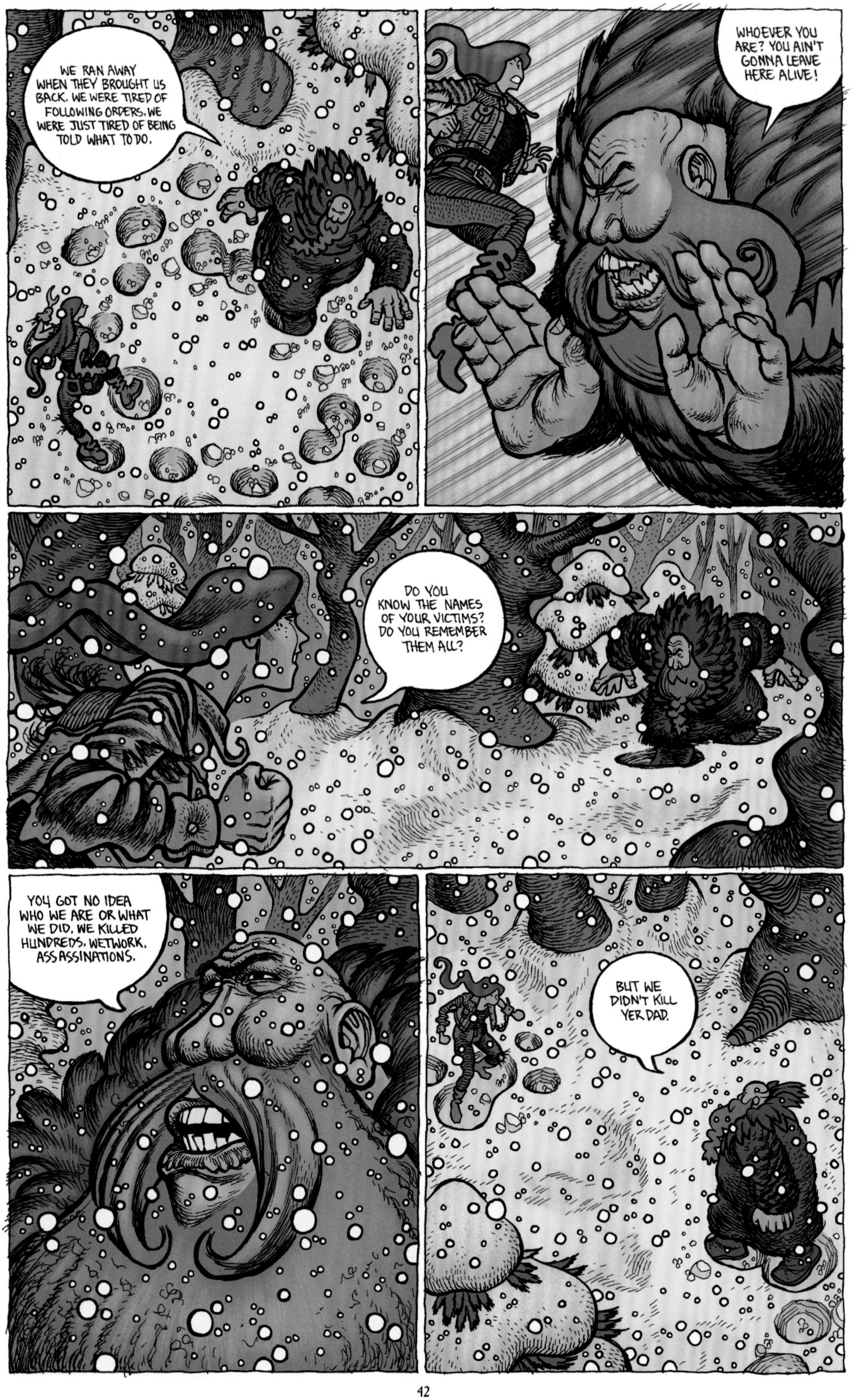
WE RAN AWAY WHEN THEY BROUGHT US BACK. WE WERE TIRED OF FOLLOWING ORDERS. WE WERE JUST TIRED OF BEING TOLD WHAT TO DO.
WHOEVER YOU ARE? YOU AIN'T GONNA LEAVE HERE ALIVE!
DO YOU KNOW THE NAMES OF YOUR VICTIMS? DO YOU REMEMBER THEM ALL?
YOU GOT NO IDEA WHO WE ARE OR WHAT WE DID. WE KILLED HUNDREDS. WETWORK. ASSASSINATIONS.
BUT WE DIDN'T KILL YER DAD.

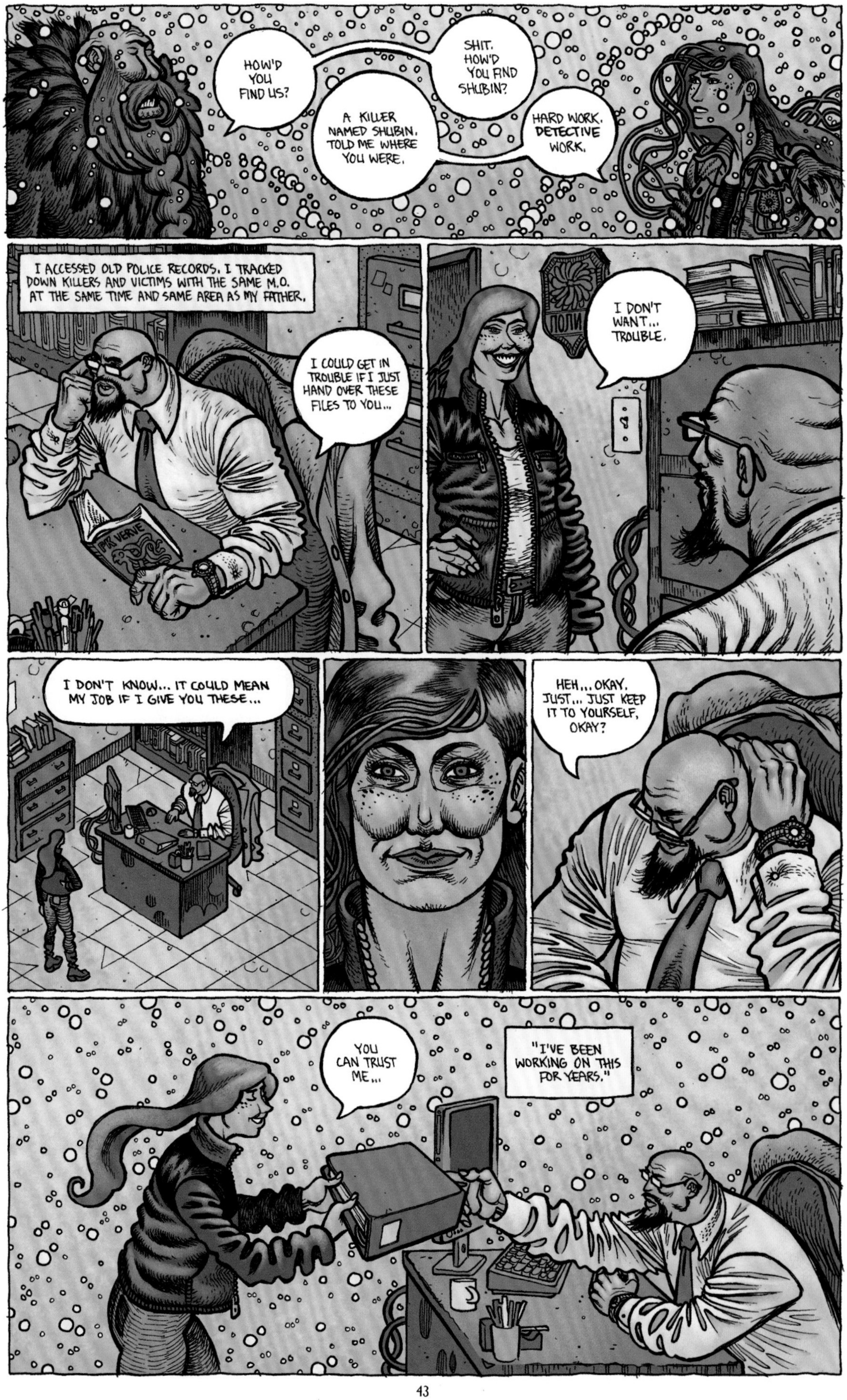
HOW'D YOU FIND US?
A KILLER NAMED SHUBIN. TOLD ME WHERE YOU WERE.
SHIT. HOW'D YOU FIND SHUBIN?
HARD WORK. DETECTIVE WORK.
I ACCESSED OLD POLICE RECORDS. I TRACKED DOWN KILLERS AND VICTIMS WITH THE SAME M.O. AT THE SAME TIME AND SAME AREA AS MY FATHER.
I COULD GET IN TROUBLE IF I JUST HAND OVER THESE FILES TO YOU...
I DON'T WANT... TROUBLE.
I DON'T KNOW... IT COULD MEAN MY JOB IF I GIVE YOU THESE...
HEH... OKAY. JUST... JUST KEEP IT TO YOURSELF, OKAY?
YOU CAN TRUST ME...
"I'VE BEEN WORKING ON THIS FOR YEARS."

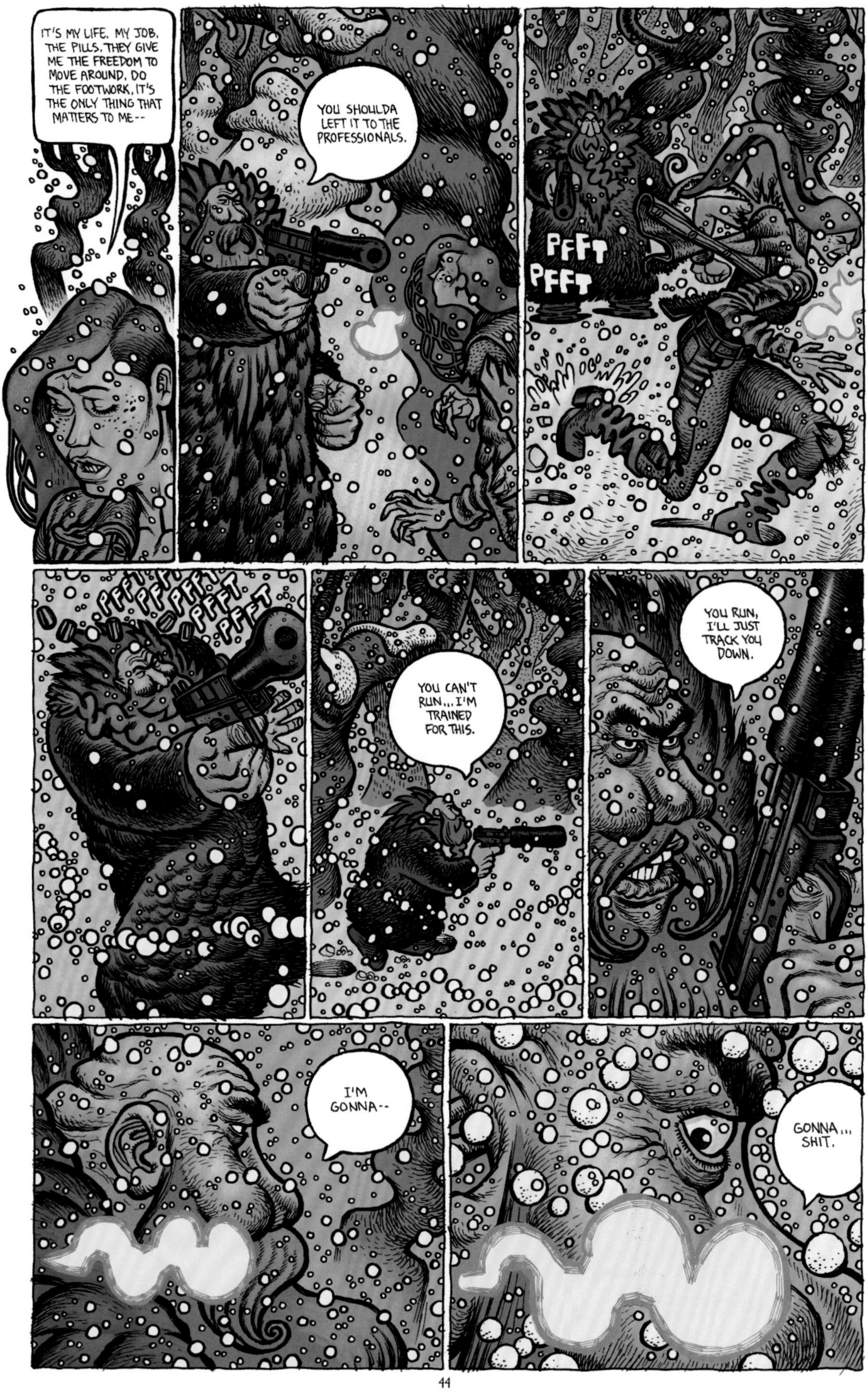
IT'S MY LIFE. MY JOB. THE PILLS. THEY GIVE ME THE FREEDOM TO MOVE AROUND, DO THE FOOTWORK. IT'S THE ONLY THING THAT MATTERS TO ME--
YOU SHOULDA LEFT IT TO THE PROFESSIONALS.
PFFT
PFFT
PFFT PFFT PFFT PFFT PFFT
YOU CAN'T RUN... I'M TRAINED FOR THIS.
YOU RUN, I'LL JUST TRACK YOU DOWN.
I'M GONNA--
GONNA... SHIT.

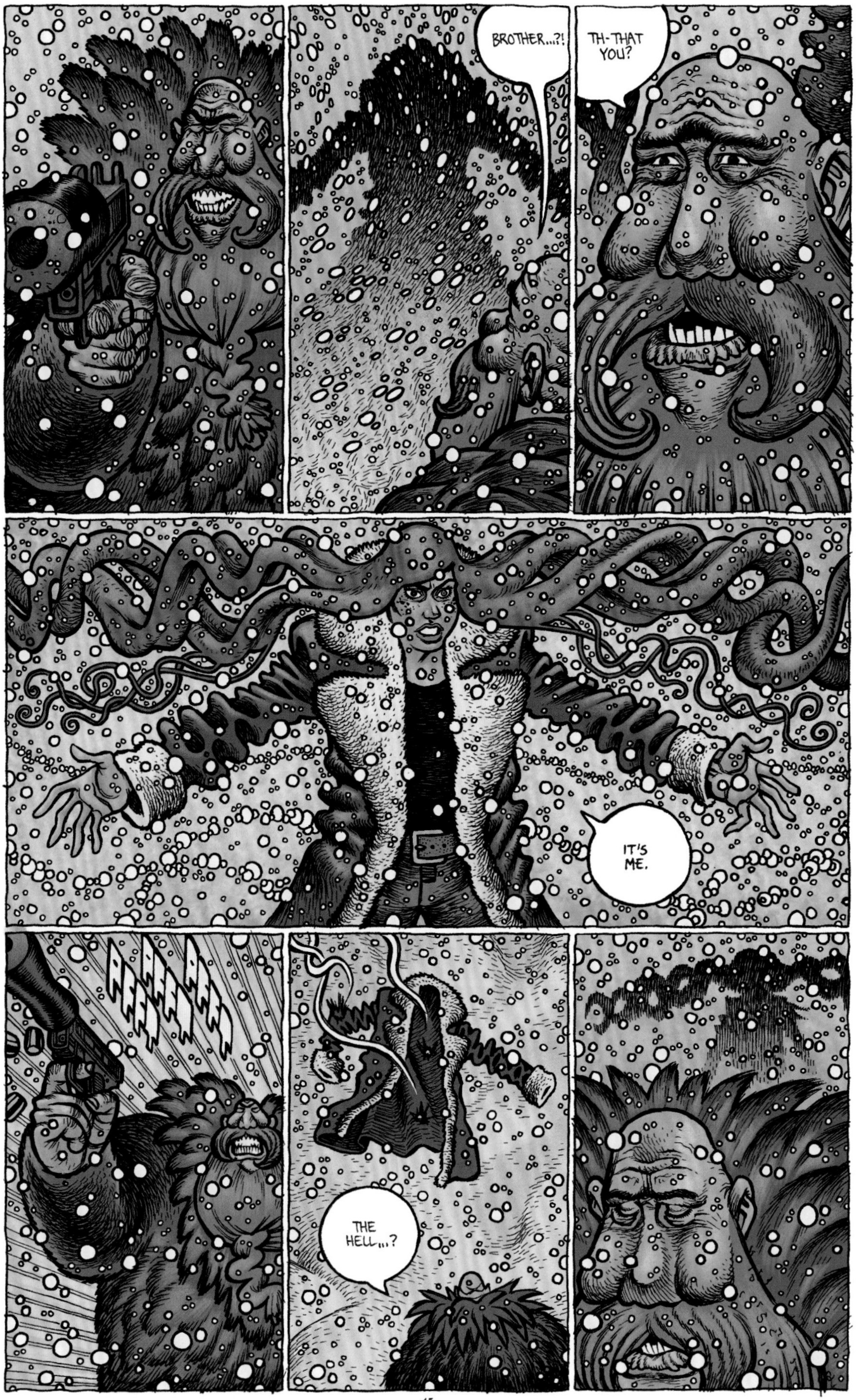
BROTHER...?!
TH-THAT YOU?
IT'S ME.
THE HELL...?

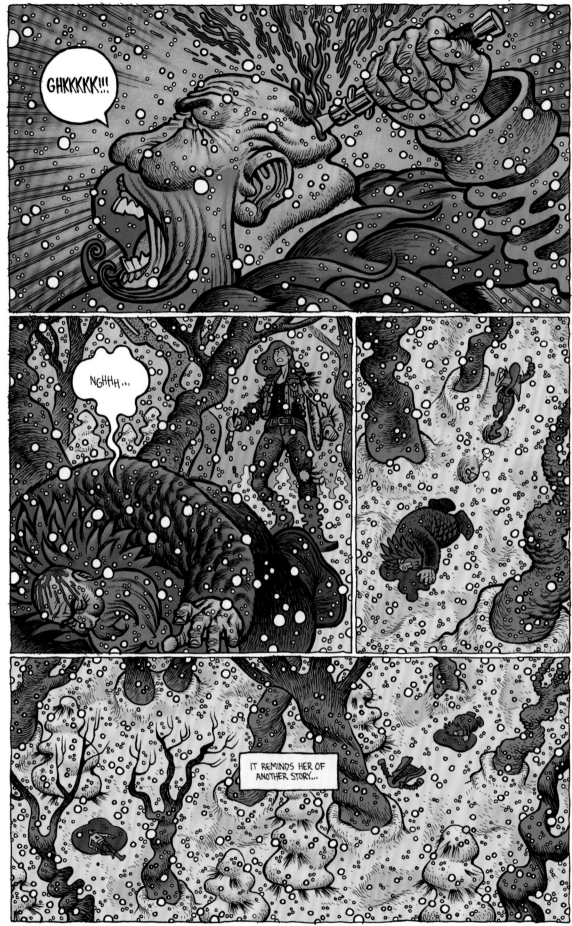

GHKKKKK!!!

NGHHH...

IT REMINDS HER OF ANOTHER STORY...

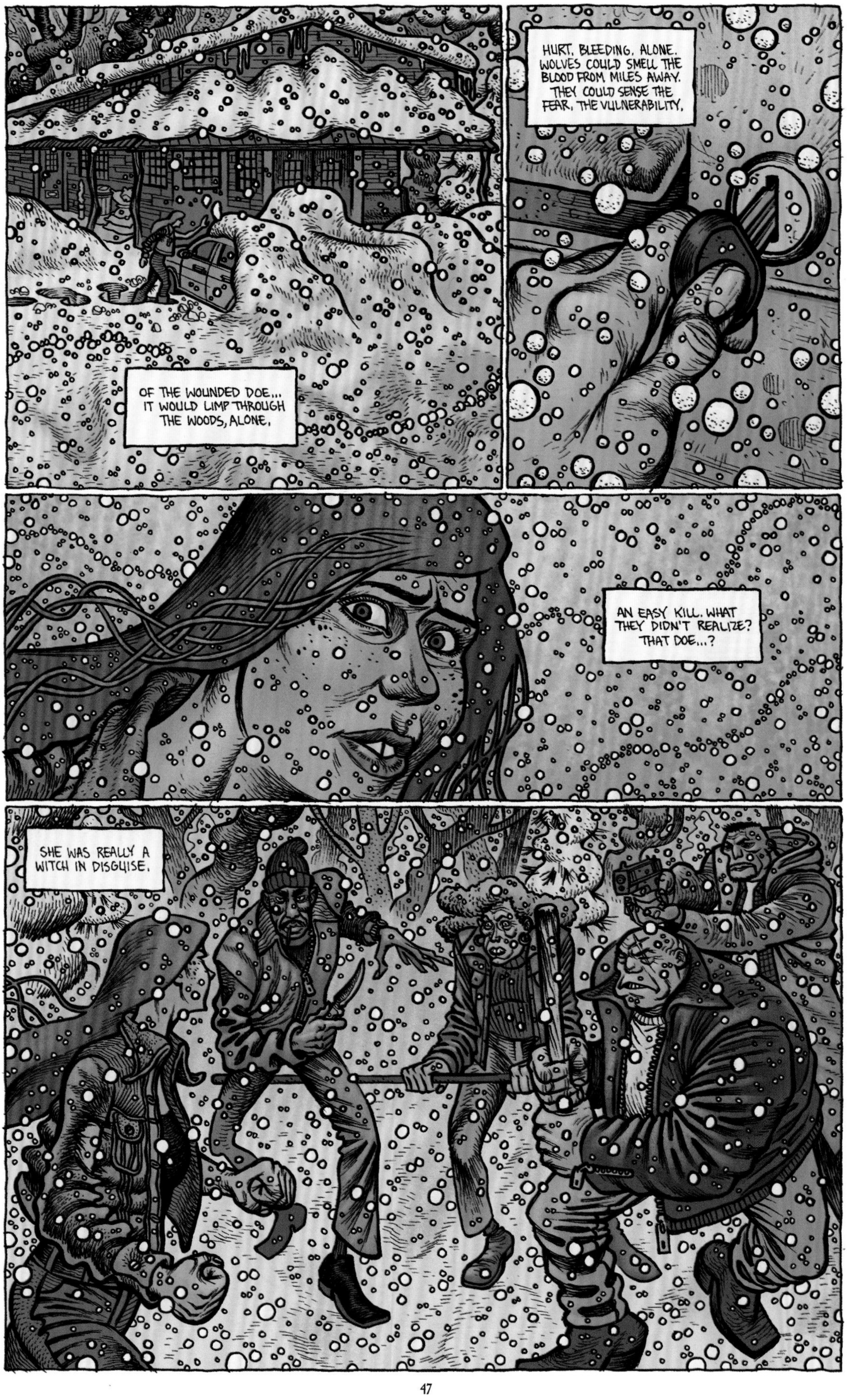
OF THE WOUNDED DOE... IT WOULD LIMP THROUGH THE WOODS, ALONE,
HURT, BLEEDING. ALONE. WOLVES COULD SMELL THE BLOOD FROM MILES AWAY. THEY COULD SENSE THE FEAR, THE VULNERABILITY,
AN EASY KILL. WHAT THEY DIDN'T REALIZE? THAT DOE...?
SHE WAS REALLY A WITCH IN DISGUISE.

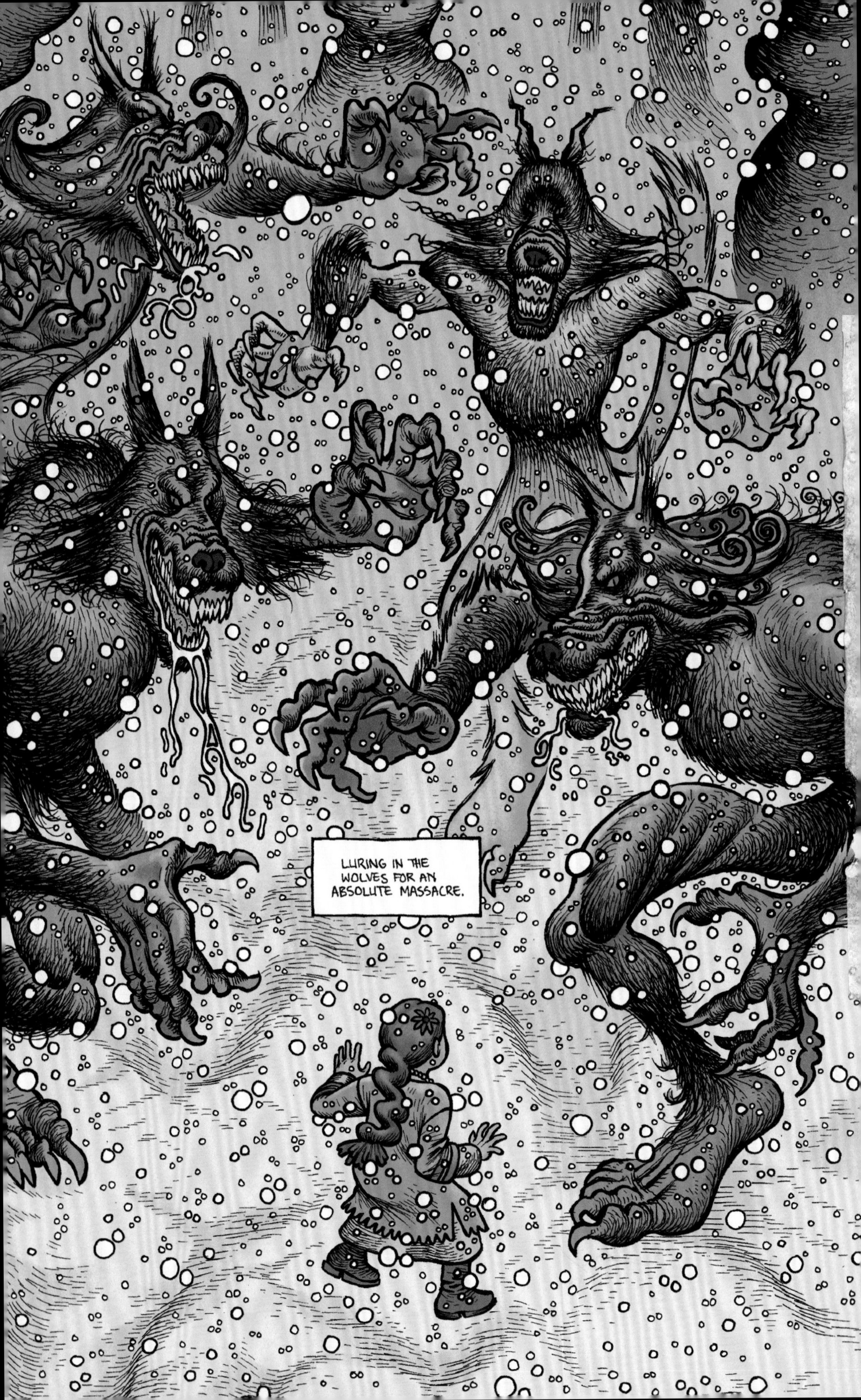
LURING IN THE WOLVES FOR AN ABSOLUTE MASSACRE.

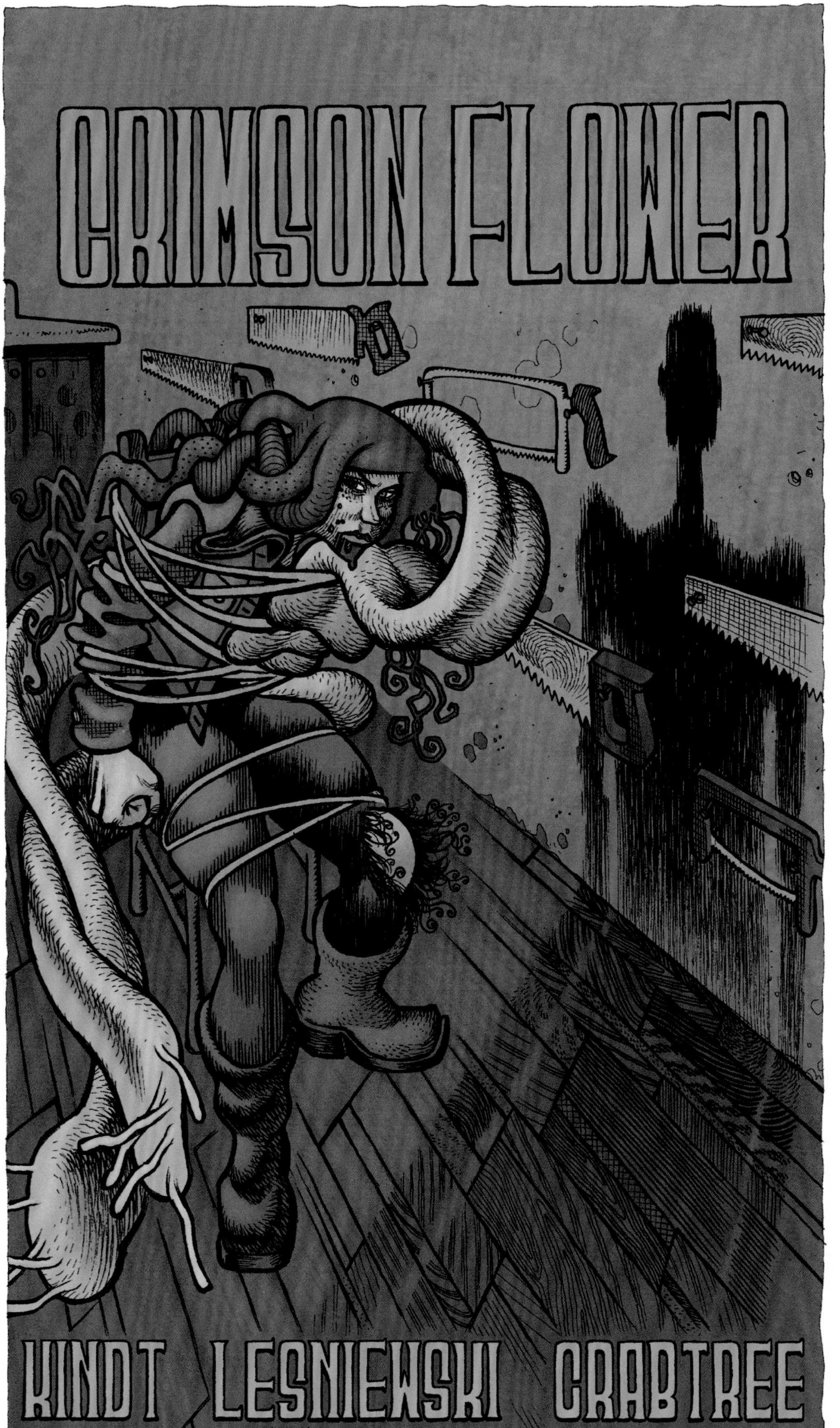
CRIMSON FLOWER
KINDT LESNIEWSKI CRABTREE

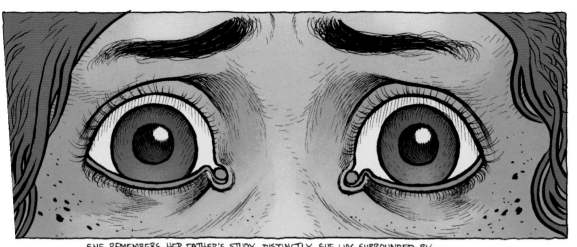

SHE REMEMBERS HER FATHER'S STUDY, DISTINCTLY, SHE WAS SURROUNDED BY...

... WOLVES. NO, THAT'S NOT IT ...

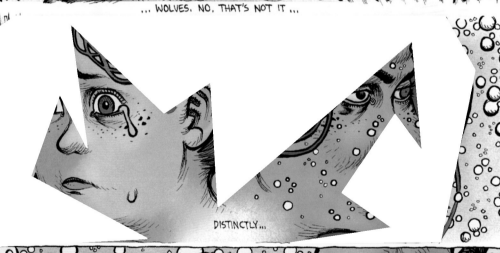

DISTINCTLY...

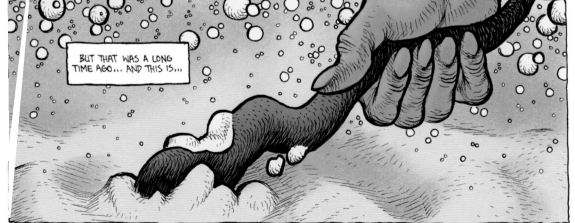

BUT THAT WAS A LONG TIME AGO... AND THIS IS...

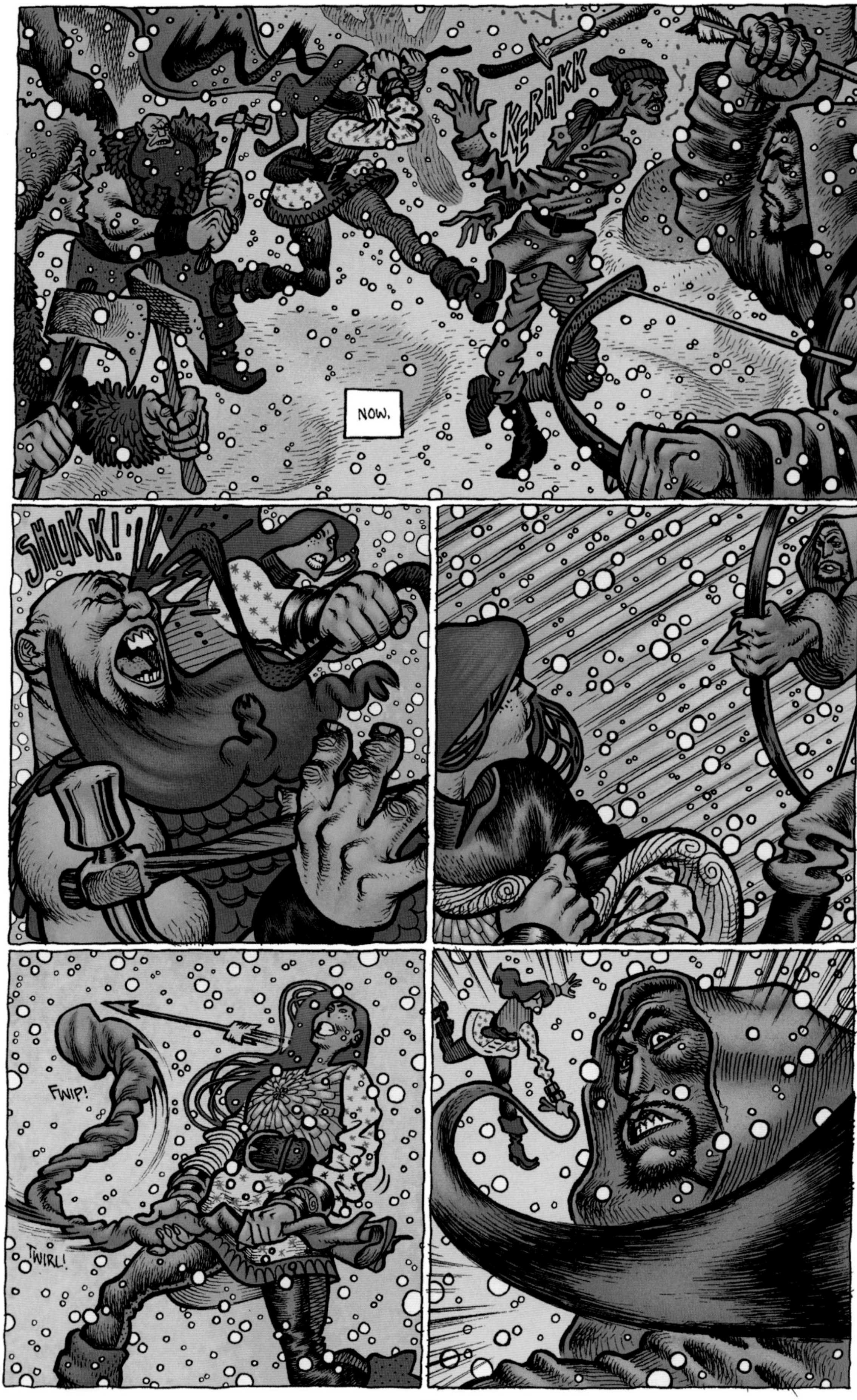

KERAKK
NOW.
SHUKK!
FWIP!
TWIRL!

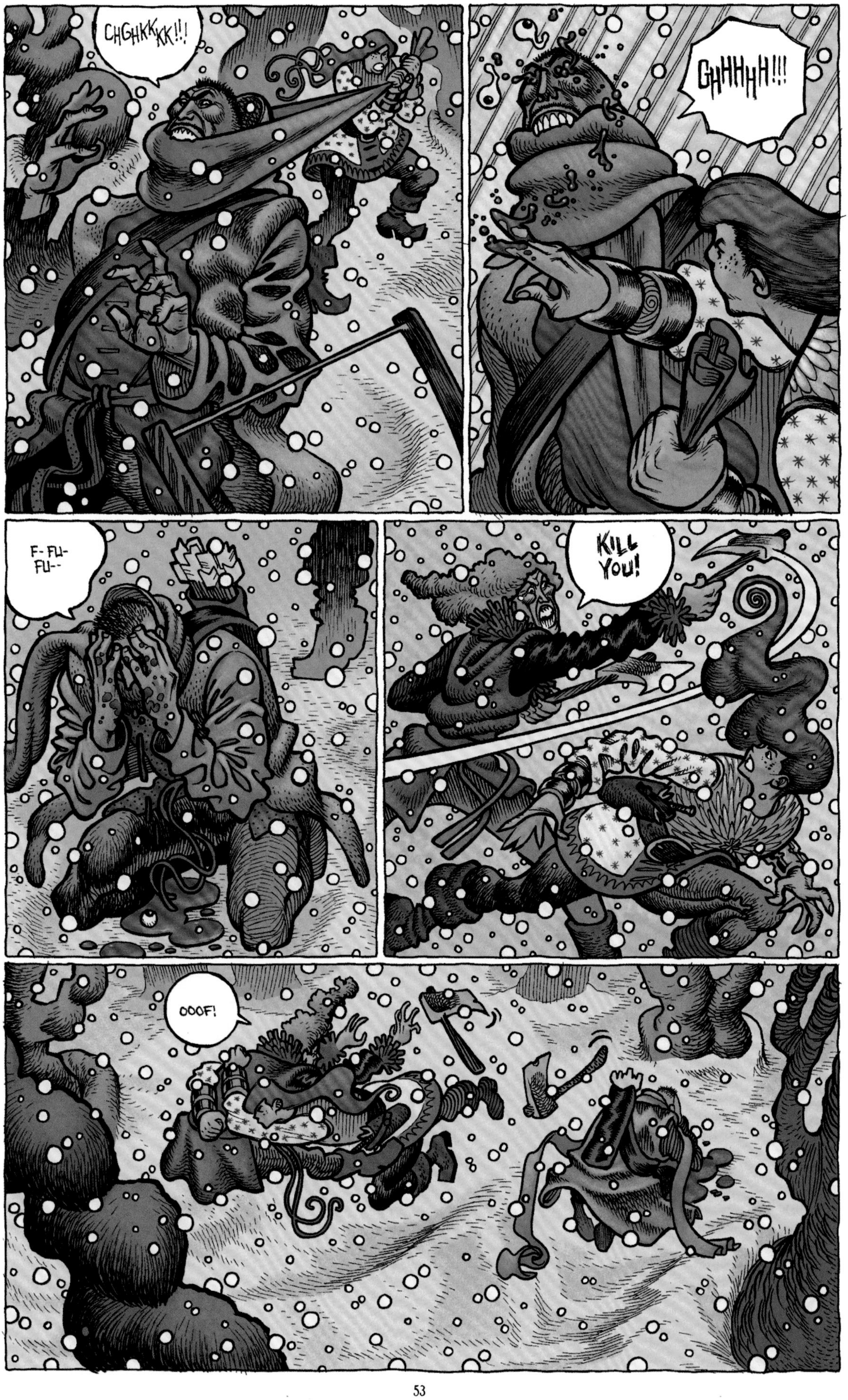
CHGHKKKK!!!
GHHHHH!!!
F- FU-
FU--
KILL
YOU!
OOOF!

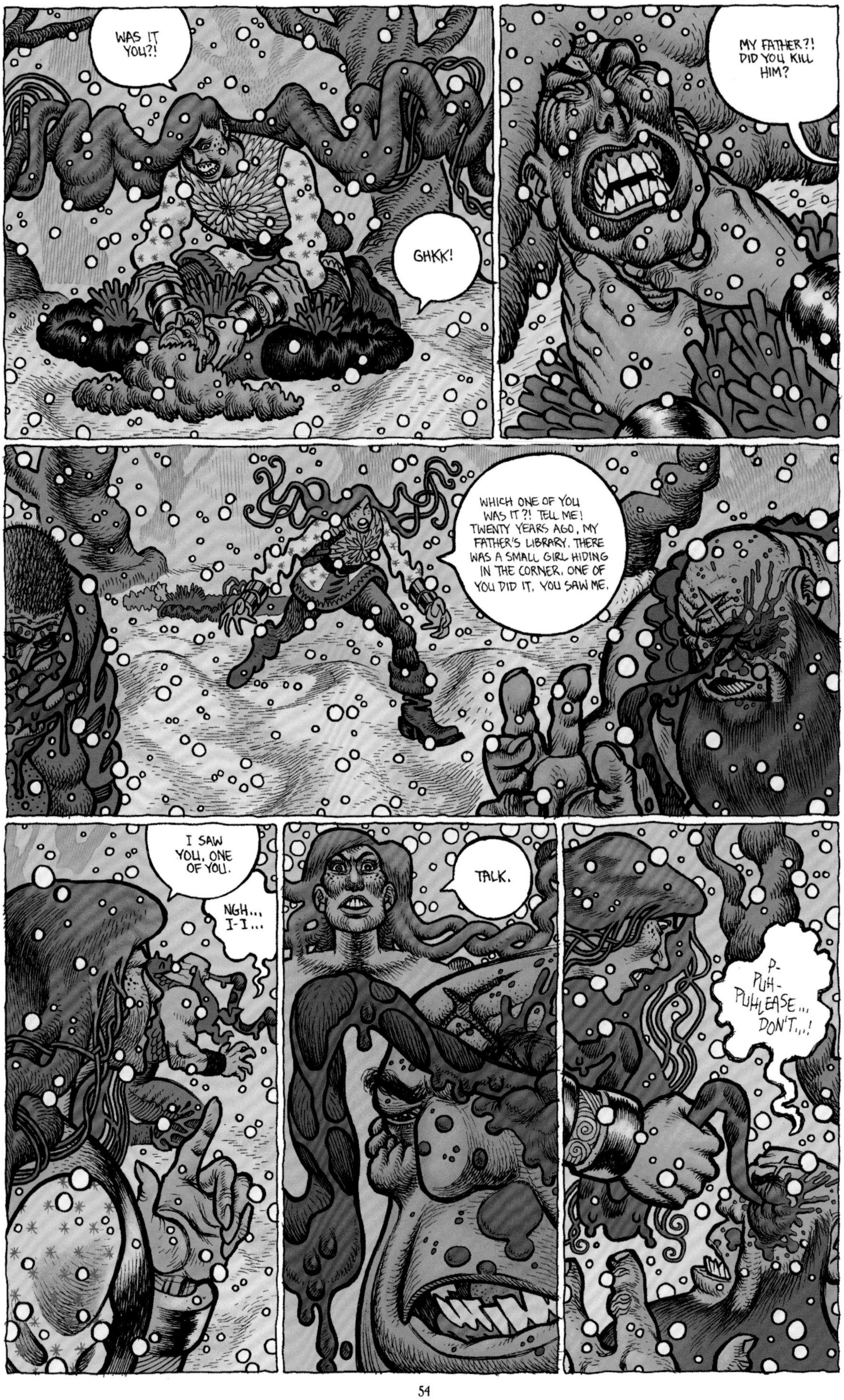
WAS IT YOU?!
GHKK!
MY FATHER?! DID YOU KILL HIM?
WHICH ONE OF YOU WAS IT?! TELL ME! TWENTY YEARS AGO, MY FATHER'S LIBRARY. THERE WAS A SMALL GIRL HIDING IN THE CORNER. ONE OF YOU DID IT. YOU SAW ME.
I SAW YOU. ONE OF YOU.
NGH... I-I...
TALK.
P-PUH-PUHLEASE... DON'T...!

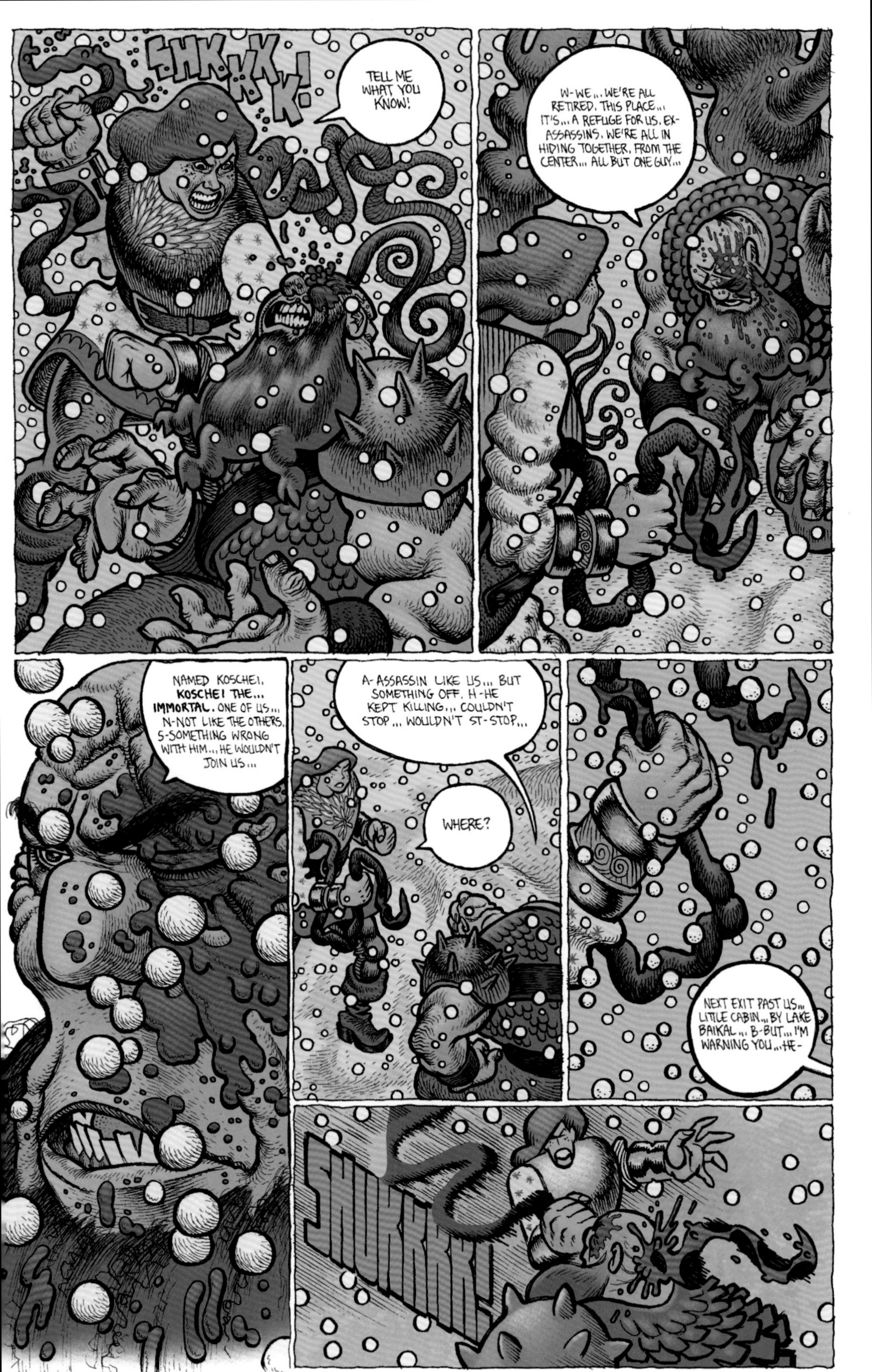
SHKKKK!
TELL ME WHAT YOU KNOW!
W-WE... WE'RE ALL RETIRED. THIS PLACE... IT'S... A REFUGE FOR US. EX-ASSASSINS. WE'RE ALL IN HIDING TOGETHER. FROM THE CENTER... ALL BUT ONE GUY...
NAMED KOSCHEI. **KOSCHEI THE... IMMORTAL.** ONE OF US... N-NOT LIKE THE OTHERS. S-SOMETHING WRONG WITH HIM... HE WOULDN'T JOIN US...
A-ASSASSIN LIKE US... BUT SOMETHING OFF. H-HE KEPT KILLING... COULDN'T STOP... WOULDN'T ST-STOP...
WHERE?
NEXT EXIT PAST US... LITTLE CABIN... BY LAKE BAIKAL... B-BUT... I'M WARNING YOU... HE-
SHUKKKK!

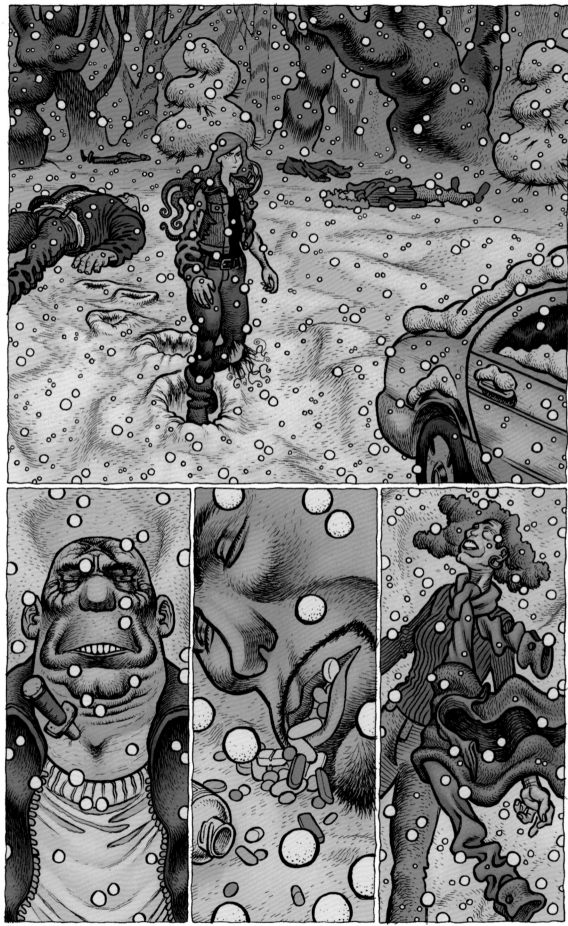

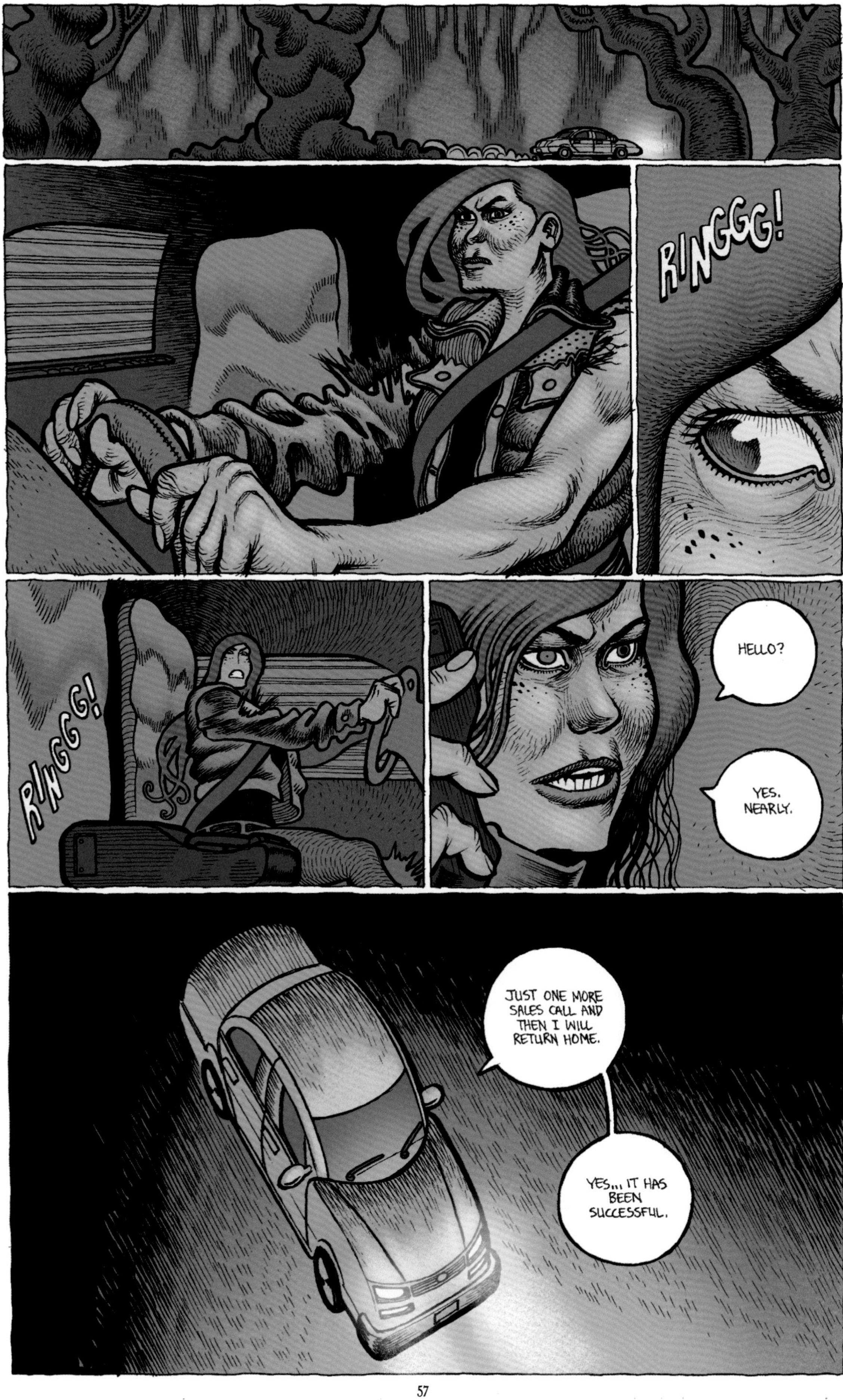
RINGGG!
RINGGG!
HELLO?
YES. NEARLY.
JUST ONE MORE SALES CALL AND THEN I WILL RETURN HOME.
YES... IT HAS BEEN SUCCESSFUL.

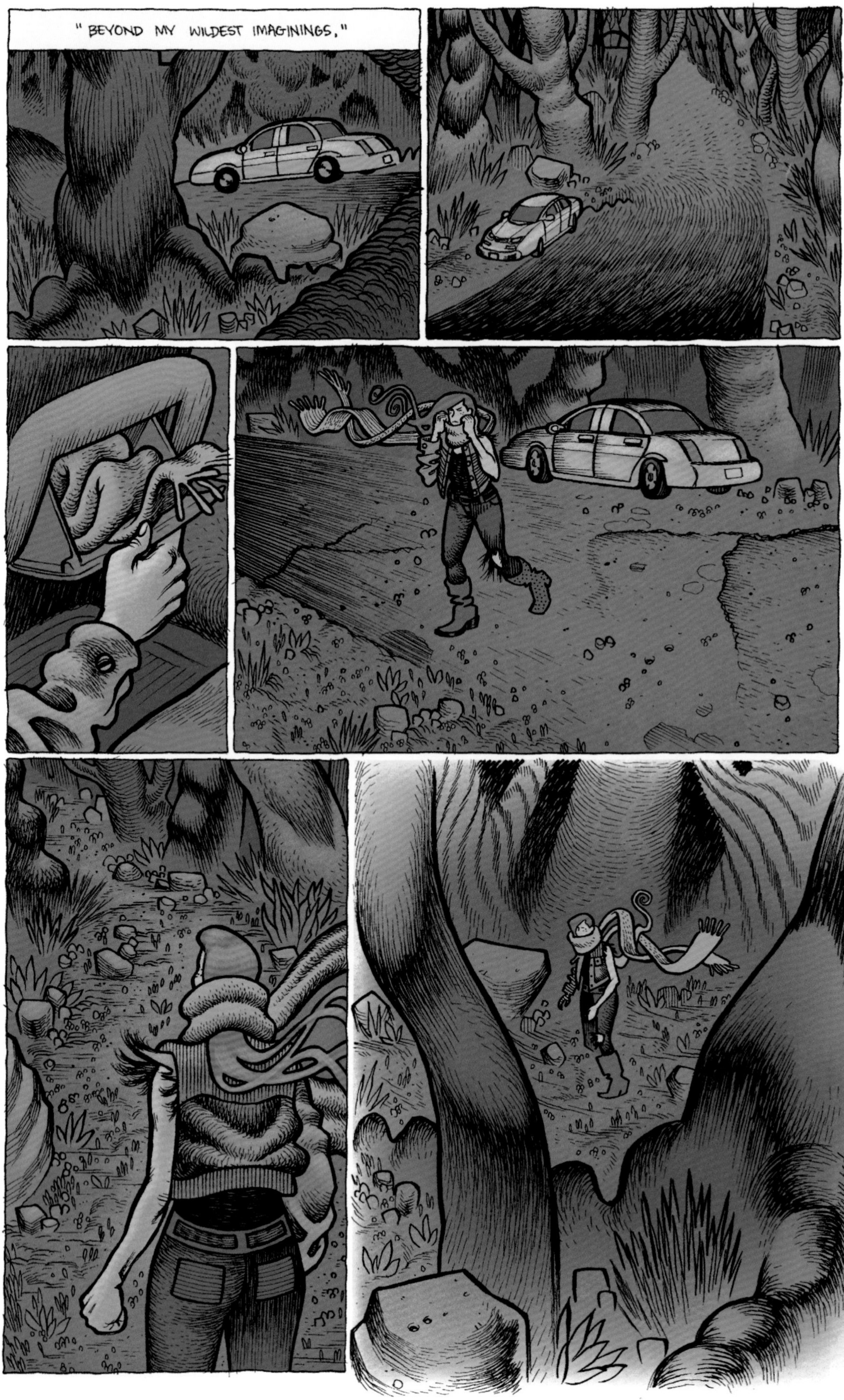
"BEYOND MY WILDEST IMAGININGS,"

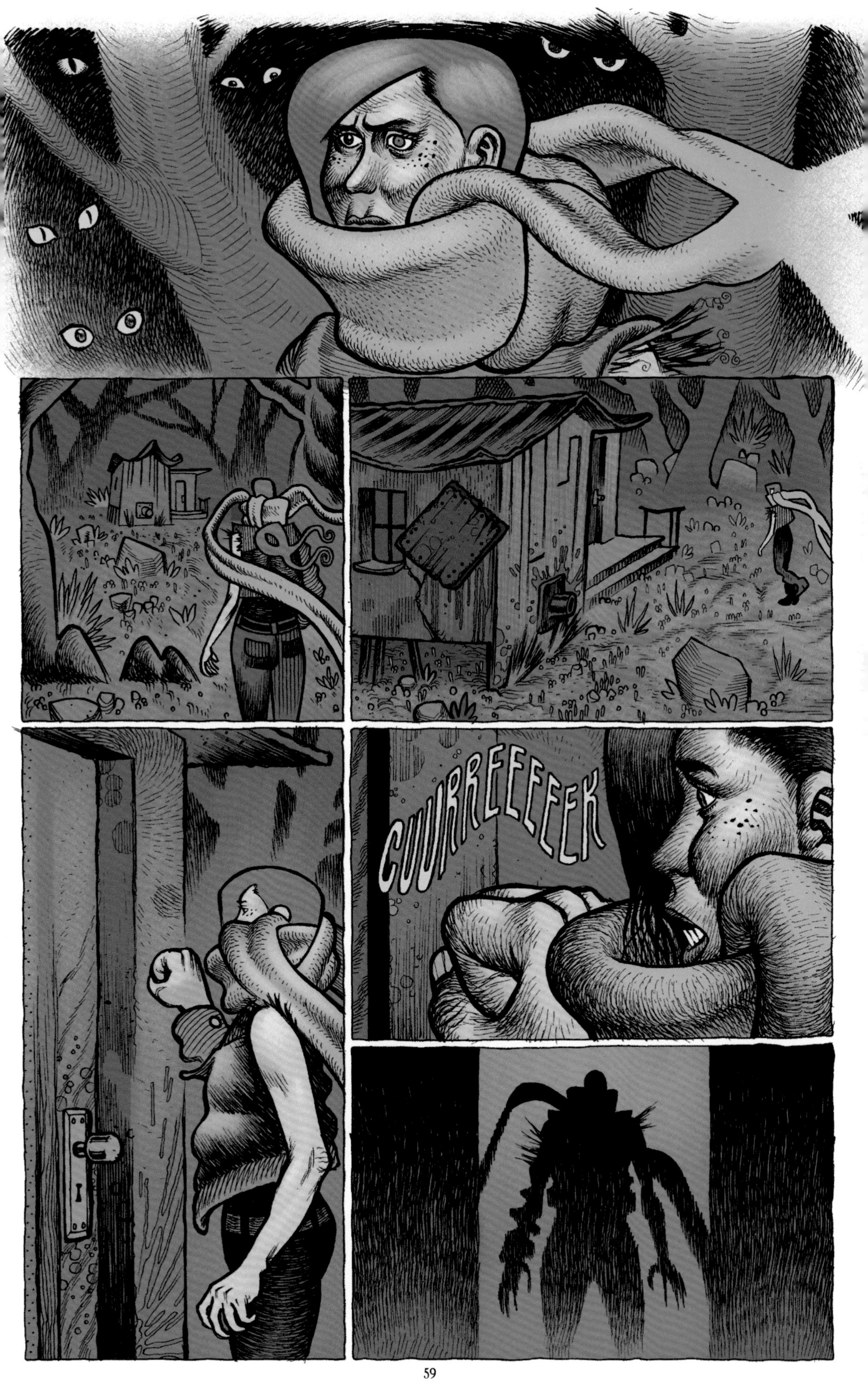
CUURREEEEK

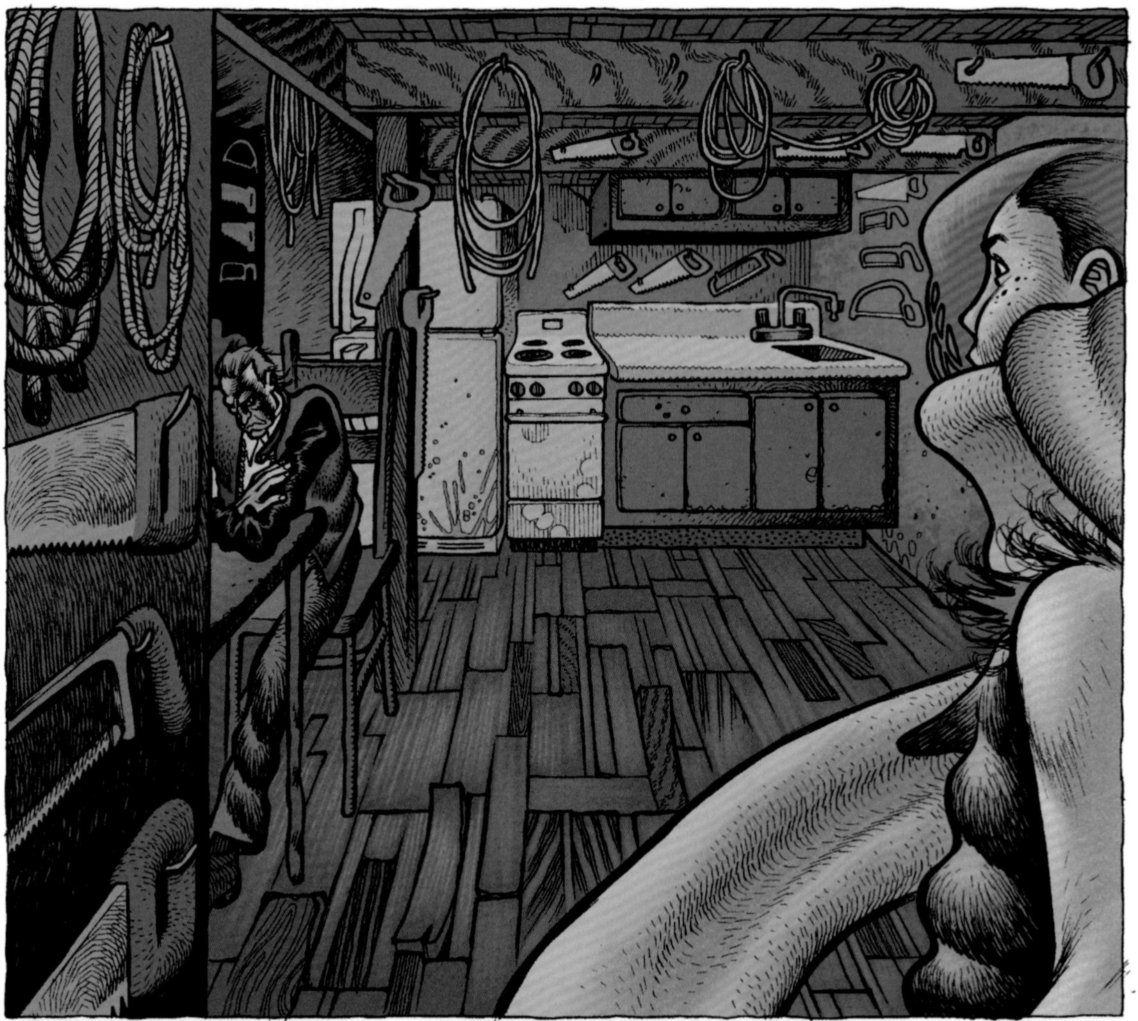

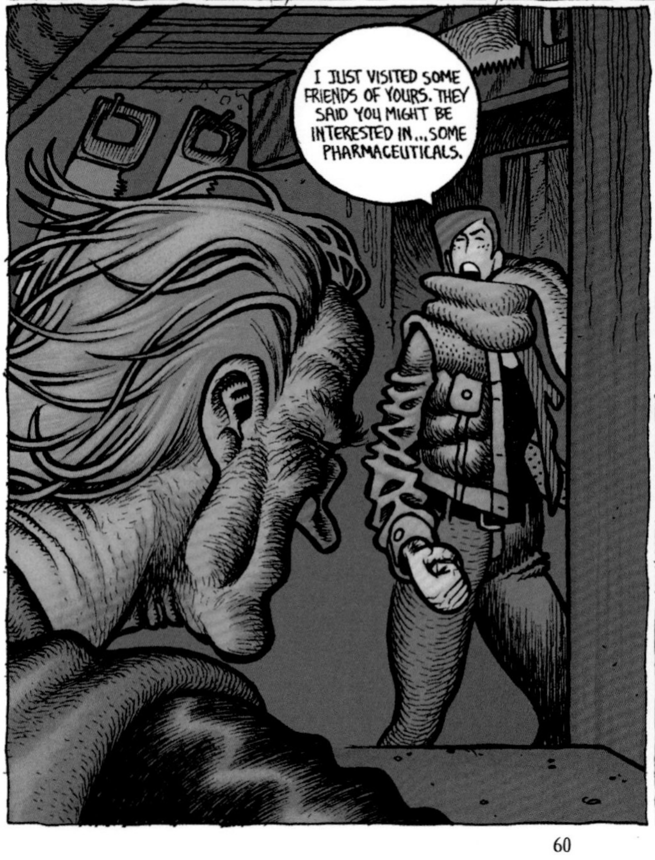
I JUST VISITED SOME FRIENDS OF YOURS. THEY SAID YOU MIGHT BE INTERESTED IN...SOME PHARMACEUTICALS.

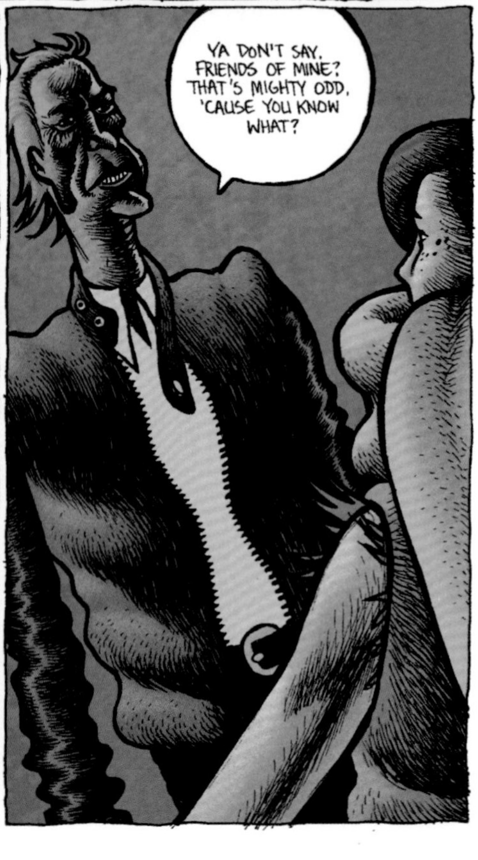
YA DON'T SAY. FRIENDS OF MINE? THAT'S MIGHTY ODD, 'CAUSE YOU KNOW WHAT?

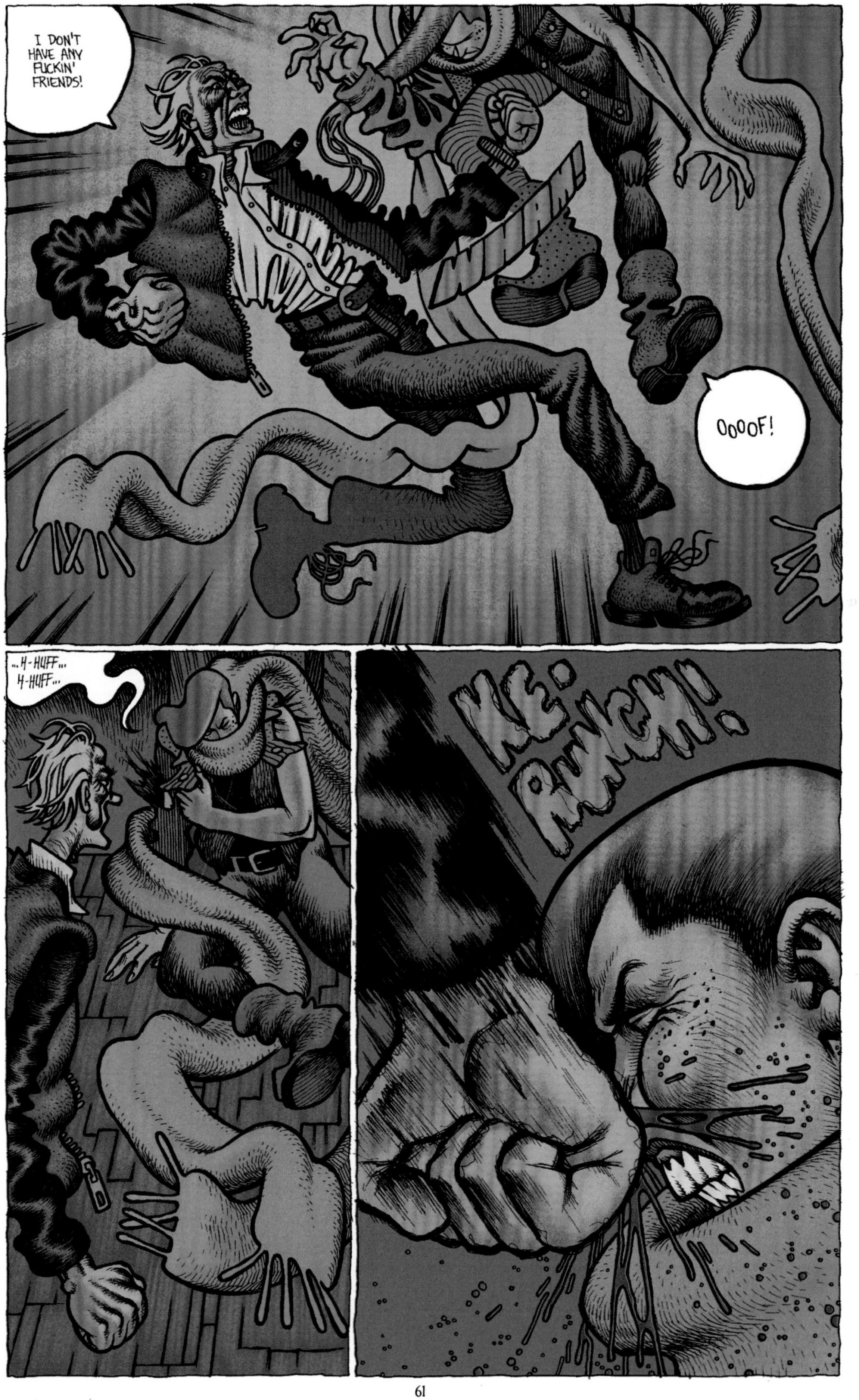
I DON'T HAVE ANY FUCKIN' FRIENDS!
WHAM!
OOOOF!
...H-HUFF... H-HUFF...
KE-RUNCH!

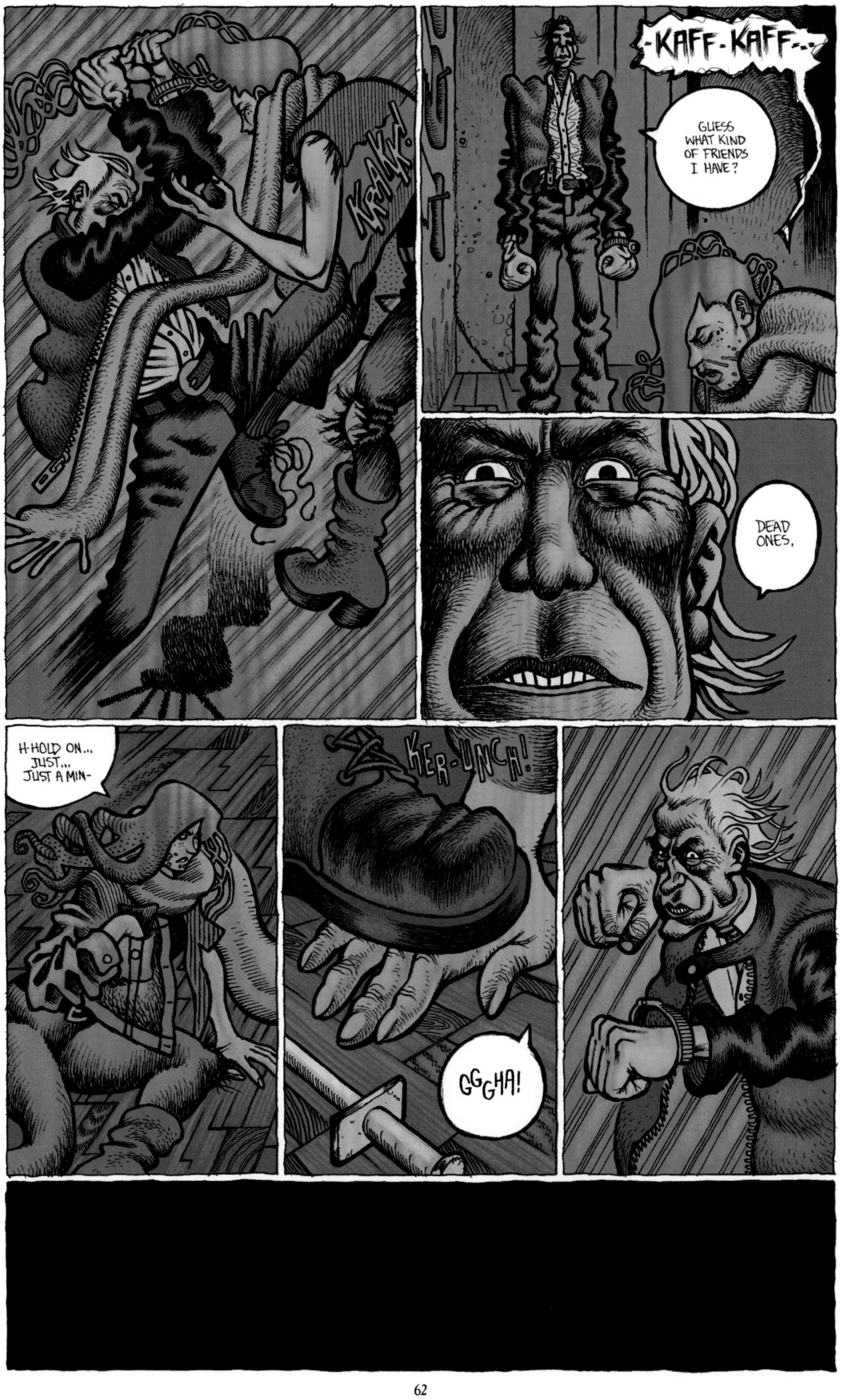
KRAKK!
-KAFF-KAFF-...
GUESS WHAT KIND OF FRIENDS I HAVE?
DEAD ONES.
H-HOLD ON... JUST... JUST A MIN-
KER-UNCH!
GGGHA!

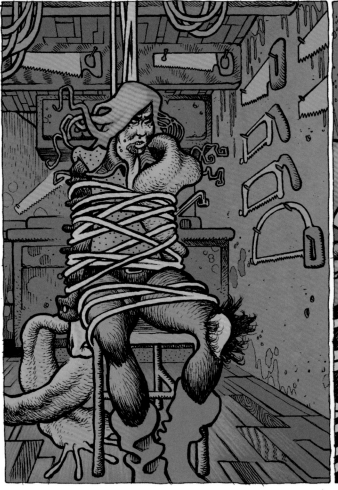

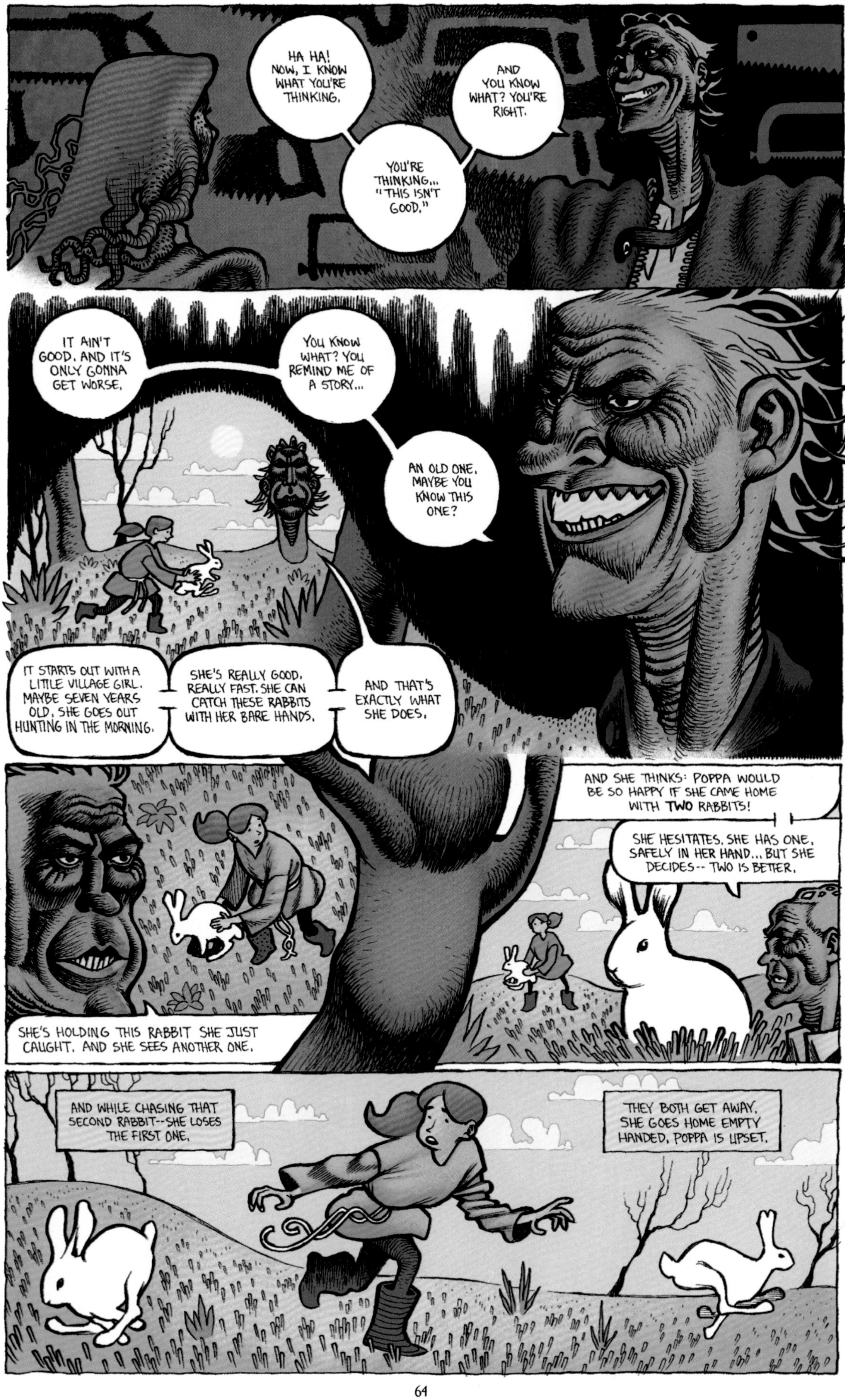
HA HA! NOW, I KNOW WHAT YOU'RE THINKING.
YOU'RE THINKING... "THIS ISN'T GOOD."
AND YOU KNOW WHAT? YOU'RE RIGHT.
IT AIN'T GOOD. AND IT'S ONLY GONNA GET WORSE.
YOU KNOW WHAT? YOU REMIND ME OF A STORY...
AN OLD ONE. MAYBE YOU KNOW THIS ONE?
IT STARTS OUT WITH A LITTLE VILLAGE GIRL. MAYBE SEVEN YEARS OLD. SHE GOES OUT HUNTING IN THE MORNING.
SHE'S REALLY GOOD. REALLY FAST. SHE CAN CATCH THESE RABBITS WITH HER BARE HANDS.
AND THAT'S EXACTLY WHAT SHE DOES.
SHE'S HOLDING THIS RABBIT SHE JUST CAUGHT. AND SHE SEES ANOTHER ONE.
AND SHE THINKS: POPPA WOULD BE SO HAPPY IF SHE CAME HOME WITH TWO RABBITS!
SHE HESITATES. SHE HAS ONE, SAFELY IN HER HAND... BUT SHE DECIDES-- TWO IS BETTER.
AND WHILE CHASING THAT SECOND RABBIT--SHE LOSES THE FIRST ONE.
THEY BOTH GET AWAY. SHE GOES HOME EMPTY HANDED. POPPA IS UPSET.

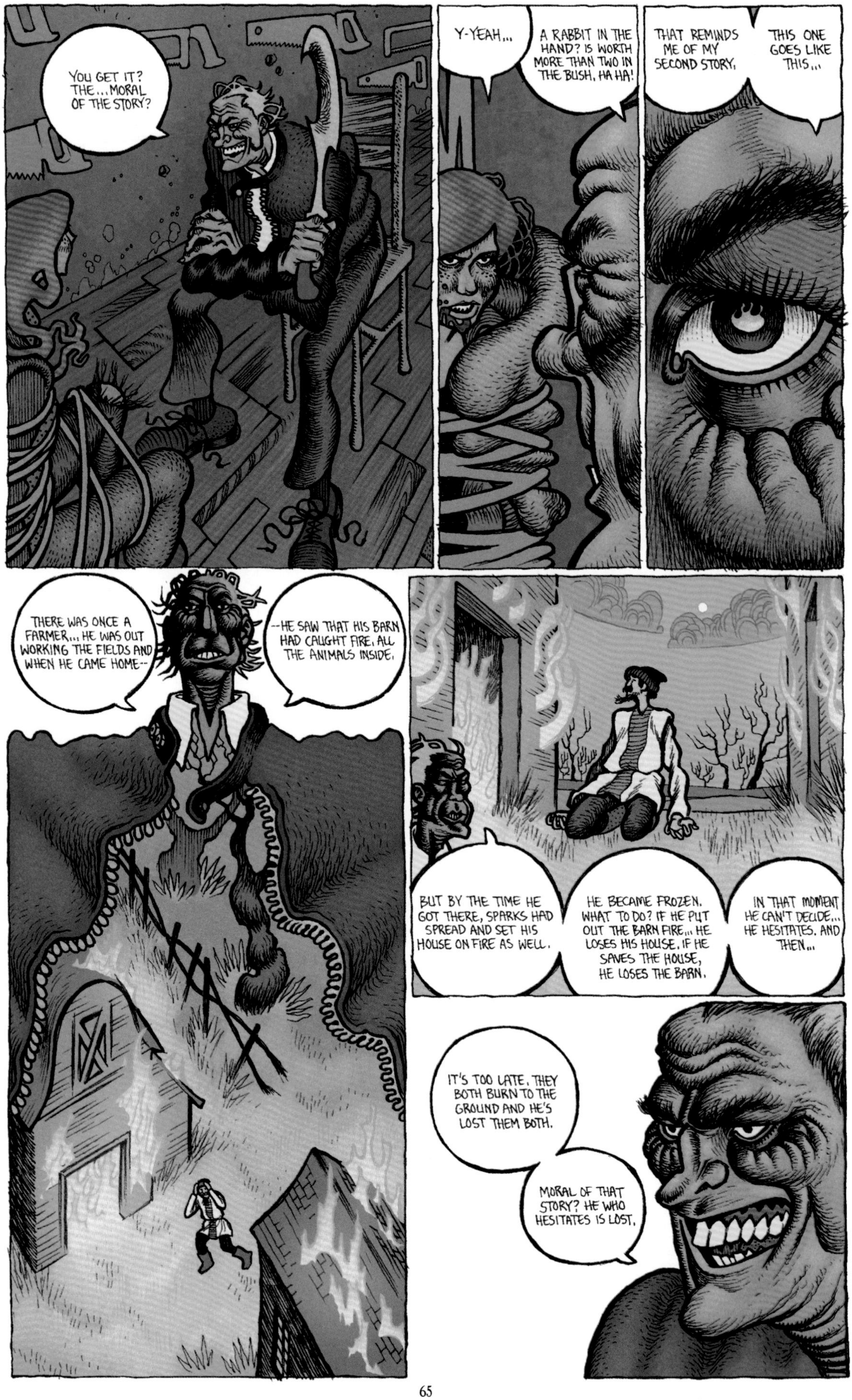
YOU GET IT? THE... MORAL OF THE STORY?
Y-YEAH...
A RABBIT IN THE HAND? IS WORTH MORE THAN TWO IN THE BUSH, HA HA!
THAT REMINDS ME OF MY SECOND STORY.
THIS ONE GOES LIKE THIS...
THERE WAS ONCE A FARMER... HE WAS OUT WORKING THE FIELDS AND WHEN HE CAME HOME--
--HE SAW THAT HIS BARN HAD CAUGHT FIRE. ALL THE ANIMALS INSIDE.
BUT BY THE TIME HE GOT THERE, SPARKS HAD SPREAD AND SET HIS HOUSE ON FIRE AS WELL.
HE BECAME FROZEN. WHAT TO DO? IF HE PUT OUT THE BARN FIRE... HE LOSES HIS HOUSE. IF HE SAVES THE HOUSE, HE LOSES THE BARN.
IN THAT MOMENT HE CAN'T DECIDE... HE HESITATES. AND THEN...
IT'S TOO LATE. THEY BOTH BURN TO THE GROUND AND HE'S LOST THEM BOTH.
MORAL OF THAT STORY? HE WHO HESITATES IS LOST.

HA HA. AND THAT? THAT REMINDS ME OF ONE MORE STORY. WANNA HEAR IT? I'LL TELL YOU.

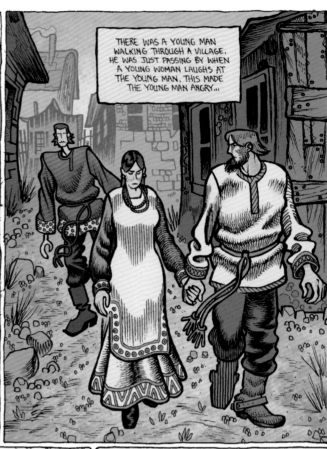

THERE WAS A YOUNG MAN WALKING THROUGH A VILLAGE. HE WAS JUST PASSING BY WHEN A YOUNG WOMAN LAUGHS AT THE YOUNG MAN. THIS MADE THE YOUNG MAN ANGRY...

SO THE YOUNG MAN KILLED THE WOMAN.

THEN THE YOUNG MAN WENT AND KILLED ALL OF THE VILLAGE'S LIVESTOCK. AND THEN?

THE YOUNG MAN WENT AND SET ALL THE HOUSES IN THE VILLAGE ON FIRE.

AS THE VILLAGE BURNED, THE VILLAGERS RAN OUT OF THEIR HOMES AND THE YOUNG MAN MURDERED THEM, CUTTING THEM DOWN AS THEY RAN BY, CHOPPING THEM TO PIECES.

AND THEN? AFTER THEY WERE ALL DEAD AND THE VILLAGE WAS NOTHING BUT A SMOKING RUIN?

THE YOUNG MAN RAPED THE CORPSES OF THAT VILLAGE.

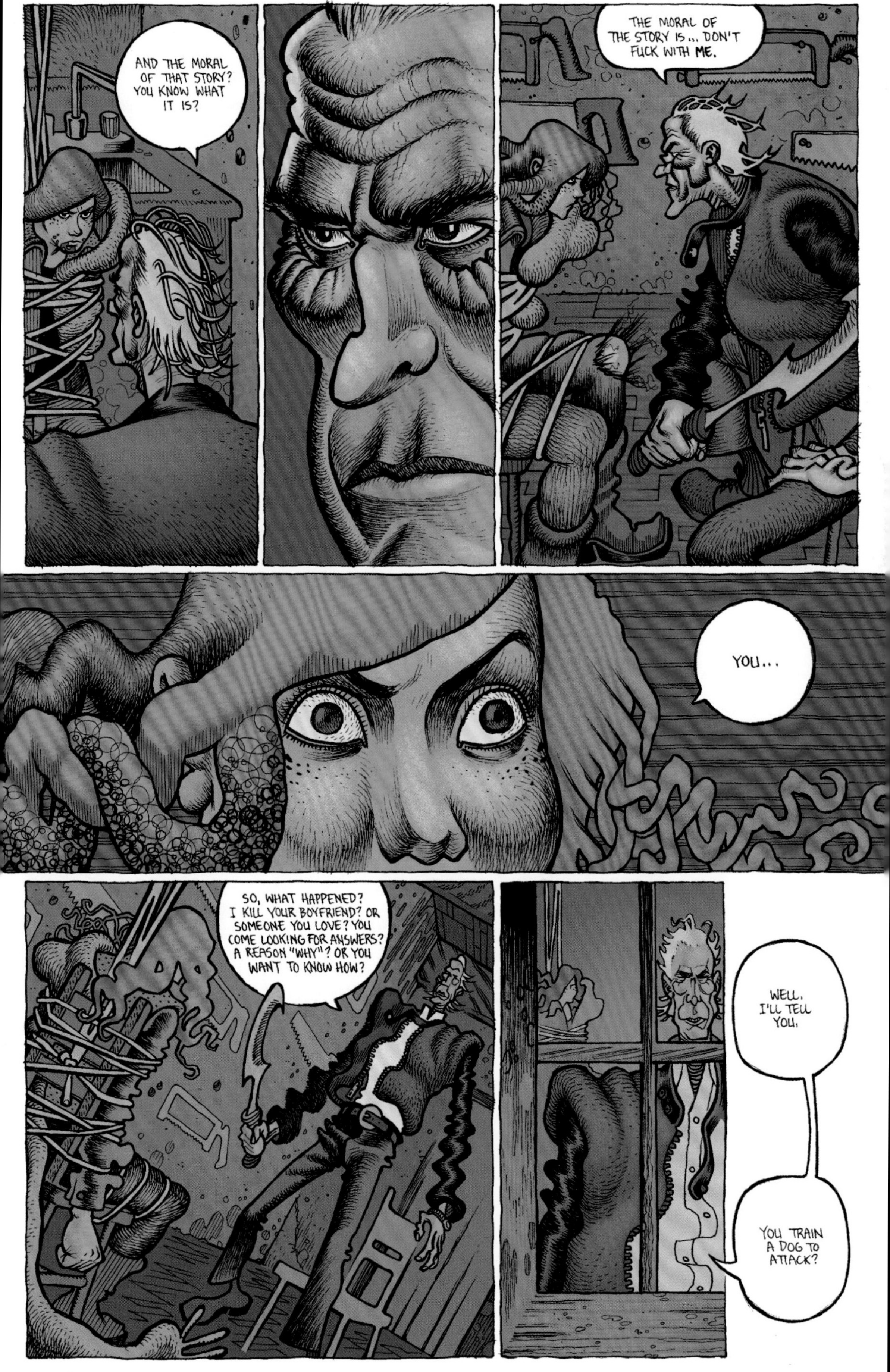
AND THE MORAL OF THAT STORY? YOU KNOW WHAT IT IS?
THE MORAL OF THE STORY IS... DON'T FUCK WITH ME.
YOU...
SO, WHAT HAPPENED? I KILL YOUR BOYFRIEND? OR SOMEONE YOU LOVE? YOU COME LOOKING FOR ANSWERS? A REASON "WHY"? OR YOU WANT TO KNOW HOW?
WELL, I'LL TELL YOU.
YOU TRAIN A DOG TO ATTACK?

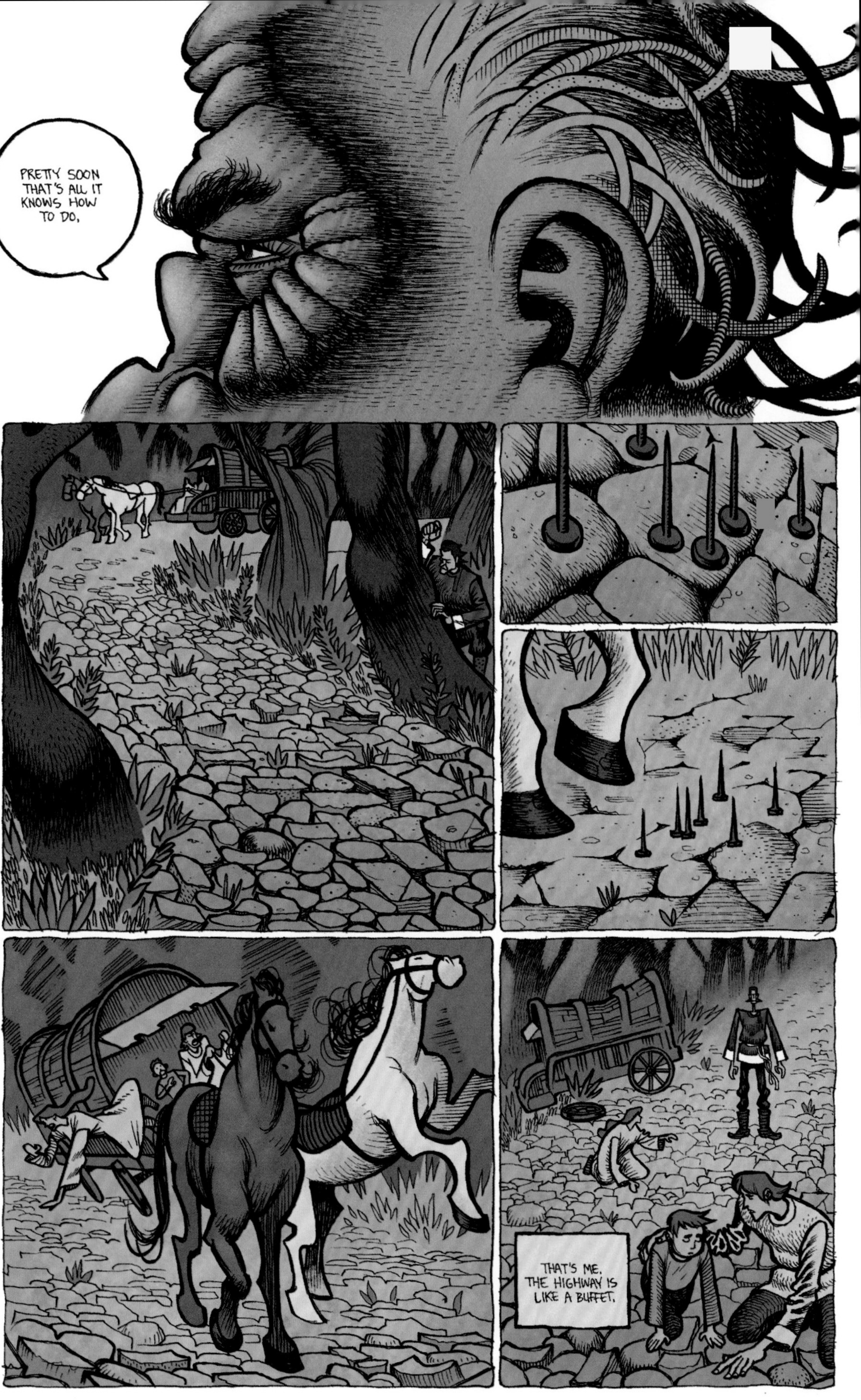
PRETTY SOON THAT'S ALL IT KNOWS HOW TO DO,
THAT'S ME. THE HIGHWAY IS LIKE A BUFFET.

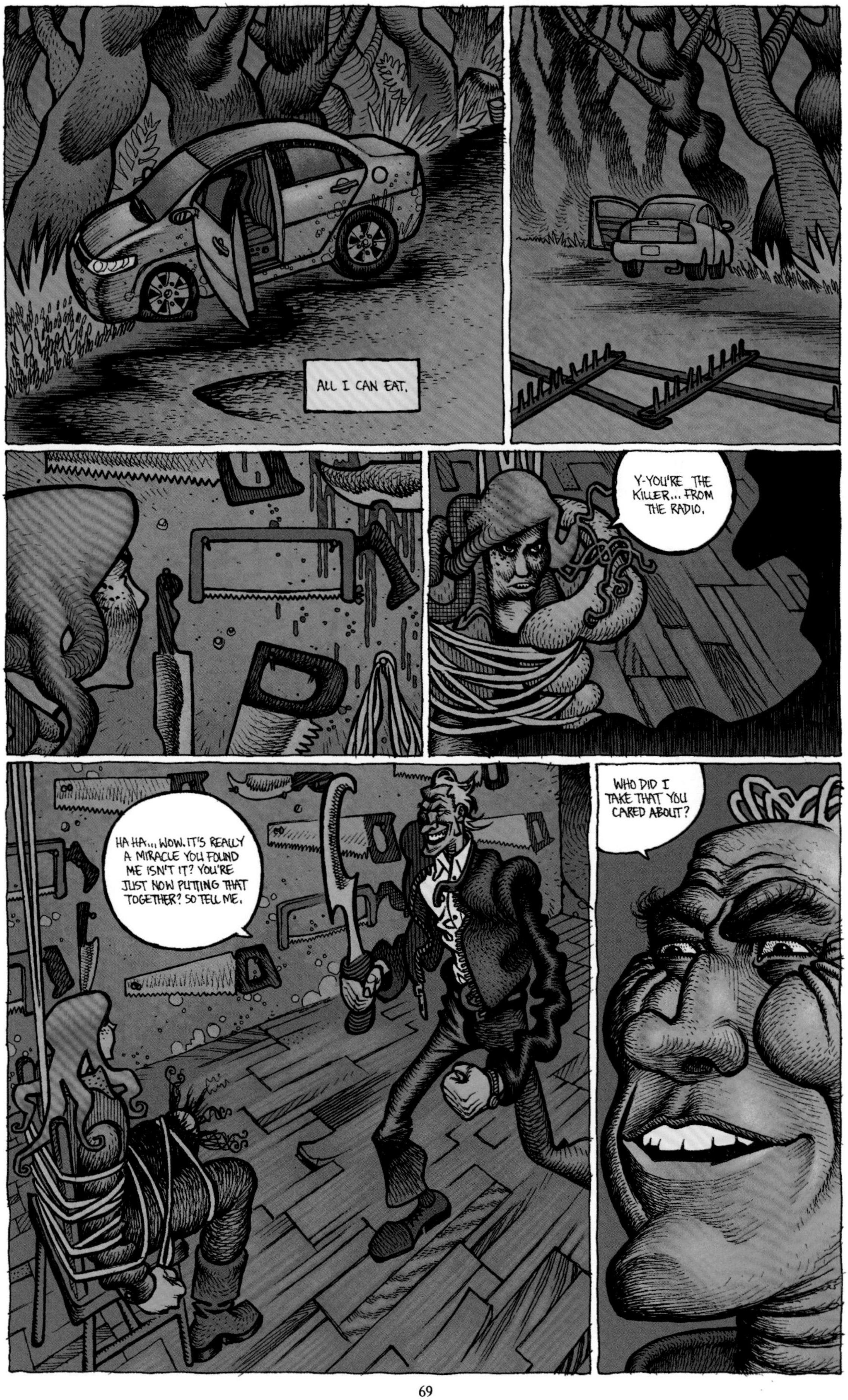
ALL I CAN EAT.
Y-YOU'RE THE KILLER... FROM THE RADIO.
HA HA... WOW. IT'S REALLY A MIRACLE YOU FOUND ME ISN'T IT? YOU'RE JUST NOW PUTTING THAT TOGETHER? SO TELL ME.
WHO DID I TAKE THAT YOU CARED ABOUT?

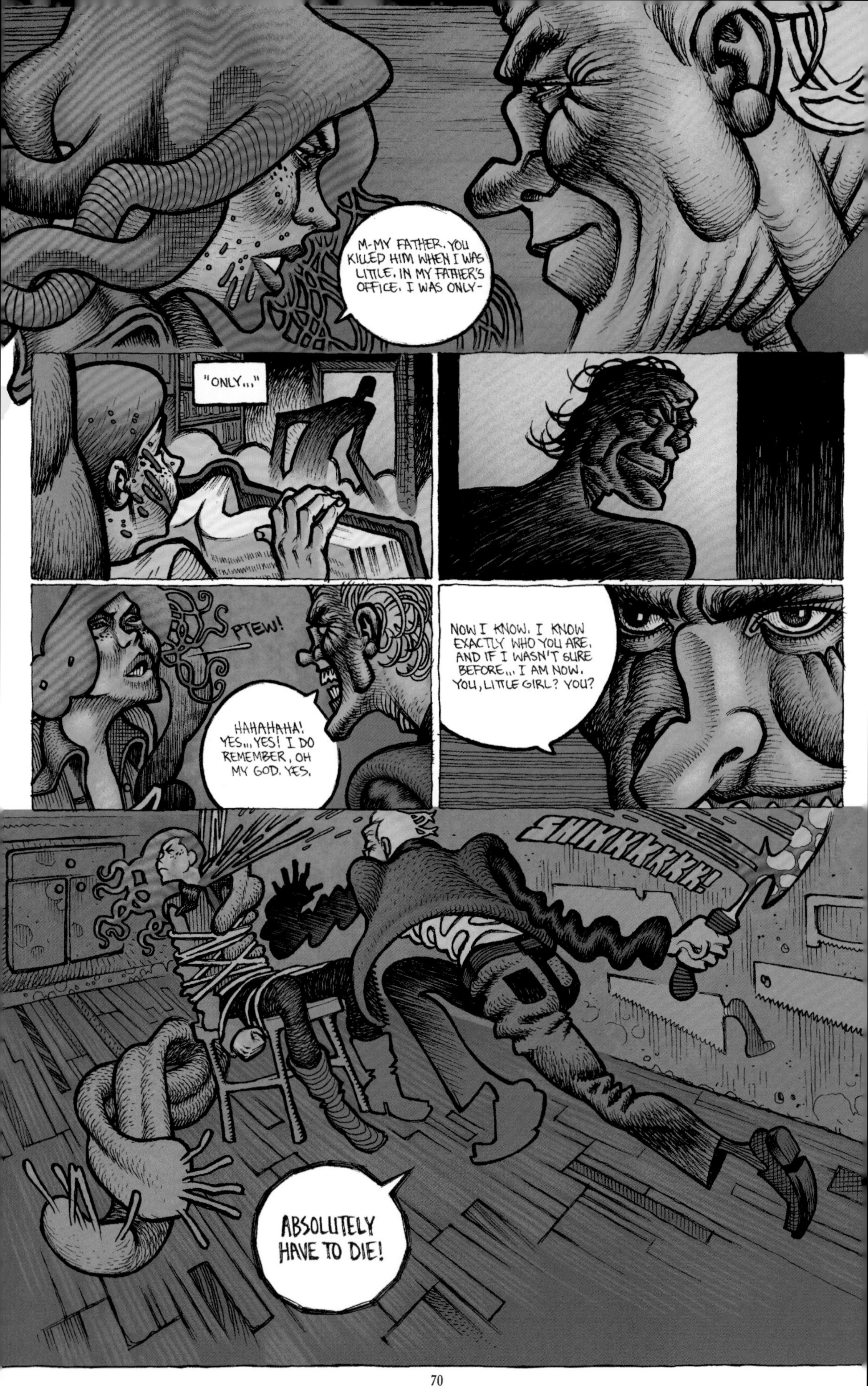
M-MY FATHER. YOU KILLED HIM WHEN I WAS LITTLE. IN MY FATHER'S OFFICE. I WAS ONLY-
"ONLY..."
PTEW!
HAHAHAHA! YES... YES! I DO REMEMBER, OH MY GOD. YES.
NOW I KNOW. I KNOW EXACTLY WHO YOU ARE. AND IF I WASN'T SURE BEFORE... I AM NOW. YOU, LITTLE GIRL? YOU?
SHINKKKKKK!
ABSOLUTELY HAVE TO DIE!

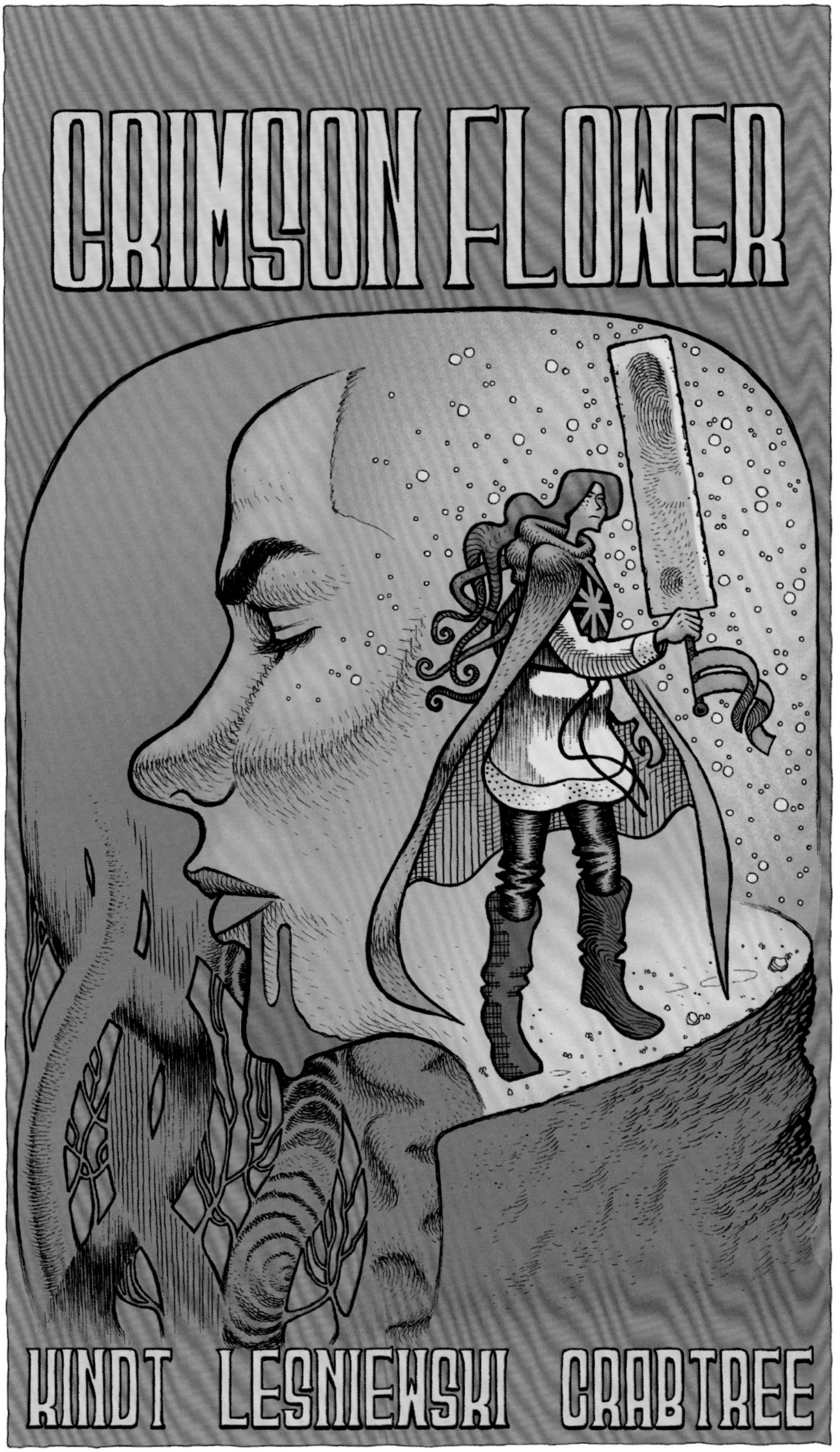
CRIMSON FLOWER
KINDT LESNIEWSKI CRABTREE

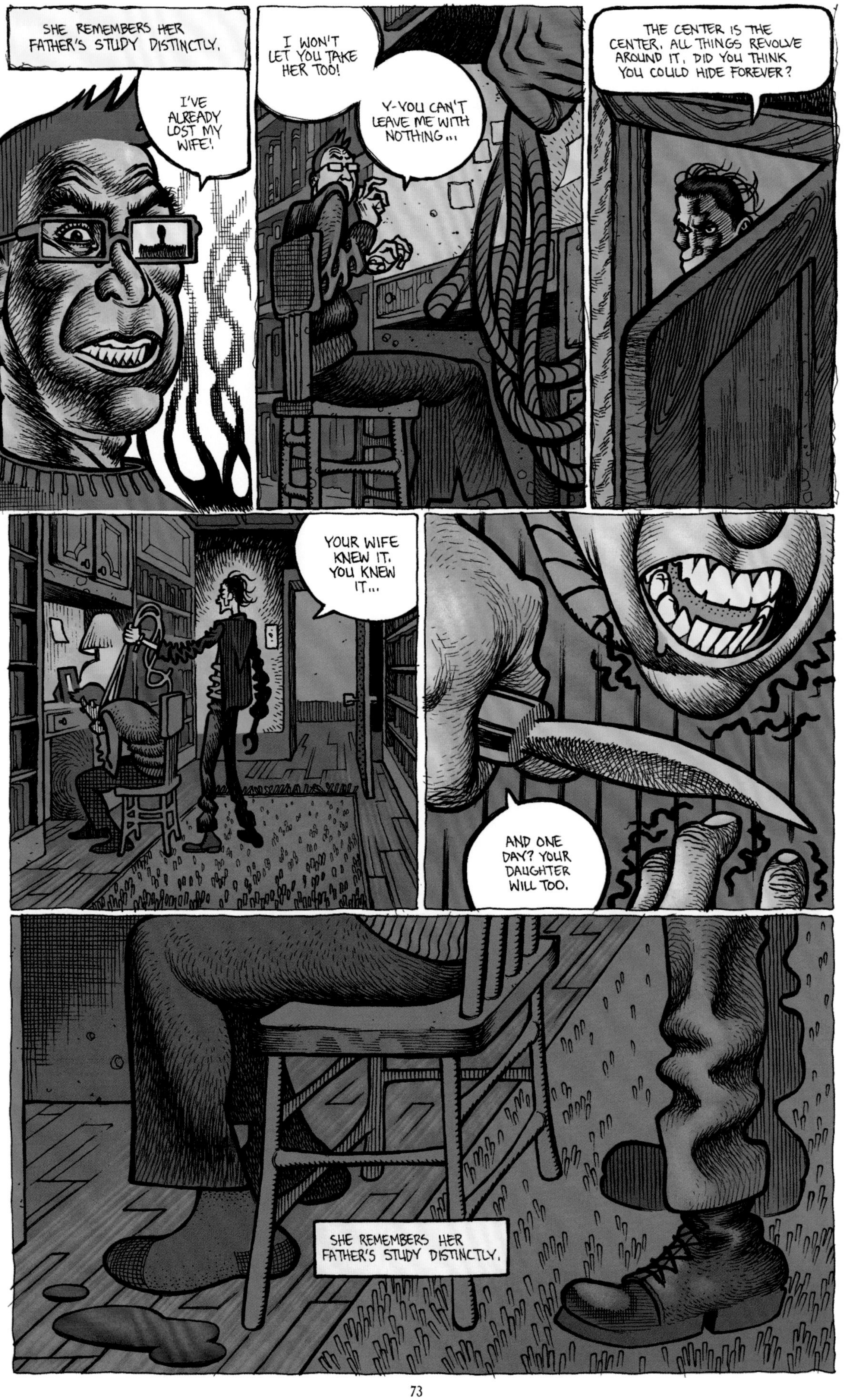
SHE REMEMBERS HER FATHER'S STUDY DISTINCTLY.
I'VE ALREADY LOST MY WIFE!
I WON'T LET YOU TAKE HER TOO!
Y-YOU CAN'T LEAVE ME WITH NOTHING...
THE CENTER IS THE CENTER. ALL THINGS REVOLVE AROUND IT. DID YOU THINK YOU COULD HIDE FOREVER?
YOUR WIFE KNEW IT. YOU KNEW IT...
AND ONE DAY? YOUR DAUGHTER WILL TOO.
SHE REMEMBERS HER FATHER'S STUDY DISTINCTLY.

IF SHE WAS QUIET, HE WOULD LET HER KEEP HIM COMPANY.

AND SHE WAS ALWAYS VERY QUIET.

IT WAS LIKE A GAME.

"ALL BUT THE GIRL, DO NOT..."

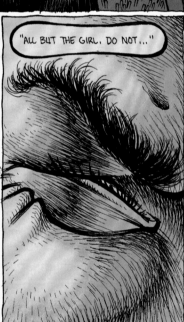

"DO NOT KILL THE GIRL,"

IT WAS LIKE A GAME.

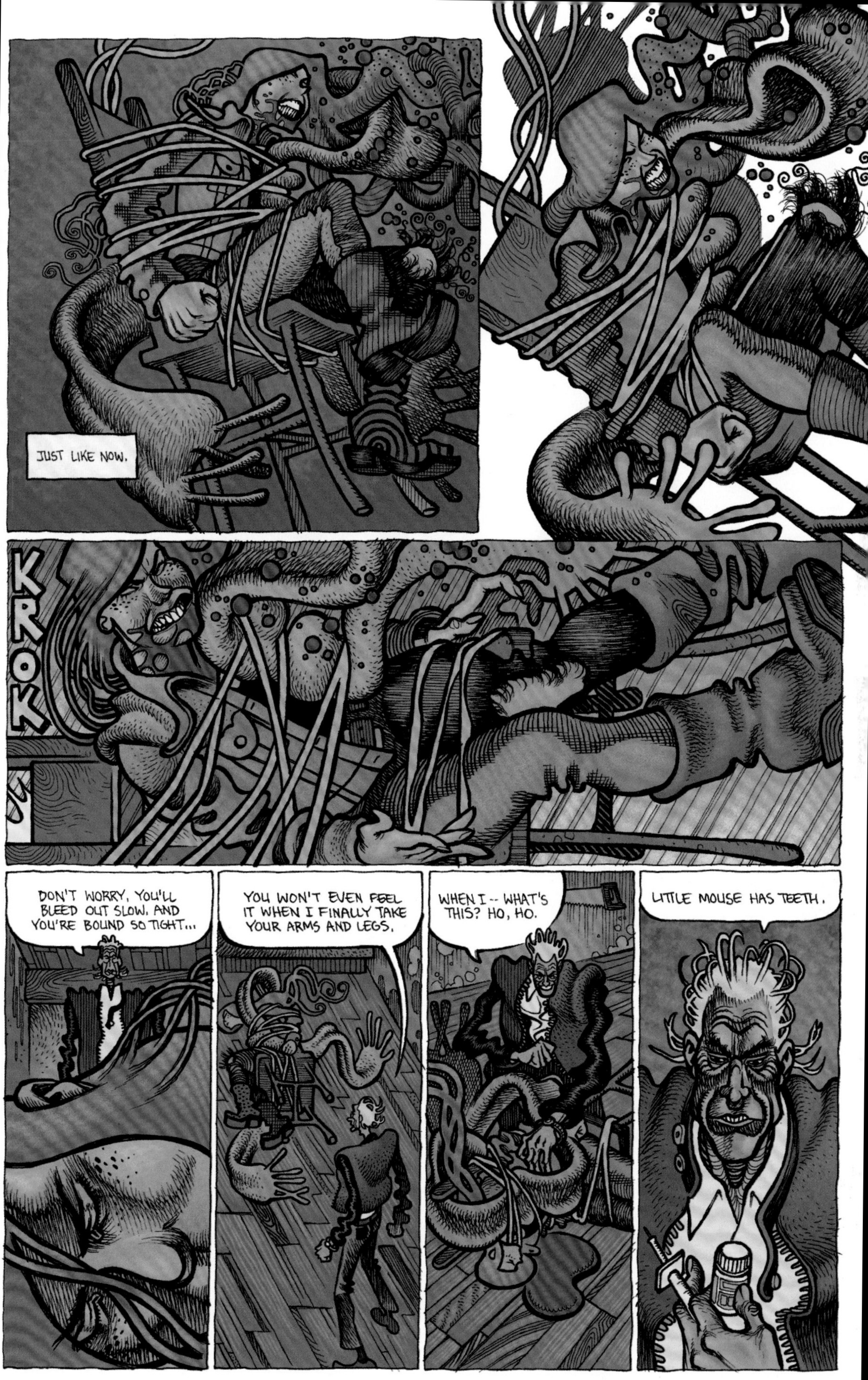
JUST LIKE NOW.
KROK
DON'T WORRY, YOU'LL BLEED OUT SLOW, AND YOU'RE BOUND SO TIGHT...
YOU WON'T EVEN FEEL IT WHEN I FINALLY TAKE YOUR ARMS AND LEGS.
WHEN I -- WHAT'S THIS? HO, HO.
LITTLE MOUSE HAS TEETH.

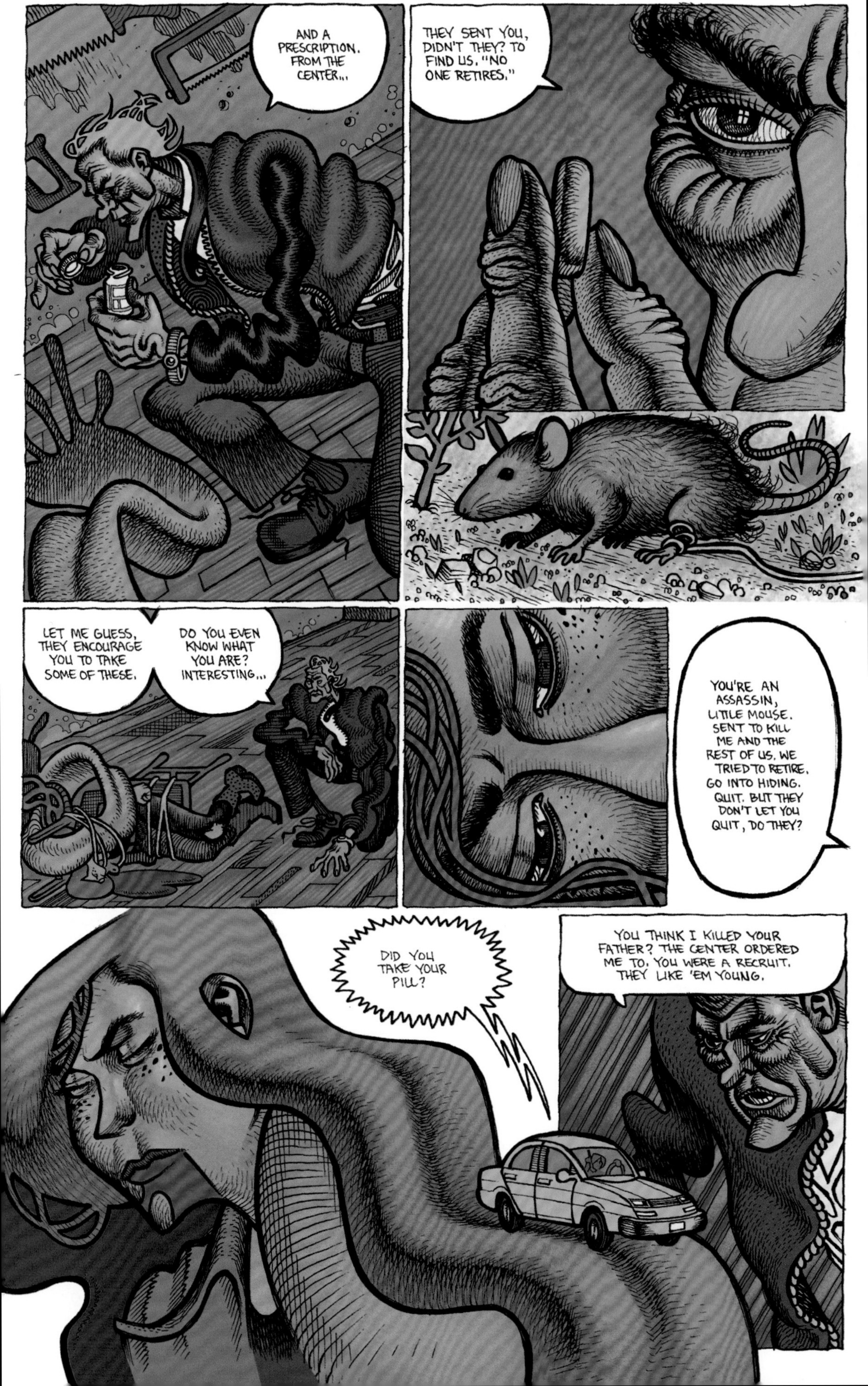
AND A PRESCRIPTION. FROM THE CENTER...
THEY SENT YOU, DIDN'T THEY? TO FIND US. "NO ONE RETIRES."
LET ME GUESS, THEY ENCOURAGE YOU TO TAKE SOME OF THESE.
DO YOU EVEN KNOW WHAT YOU ARE? INTERESTING...
YOU'RE AN ASSASSIN, LITTLE MOUSE. SENT TO KILL ME AND THE REST OF US. WE TRIED TO RETIRE. GO INTO HIDING. QUIT. BUT THEY DON'T LET YOU QUIT, DO THEY?
DID YOU TAKE YOUR PILL?
YOU THINK I KILLED YOUR FATHER? THE CENTER ORDERED ME TO. YOU WERE A RECRUIT. THEY LIKE 'EM YOUNG.

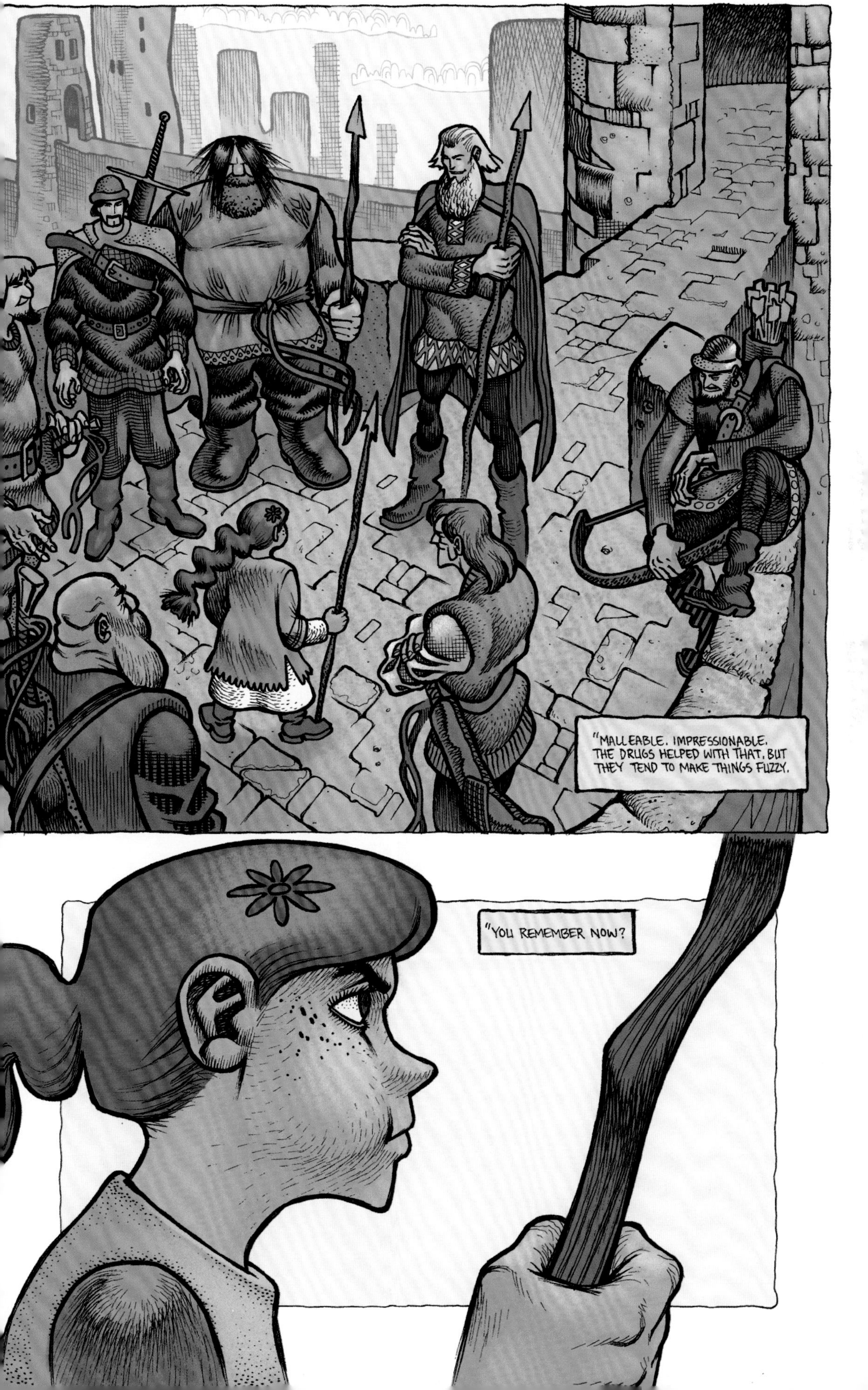
"MALLEABLE. IMPRESSIONABLE. THE DRUGS HELPED WITH THAT, BUT THEY TEND TO MAKE THINGS FUZZY.
"YOU REMEMBER NOW?

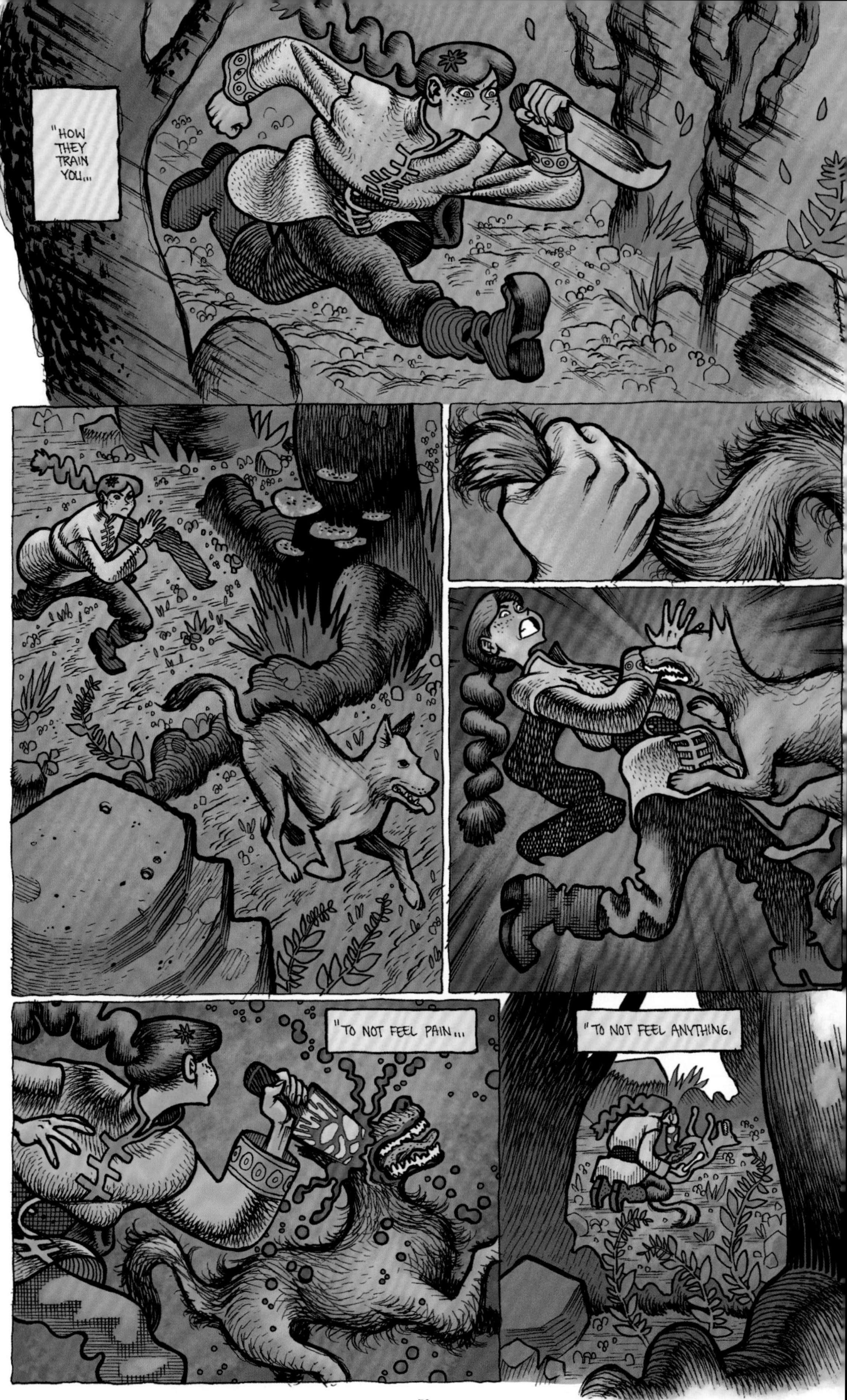
"HOW THEY TRAIN YOU...
"TO NOT FEEL PAIN...
"TO NOT FEEL ANYTHING.

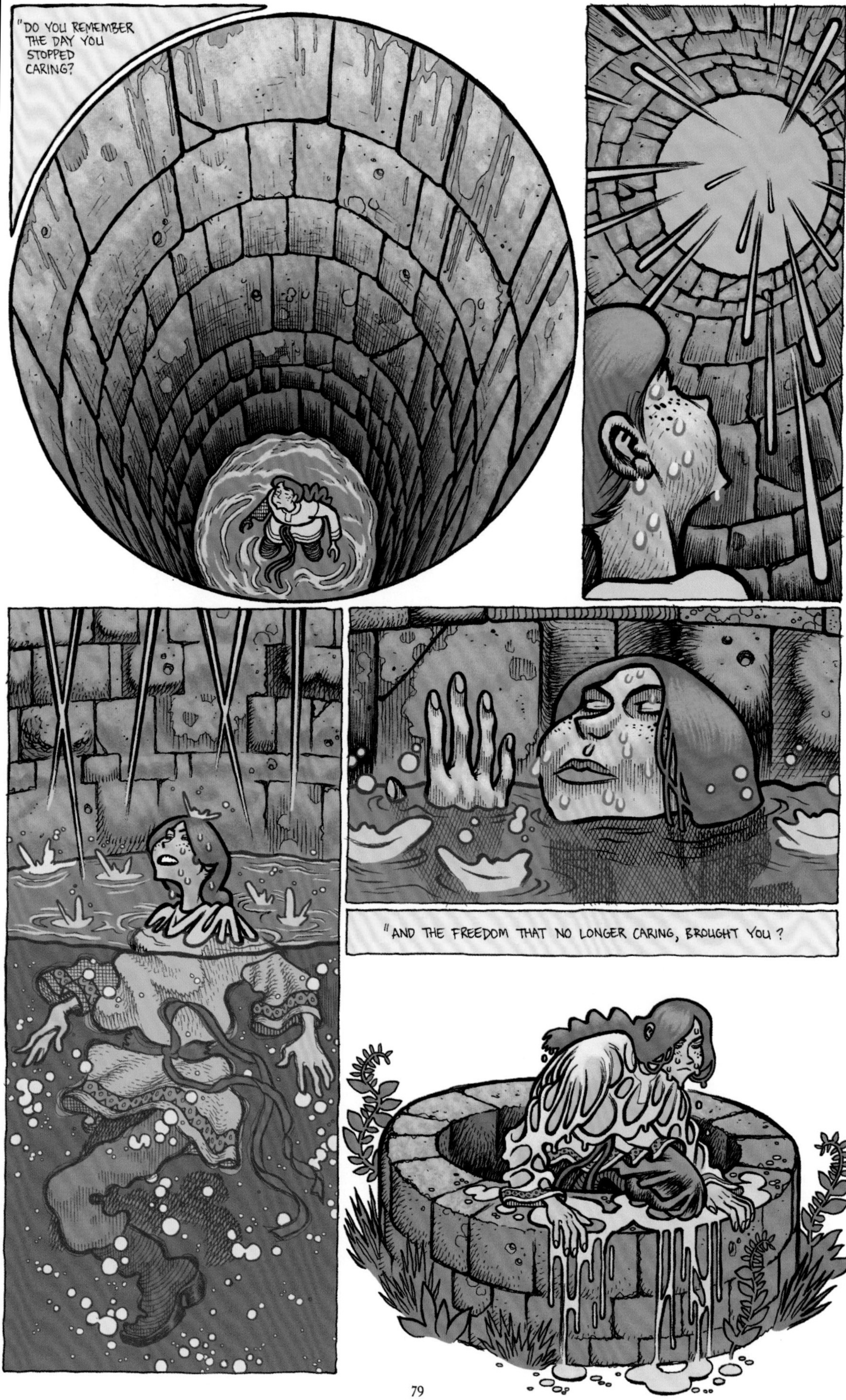
"DO YOU REMEMBER THE DAY YOU STOPPED CARING?
"AND THE FREEDOM THAT NO LONGER CARING, BROUGHT YOU?

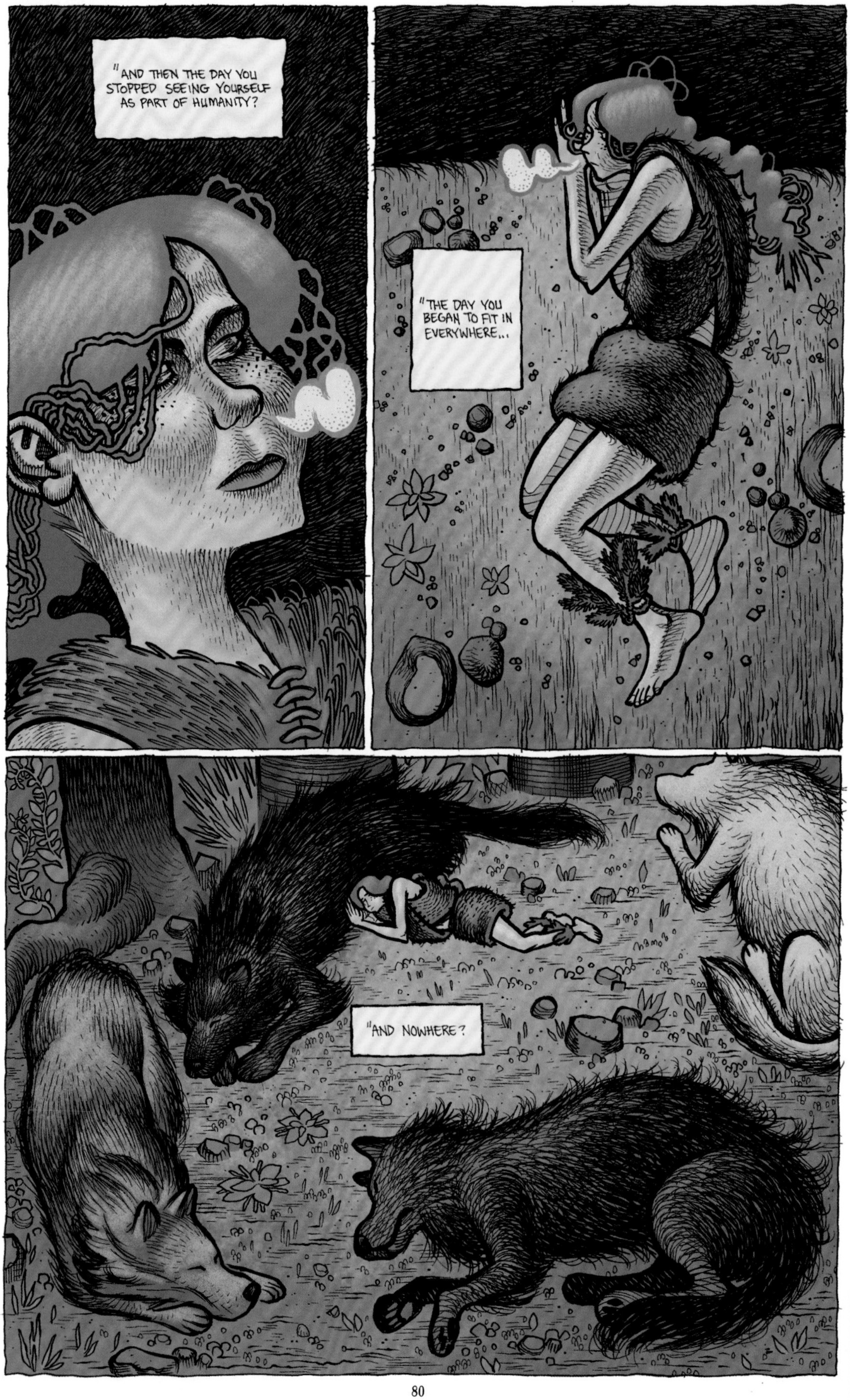
"AND THEN THE DAY YOU STOPPED SEEING YOURSELF AS PART OF HUMANITY?
"THE DAY YOU BEGAN TO FIT IN EVERYWHERE...
"AND NOWHERE?

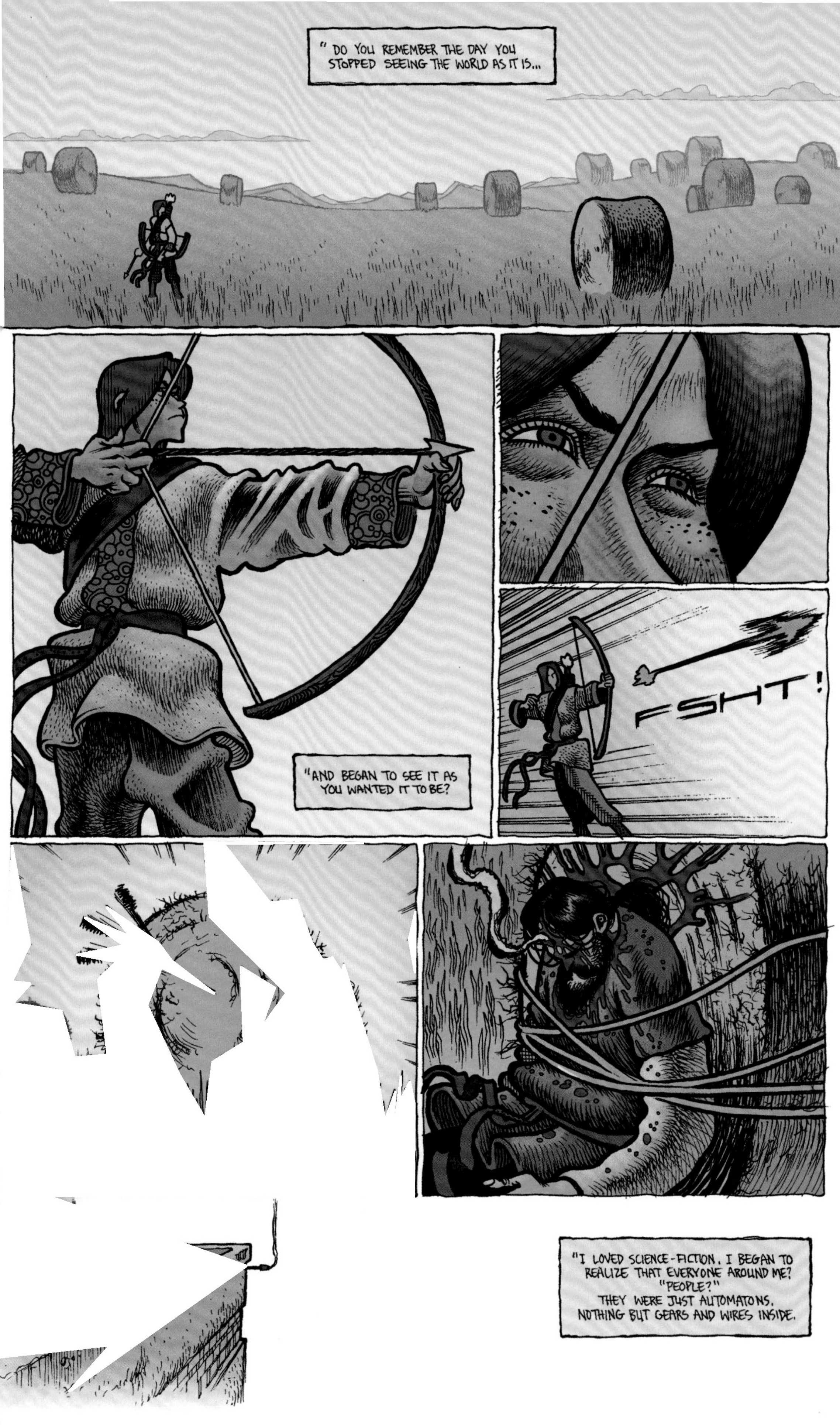
"DO YOU REMEMBER THE DAY YOU STOPPED SEEING THE WORLD AS IT IS...
"AND BEGAN TO SEE IT AS YOU WANTED IT TO BE?
FSHT!
"I LOVED SCIENCE-FICTION. I BEGAN TO REALIZE THAT EVERYONE AROUND ME? "PEOPLE?" THEY WERE JUST AUTOMATONS. NOTHING BUT GEARS AND WIRES INSIDE.

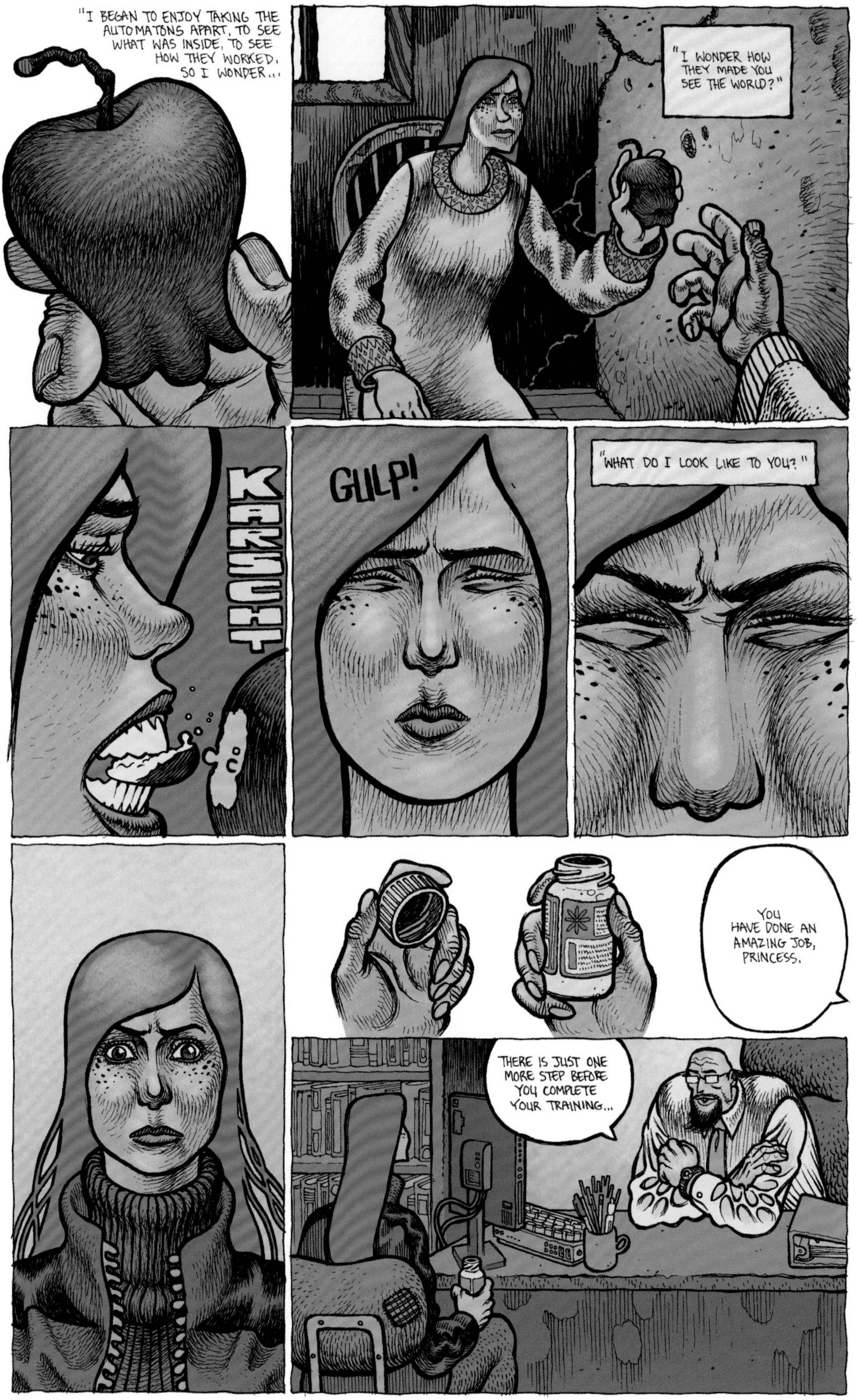
"I BEGAN TO ENJOY TAKING THE AUTOMATONS APART, TO SEE WHAT WAS INSIDE, TO SEE HOW THEY WORKED. SO I WONDER...
"I WONDER HOW THEY MADE YOU SEE THE WORLD?"
KARSCHT
GULP!
"WHAT DO I LOOK LIKE TO YOU?"
YOU HAVE DONE AN AMAZING JOB, PRINCESS.
THERE IS JUST ONE MORE STEP BEFORE YOU COMPLETE YOUR TRAINING...

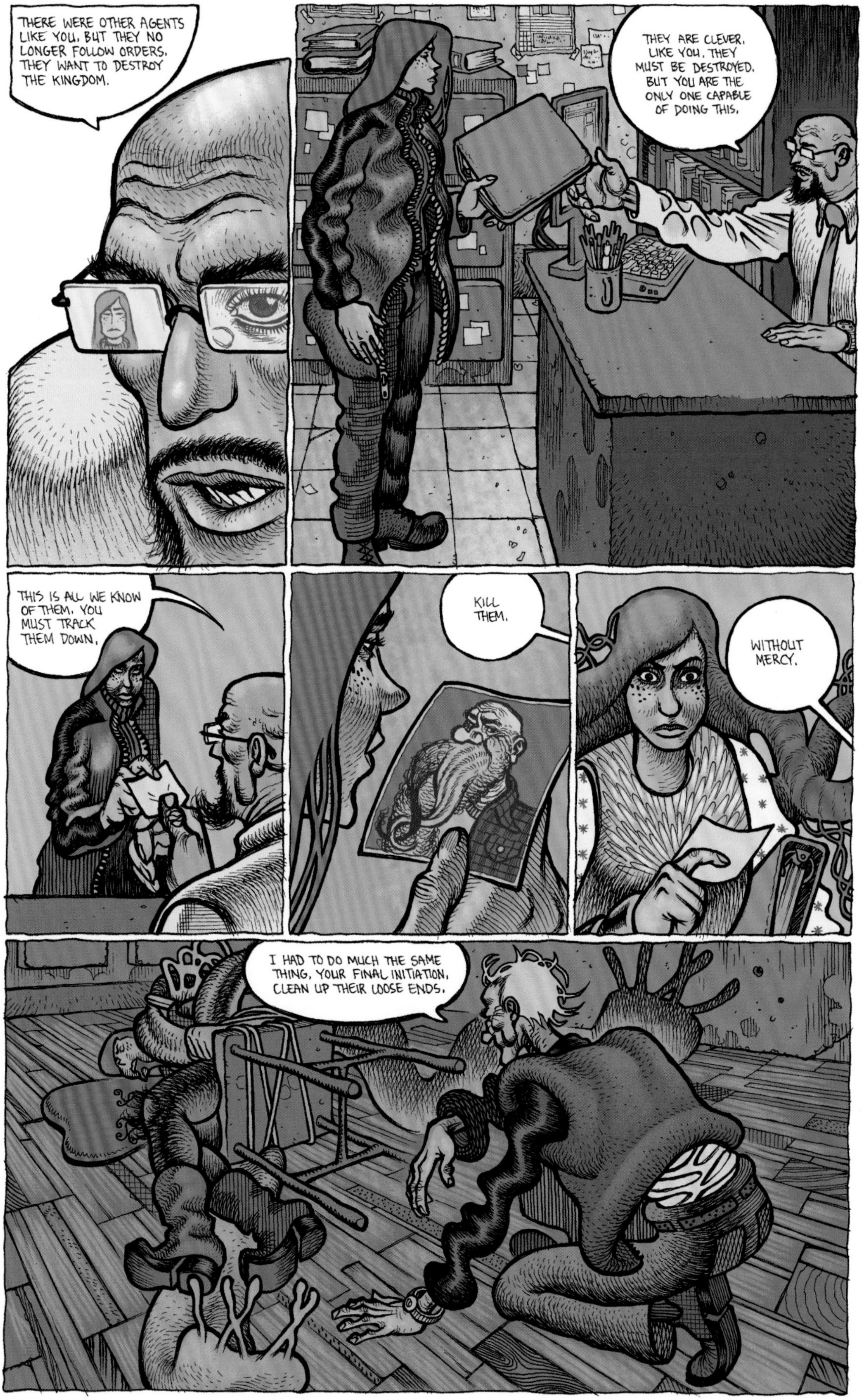
THERE WERE OTHER AGENTS LIKE YOU, BUT THEY NO LONGER FOLLOW ORDERS. THEY WANT TO DESTROY THE KINGDOM.
THEY ARE CLEVER, LIKE YOU. THEY MUST BE DESTROYED. BUT YOU ARE THE ONLY ONE CAPABLE OF DOING THIS.
THIS IS ALL WE KNOW OF THEM. YOU MUST TRACK THEM DOWN.
KILL THEM.
WITHOUT MERCY.
I HAD TO DO MUCH THE SAME THING, YOUR FINAL INITIATION. CLEAN UP THEIR LOOSE ENDS.

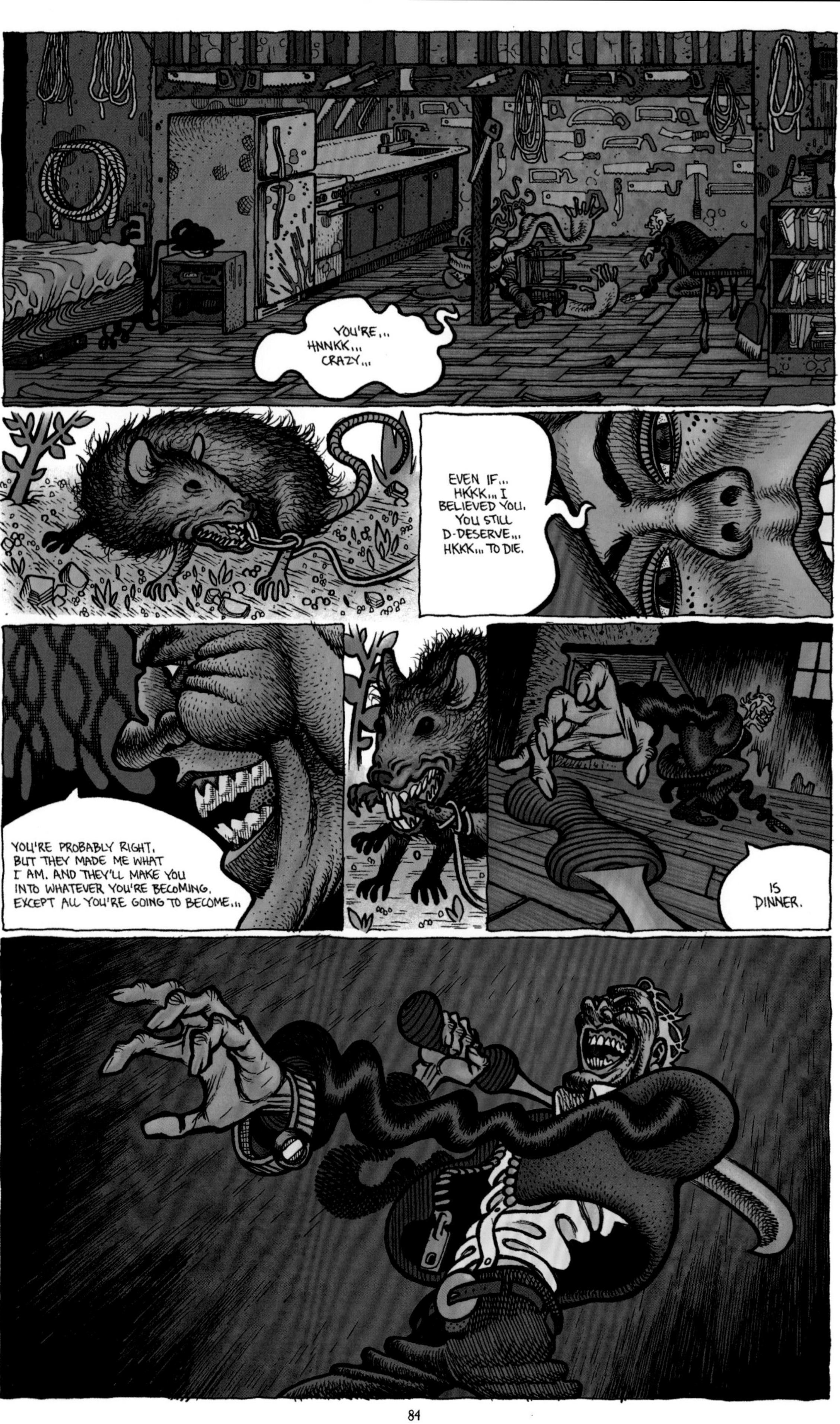
YOU'RE... HNNKK... CRAZY...
EVEN IF... HKKK... I BELIEVED YOU, YOU STILL D-DESERVE... HKKK... TO DIE.
YOU'RE PROBABLY RIGHT, BUT THEY MADE ME WHAT I AM. AND THEY'LL MAKE YOU INTO WHATEVER YOU'RE BECOMING. EXCEPT ALL YOU'RE GOING TO BECOME...
IS DINNER.

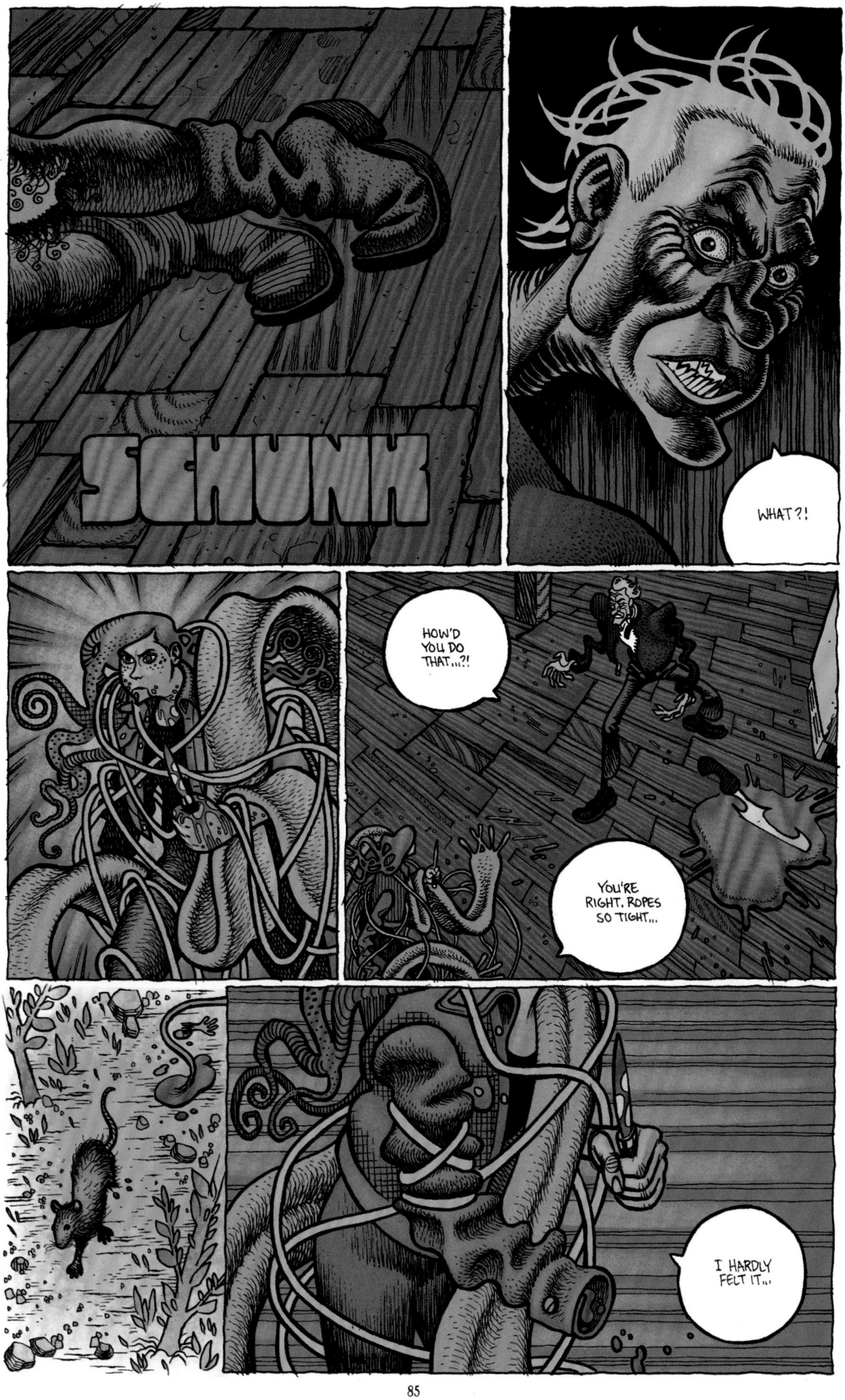
SCHUNK
WHAT?!
HOW'D YOU DO THAT...?!
YOU'RE RIGHT. ROPES SO TIGHT...
I HARDLY FELT IT...

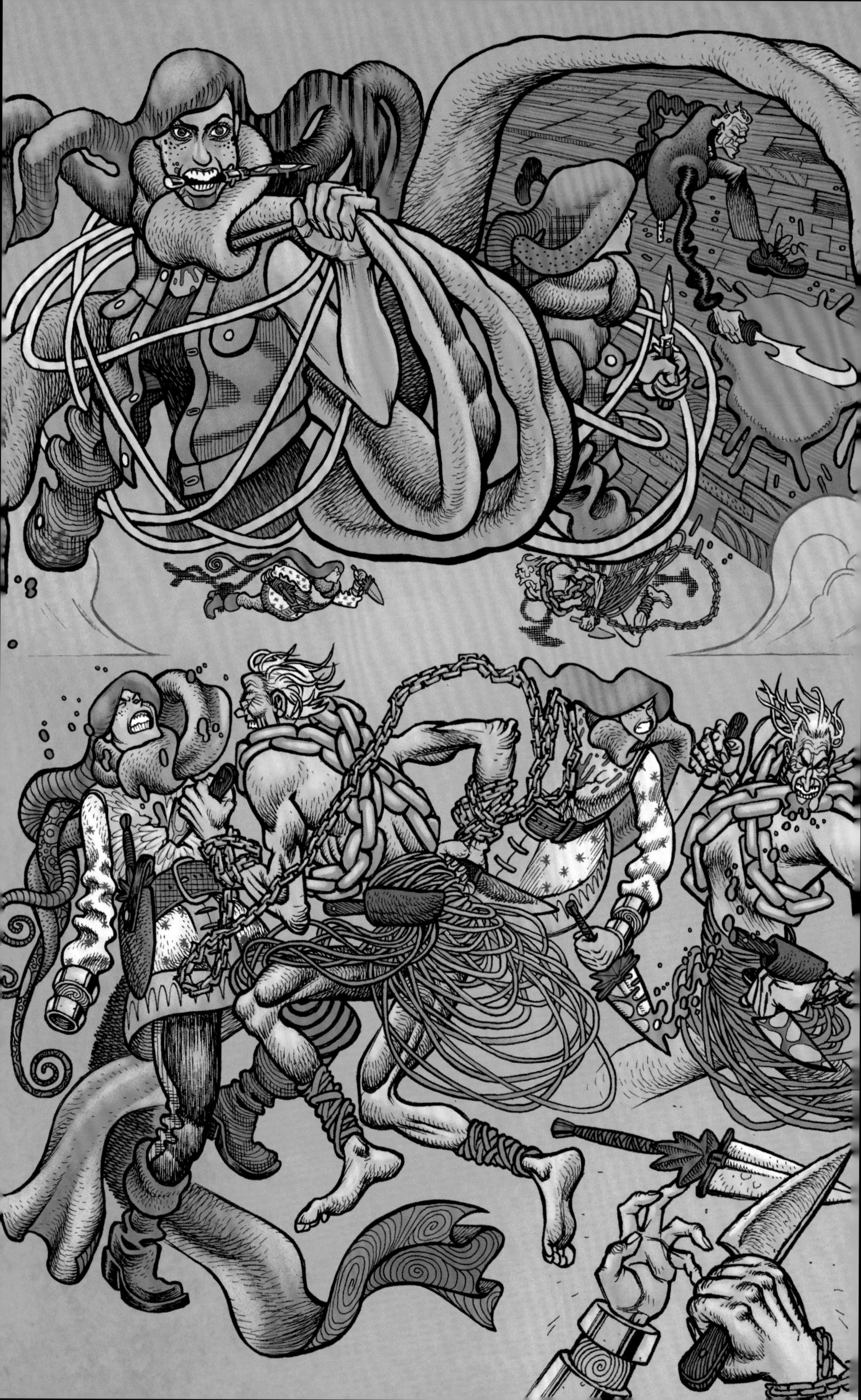

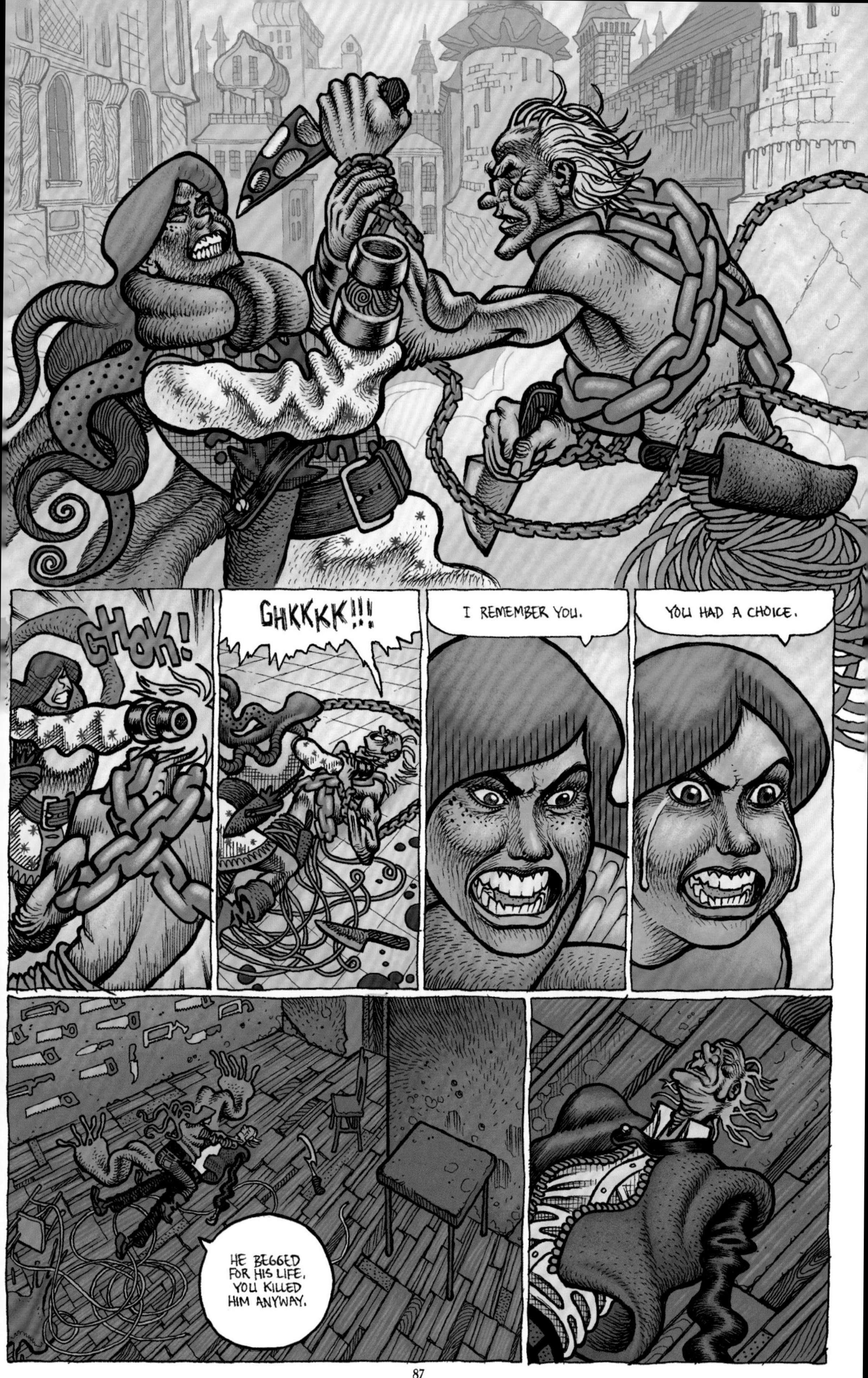
CHOK!
GHKKKK!!!
I REMEMBER YOU.
YOU HAD A CHOICE.
HE BEGGED FOR HIS LIFE. YOU KILLED HIM ANYWAY.

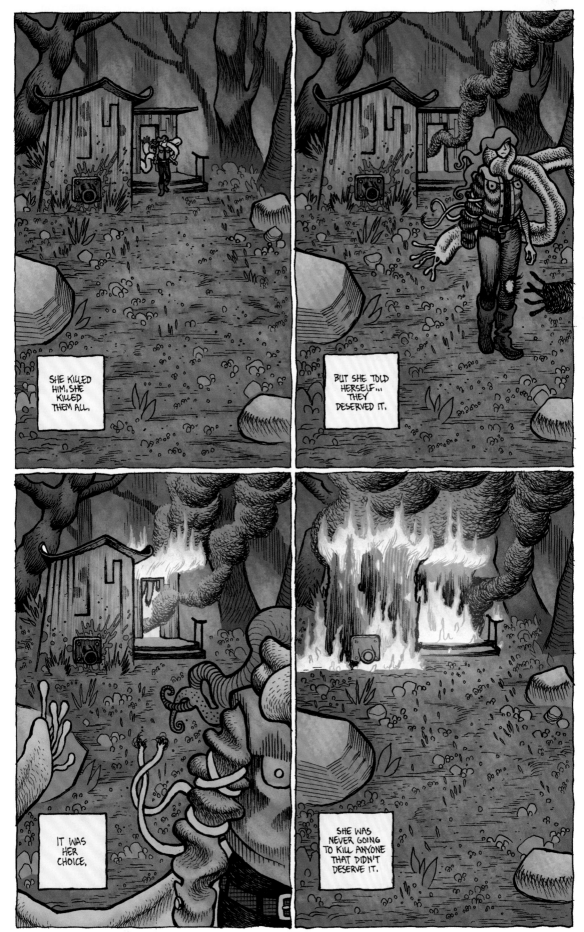

SHE KILLED HIM, SHE KILLED THEM ALL,

BUT SHE TOLD HERSELF... THEY DESERVED IT,

IT WAS HER CHOICE,

SHE WAS NEVER GOING TO KILL ANYONE THAT DIDN'T DESERVE IT.

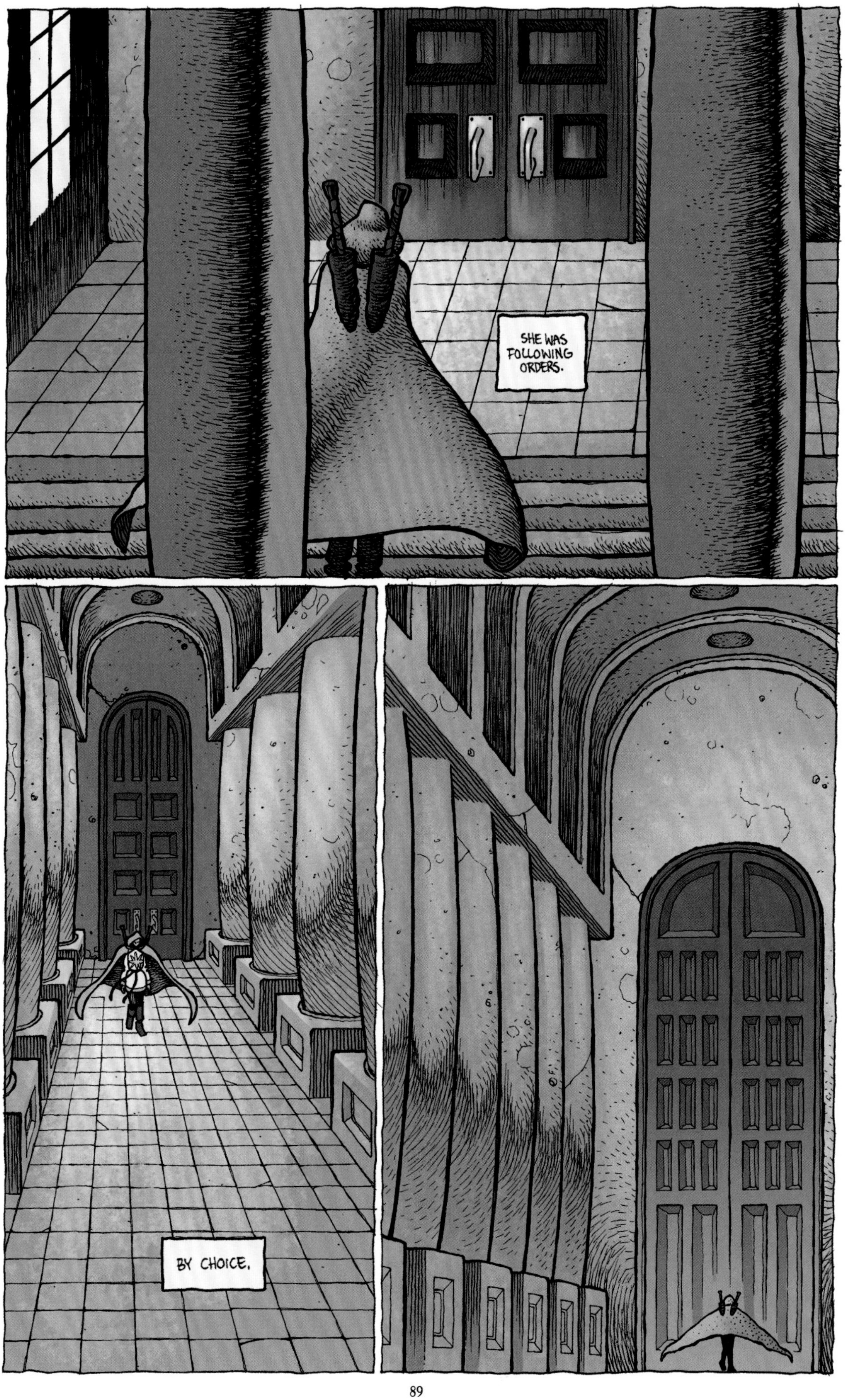
SHE WAS FOLLOWING ORDERS.
BY CHOICE.

RISE. APPROACH US.

YOU HAVE DONE WELL.

RECEIVE YOUR COMMUNION. YOU ARE A TRUSTED LADY OF THE COURT.

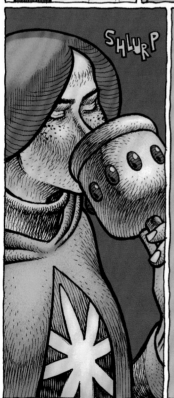

SHLURP

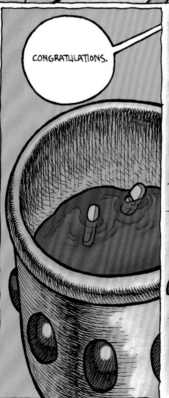

CONGRATULATIONS.

WE DUB YOU FULL LADY OF THE COURT. YOUR CODENAME...

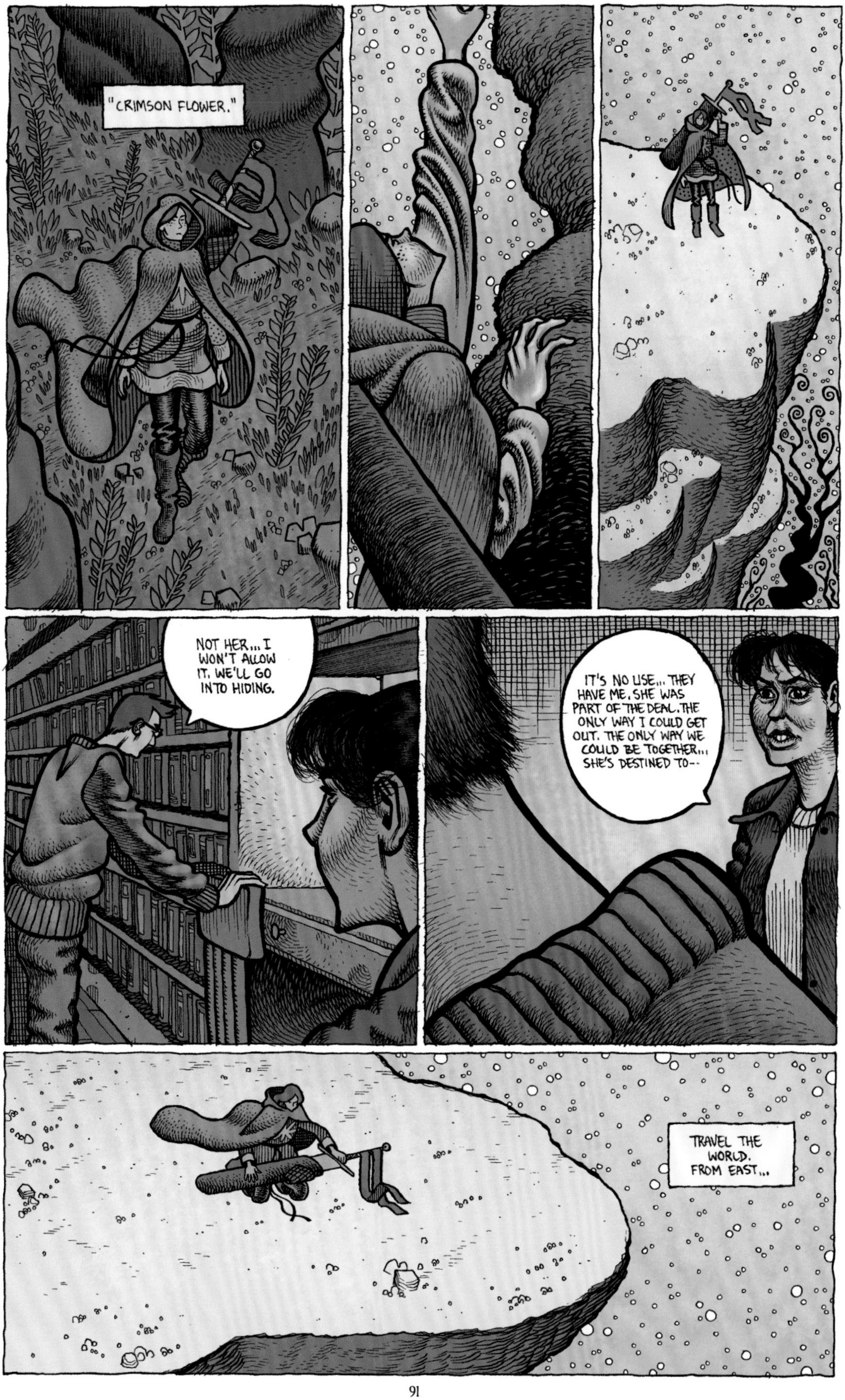
"CRIMSON FLOWER."
NOT HER... I WON'T ALLOW IT. WE'LL GO INTO HIDING.
IT'S NO USE... THEY HAVE ME. SHE WAS PART OF THE DEAL. THE ONLY WAY I COULD GET OUT. THE ONLY WAY WE COULD BE TOGETHER... SHE'S DESTINED TO--
TRAVEL THE WORLD. FROM EAST...

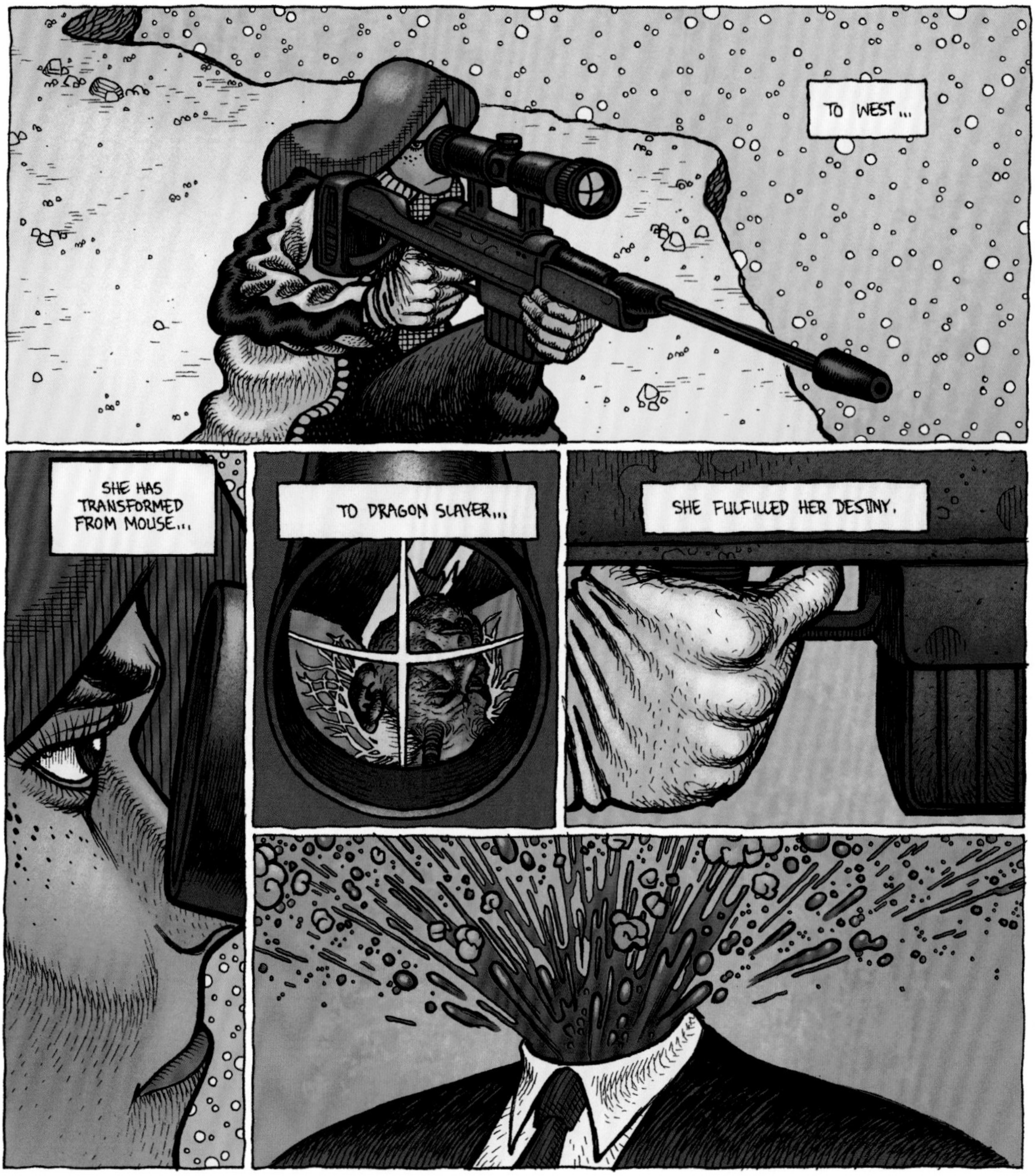
TO WEST...
SHE HAS TRANSFORMED FROM MOUSE...
TO DRAGON SLAYER...
SHE FULFILLED HER DESTINY.

SHE LIVED HAPPILY EVER AFTER.

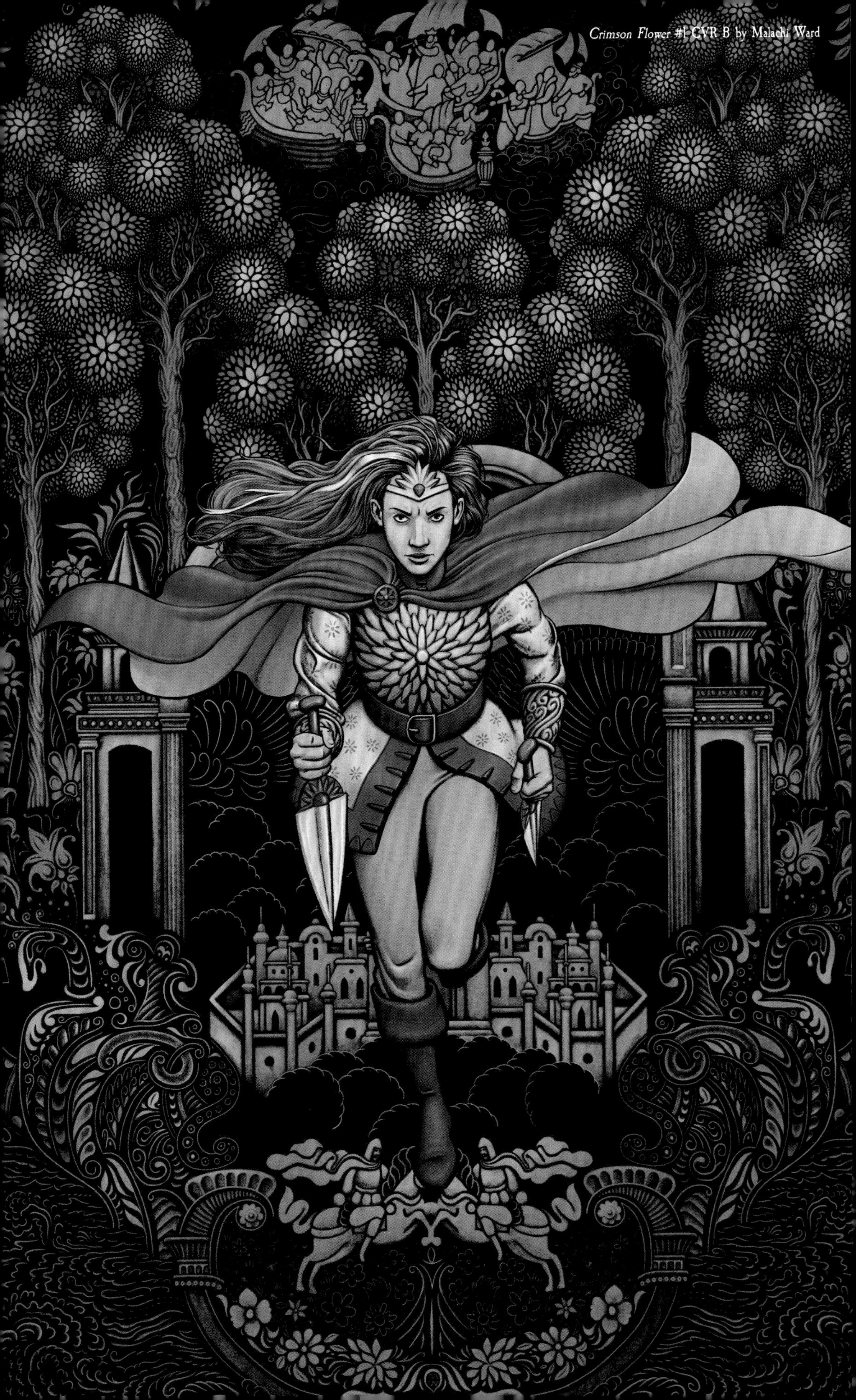

Crimson Flower #1 CVR B by Malachi Ward

Crimson Flower #1 FOC Cover by Jill Thompson

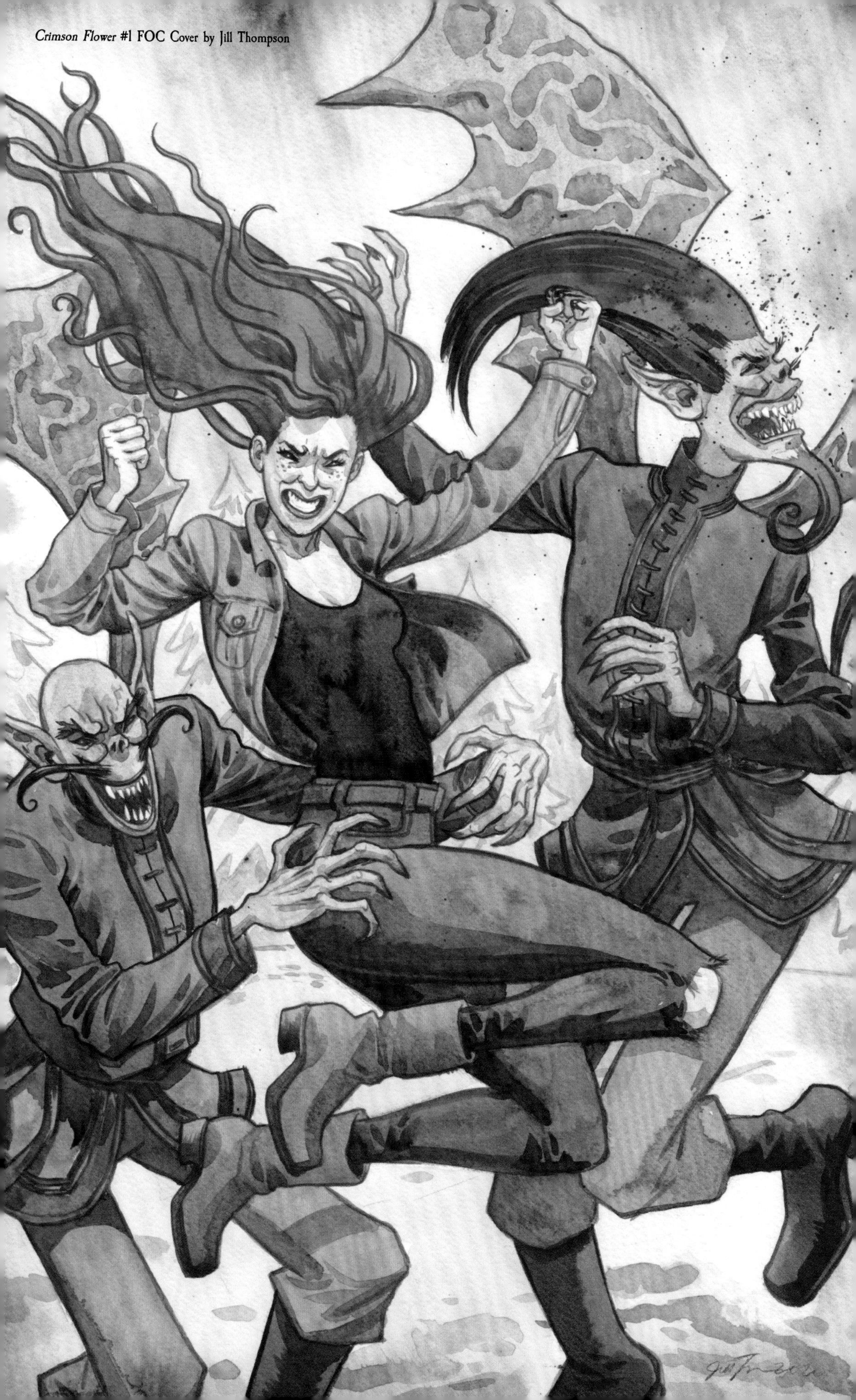

Crimson Flower #2 CVR B by Patric Reynolds with Lee Loughridge

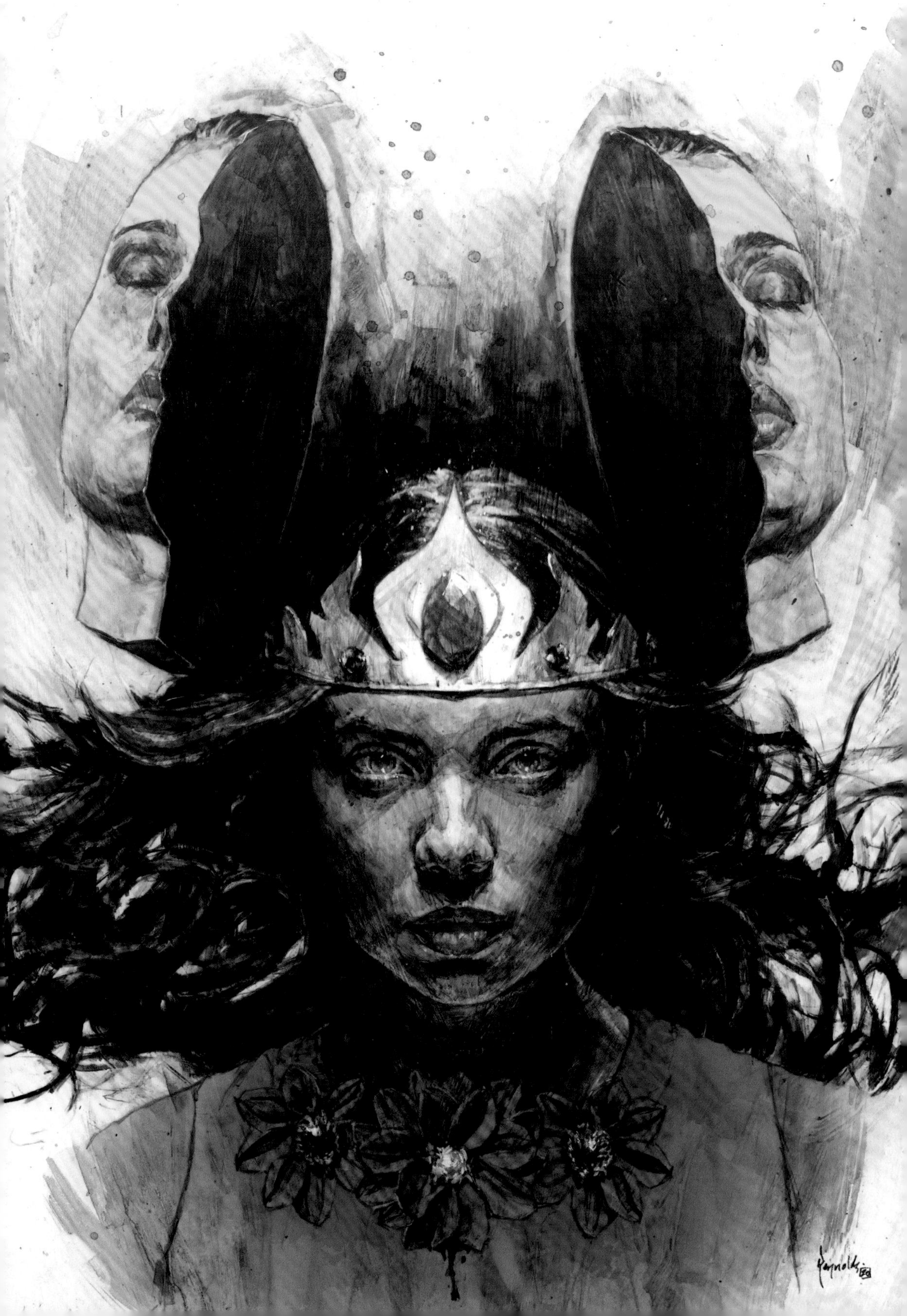

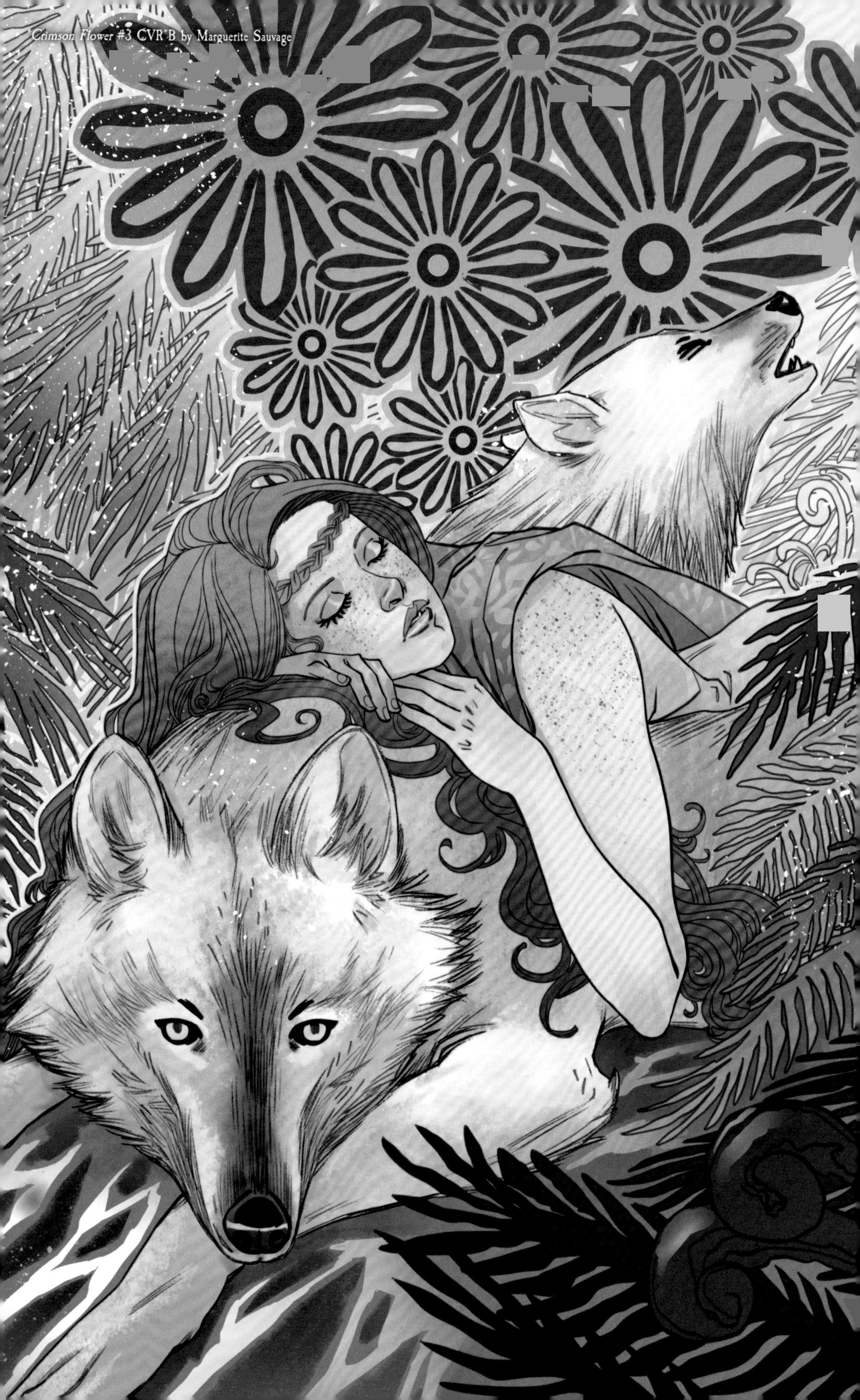

Crimson Flower #3 CVR B by Marguerite Sauvage

Crimson Flower #4 CVR B by Tyler Bence with Bill Crabtree

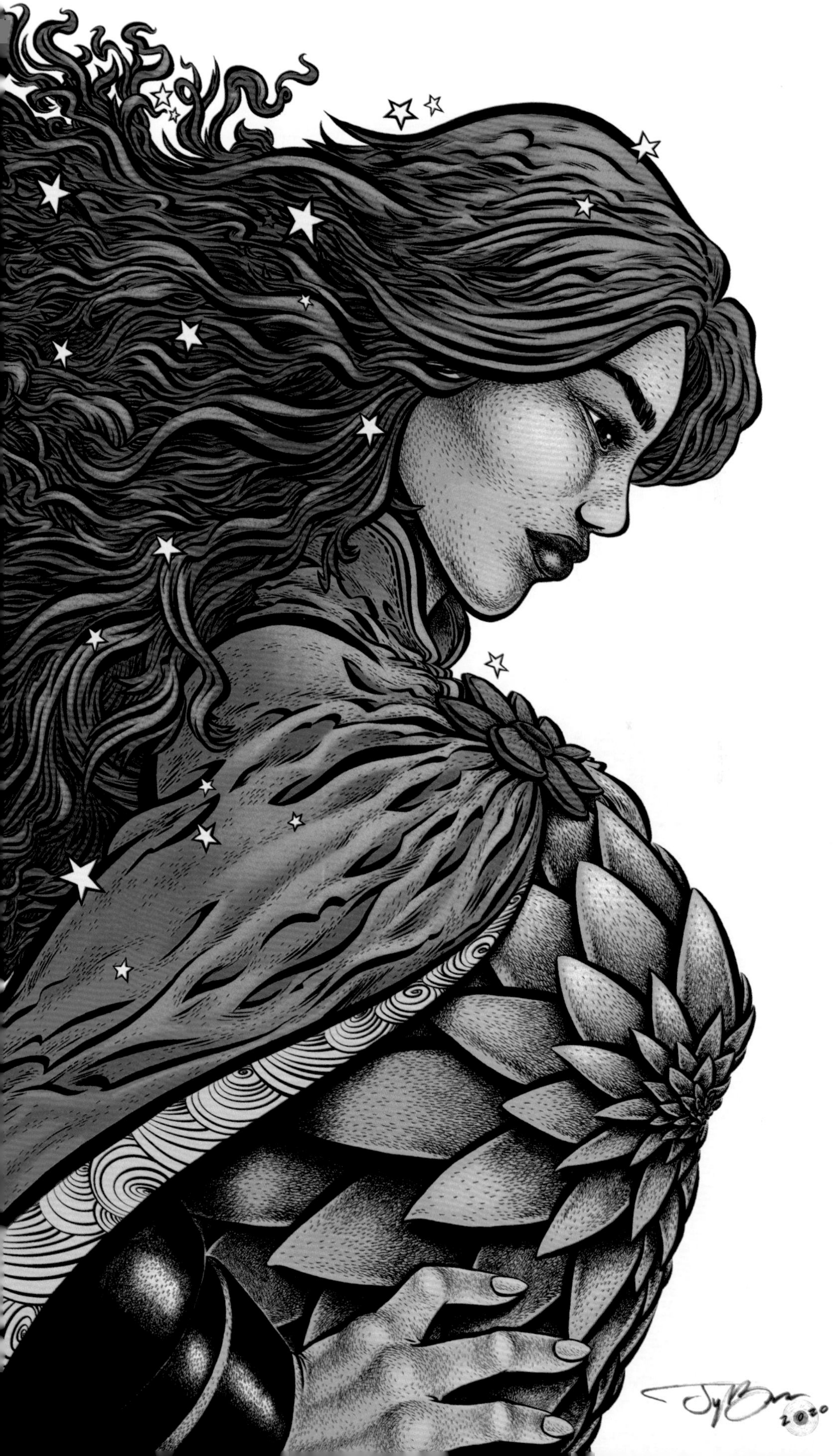

CRIMSON FLOWER

SKETCHBOOK

Notes by Matt Lesniewski

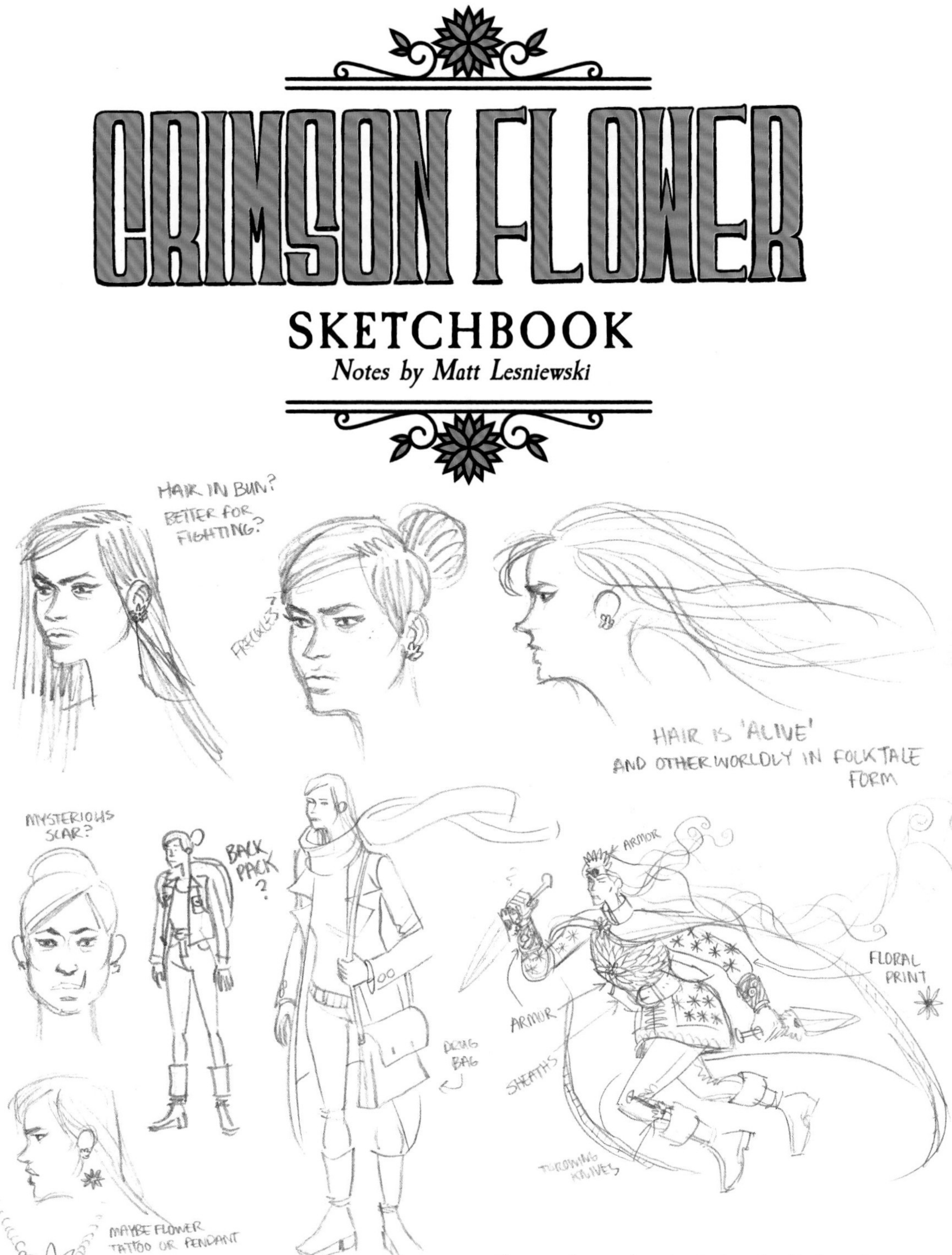

HAIR IN BUN?
BETTER FOR FIGHTING?
FRECKLES?
HAIR IS 'ALIVE'
AND OTHERWORLDLY IN FOLKTALE FORM
MYSTERIOUS SCAR?
BACK PACK ?
ARMOR
FLORAL PRINT
ARMOR
SHEATHS
DRUG BAG
THROWING KNIVES
MAYBE FLOWER TATTOO OR PENDANT

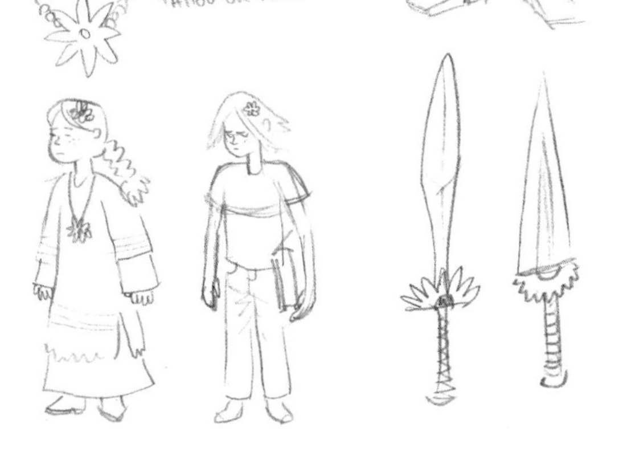

Getting down a bunch of ideas for Rodion. I remember being influenced by the *Tomb Raider* game from 2012, which I had first picked up and played just before I knew I was even going to draw this book. Also, it's hard to deny her hair coming "alive" when she's turning folk mode isn't at least partially a nod to *Dragonball Z* and the fighters turning super saiyan. Other than the shift in her eyes, I wanted there to be a clear difference between "regular" Rodion, and the "folk" version, but with my own way of doing that.

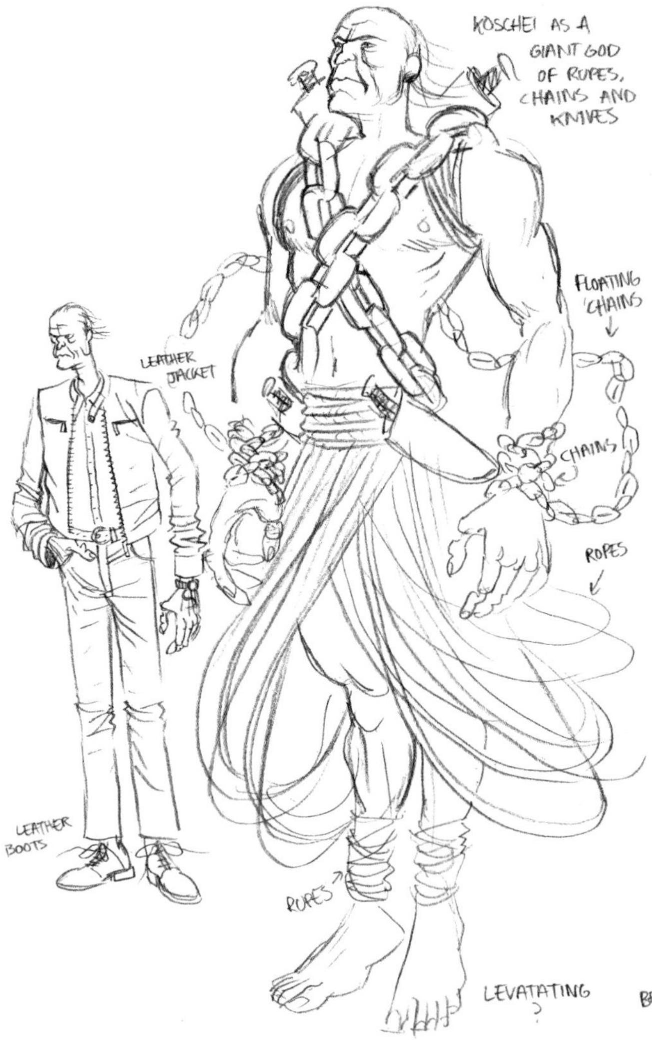
KOSCHEI AS A GIANT GOD OF ROPES, CHAINS AND KNIVES
LEATHER JACKET
FLOATING CHAINS
CHAINS
ROPES
LEATHER BOOTS
ROPES
LEVATATING ?

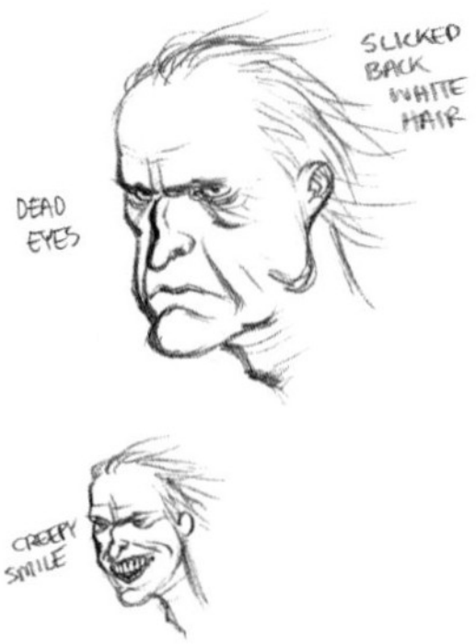
SLICKED BACK WHITE HAIR
DEAD EYES
CREEPY SMILE

Koschei being the real killer, I wanted him to read as ruthless and as empty as it gets. I tried to pull that off with just his face alone—something anyone would quickly pick up on if you just saw him at the grocery store. One look at him, and you know he's a terrible person inside, and not shocking at all that he's a brutal individual.

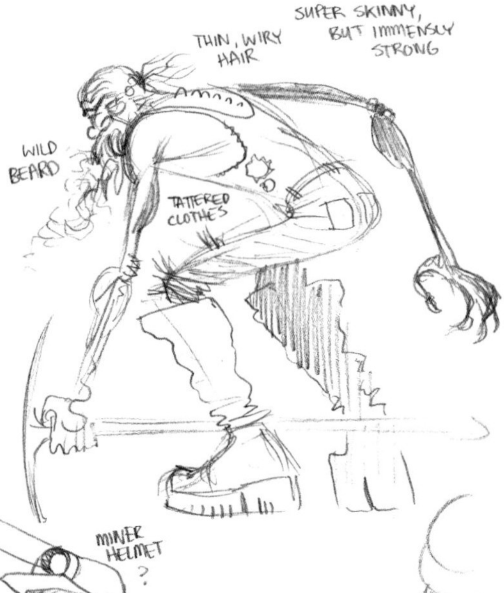
SUPER SKINNY, BUT IMMENSLY STRONG
THIN, WIRY HAIR
WILD BEARD
TATTERED CLOTHES

Shubin might even seem darker than Koschei overall, but I wanted that on purpose. He's the first assassin we see, so I wanted him to seem like he could be the guy Rodion's after. Turns out he is a killer, but he just looks worse than the ultimate badass Rodion is searching for.

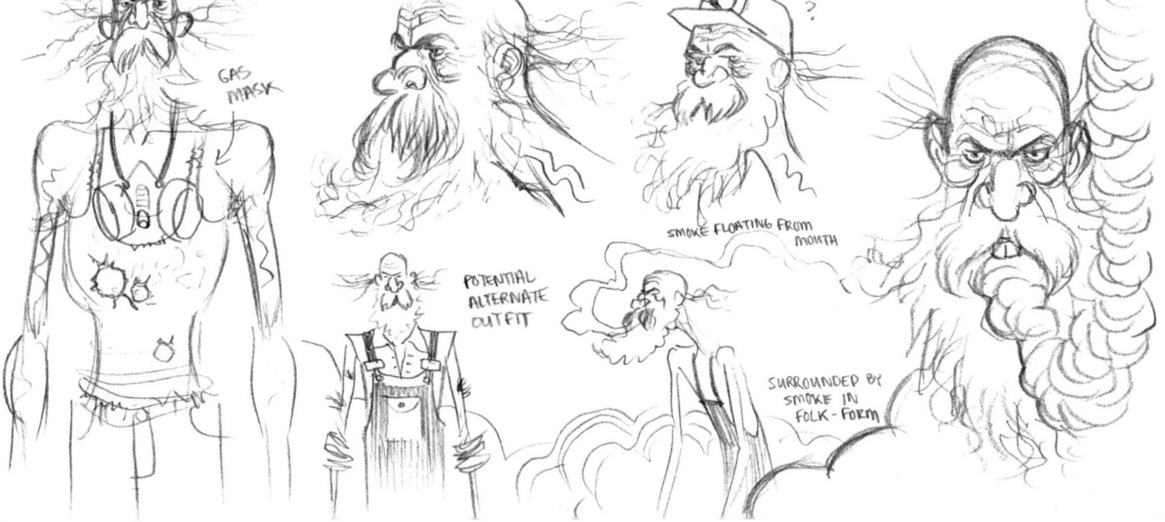
GAS MASK
MINER HELMET ?
SMOKE FLOATING FROM MOUTH
POTENTIAL ALTERNATE OUTFIT
SURROUNDED BY SMOKE IN FOLK-FORM

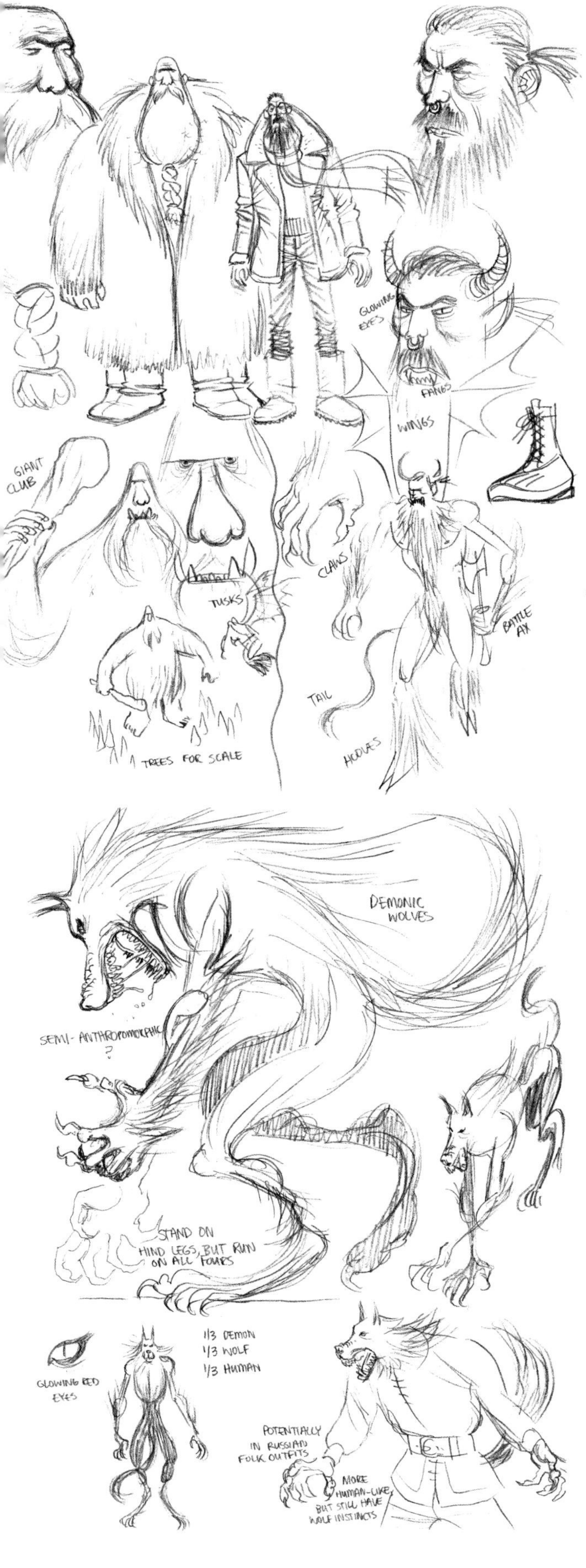
GIANT CLUB
GLOWING EYES
FANGS
WINGS
TUSKS
CLAWS
BATTLE AX
TAIL
HOOVES
TREES FOR SCALE
DEMONIC WOLVES
SEMI-ANTHROPOMORPHIC ?
STAND ON HIND LEGS, BUT RUN ON ALL FOURS
1/3 DEMON
1/3 WOLF
1/3 HUMAN
GLOWING RED EYES
POTENTIALLY IN RUSSIAN FOLK OUTFITS
MORE HUMAN-LIKE, BUT STILL HAVE WOLF INSTINCTS

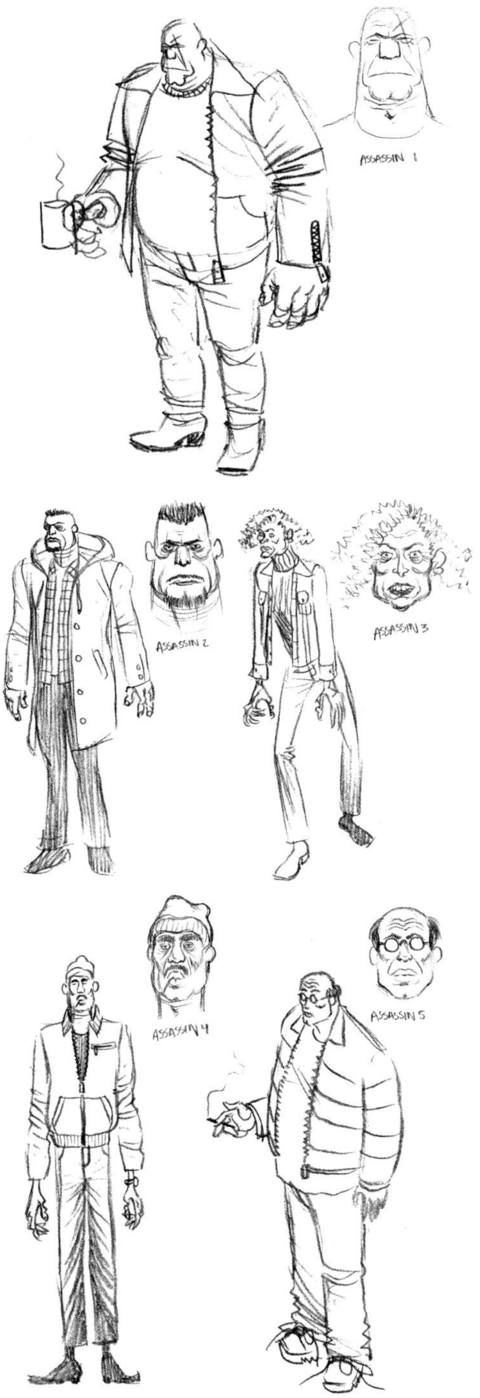
ASSASSIN 1
ASSASSIN 2
ASSASSIN 3
ASSASSIN 4
ASSASSIN 5

A bunch of retired assassins. A community of killers. I wanted each of them to feel like they were unique in their own way and all have dark, dark pasts. It would take days to tell you all the wrong they've done in their lives. As for the wolves, you can see how I broke them down in my head: 1/3 demon, 1/3 wolf, 1/3 human. The perfect mix from folklore hell.

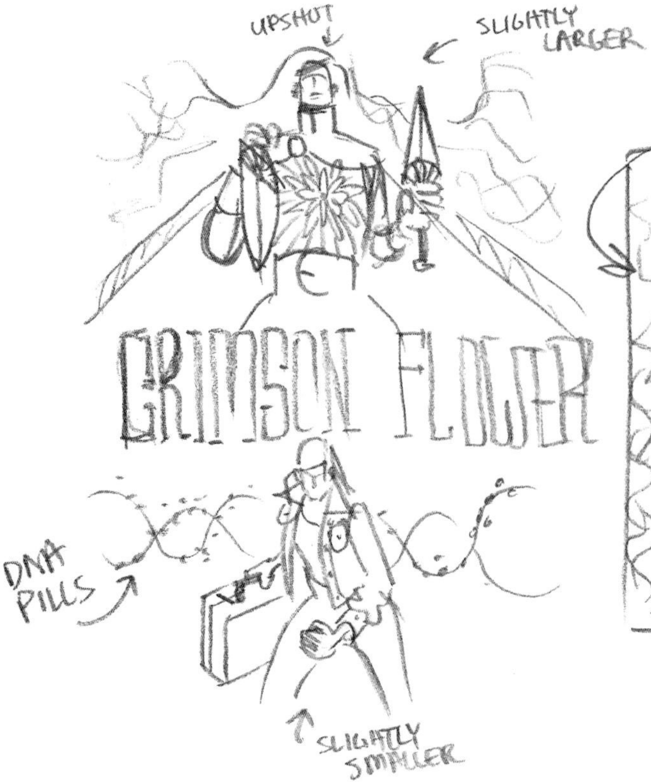
UPSHOT
SLIGHTLY LARGER
CRIMSON FLOWER
DNA PILLS
SLIGHTLY SMALLER

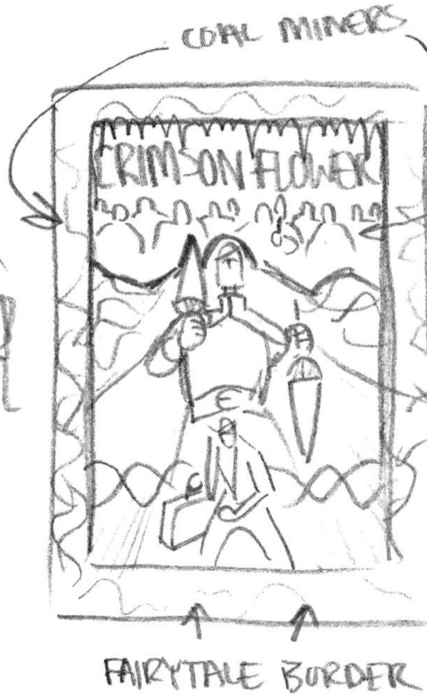
COAL MINERS
CRIMSON FLOWER
FAIRYTALE BORDER

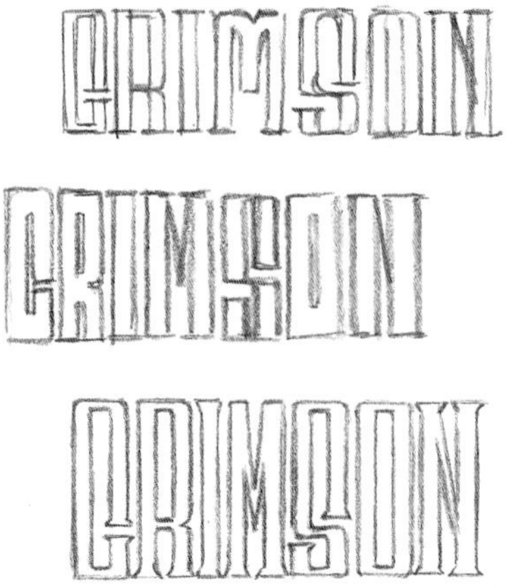
CRIMSON
CRIMSON
CRIMSON

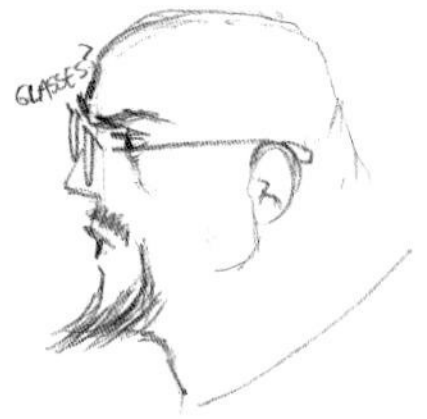
GLASSES?

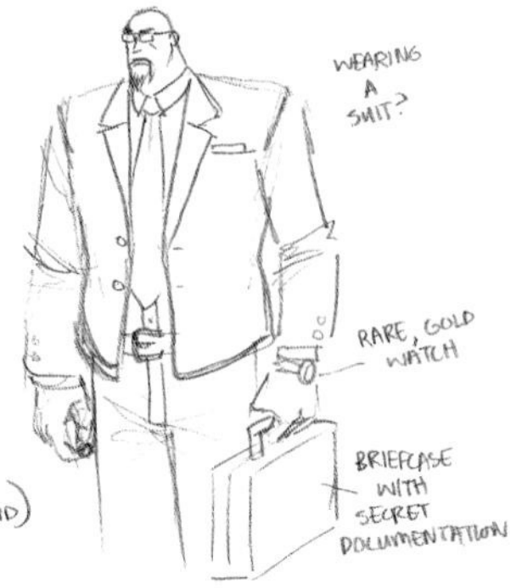
WEARING A SUIT?
RARE, GOLD WATCH
BRIEFCASE WITH SECRET DOCUMENTATION

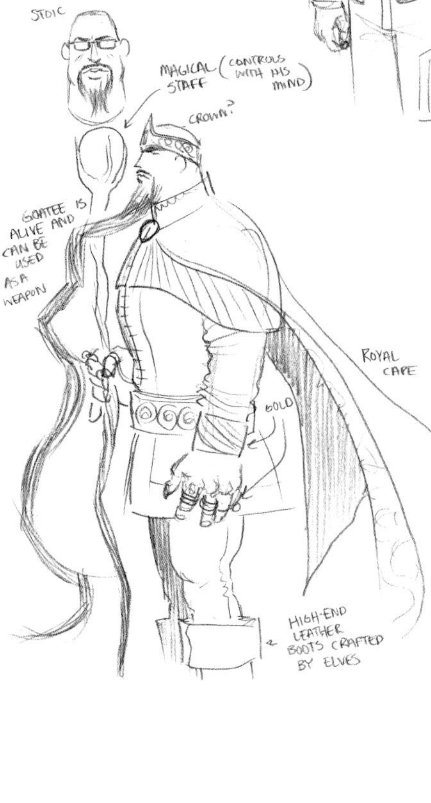
STOIC
MAGICAL STAFF
(CONTROLS WITH HIS MIND)
CROWN?
GOATEE IS ALIVE AND CAN BE USED AS A WEAPON
ROYAL CAPE
GOLD
HIGH-END LEATHER BOOTS CRAFTED BY ELVES

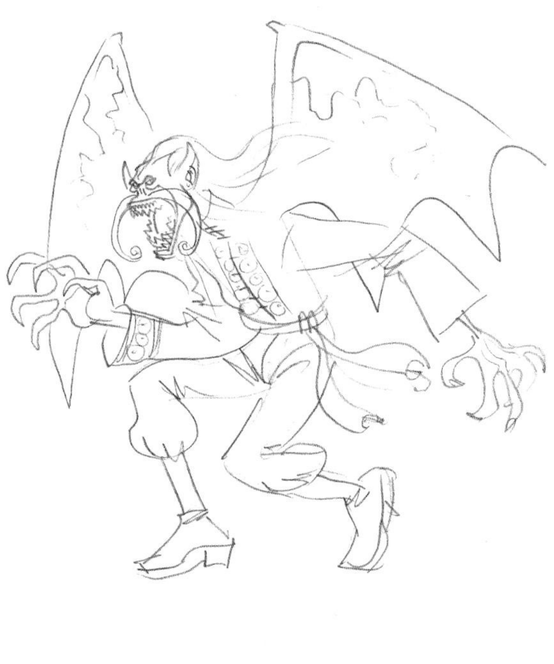

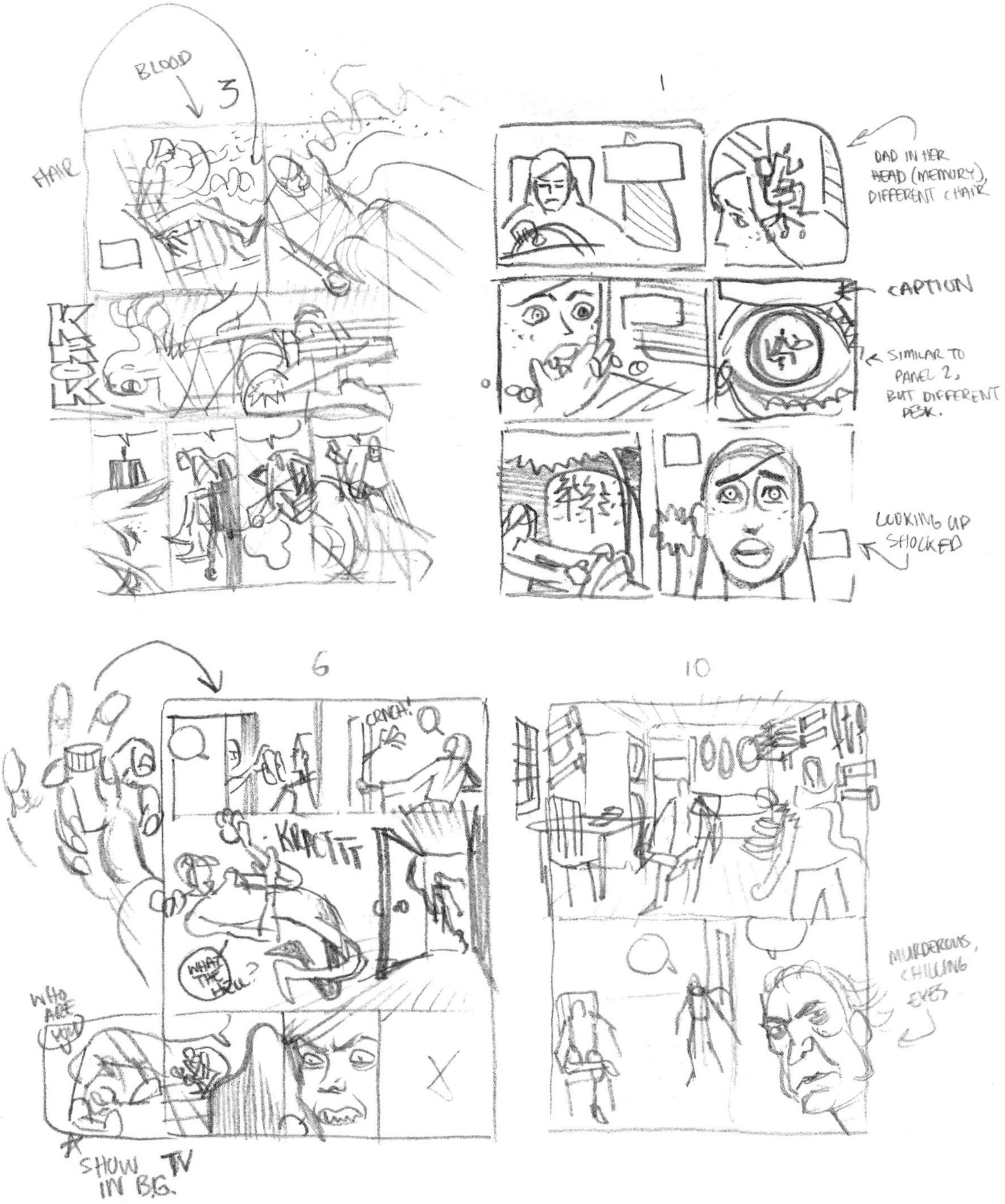
BLOOD
HAIR
DAD IN HER HEAD (MEMORY), DIFFERENT CHAIR
CAPTION
SIMILAR TO PANEL 2, BUT DIFFERENT DESK.
LOOKING UP SHOCKED
WHAT THE HELL?
WHO ARE YOU
SHOW TV IN B.G.
MURDEROUS, CHILLING EYES

Above: Some of the thumbnails I did for the comic. Part of my process and something for me to follow before I draw the actual page. Working out a lot of the storytelling here.

Facing Page: Fun fact: the logo and credits were hand drawn. I always think that's a nice touch to a comic. Also, you might notice I had the idea for a fairytale border, but we ultimately decide it would make things too "busy," which explains the white border on the covers.

matt kindt

"I'll read anything Kindt does."—Douglas Wolk, author of *Reading Comics*

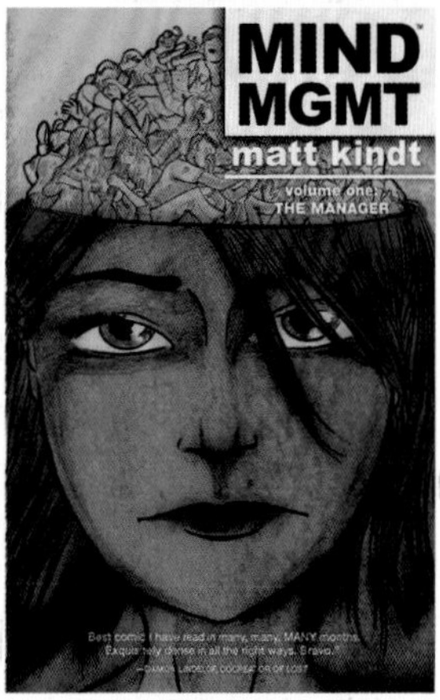

MIND MGMT
matt kindt
volume one: THE MANAGER

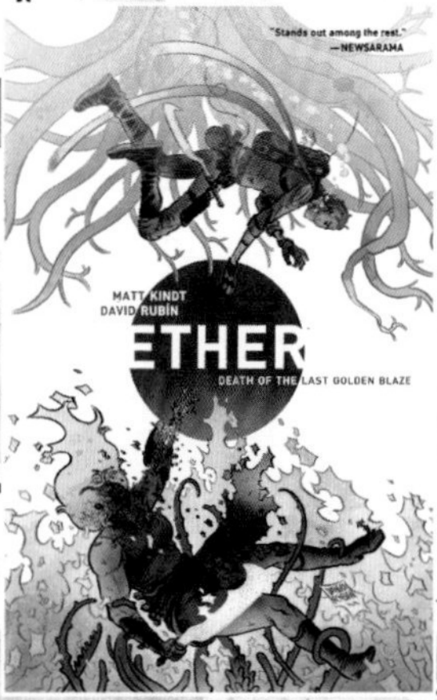

"Stands out among the rest." —NEWSARAMA
MATT KINDT
DAVID RUBÍN
ETHER
DEATH OF THE LAST GOLDEN BLAZE

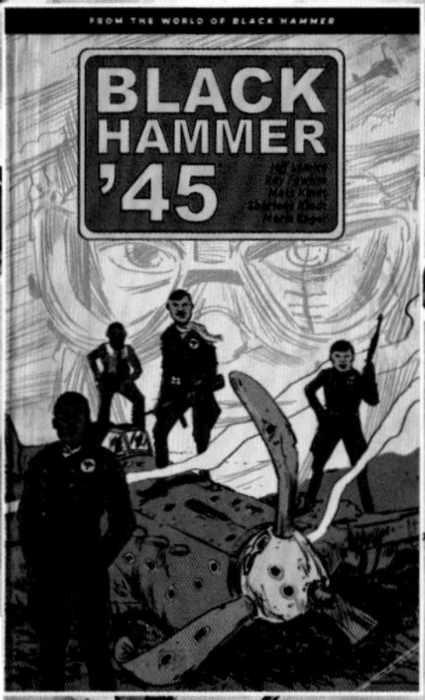

FROM THE WORLD OF BLACK HAMMER
BLACK HAMMER '45

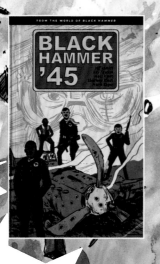

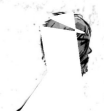

MIND MGMT OMNIBUS
VOLUME 1: THE MANAGER AND THE FUTURIST
ISBN 978-1-50670-460-9
$24.99

VOLUME 2: THE HOME MAKER AND THE MAGICIAN
ISBN 978-1-50670-461-6
$24.99

VOLUME 3: THE ERASER AND THE IMMORTALS
ISBN 978-1-50670-462-3
$24.99

DEPT. H OMNIBUS
VOLUME 1
ISBN 978-1-50671-093-8
$24.99

VOLUME 2
ISBN 978-1-50671-094-5
$24.99

POPPY! AND THE LOST LAGOON
With Brian Hurtt
ISBN 978-1-61655-943-4
$14.99

PAST AWAYS
With Scott Kolins
ISBN 978-1-61655-792-8
$19.99

THE COMPLETE PISTOLWHIP
With Jason Hall
ISBN 978-1-61655-720-1
$27.99

3 STORY: THE SECRET HISTORY OF THE GIANT MAN NEW EXPANDED EDITION
ISBN 978-1-50670-622-1
$19.99

2 SISTERS
ISBN 978-1-61655-721-8
$27.99

BANG!
ISBN 978-1-50671-616-9
$19.99

ETHER
With David Rubín

VOLUME 1: DEATH OF THE LAST GOLDEN BLAZE
ISBN 978-1-50670-174-5
$14.99

VOLUME 2: COPPER GOLEMS
ISBN 978-1-61655-991-5
$19.99

VOLUME 3: THE DISAPPEARANCE OF VIOLET BELL
ISBN 978-1-50671-151-5
$19.99

ETHER LIBRARY EDITION
ISBN 978-1-50671-152-2
$59.99

FEAR CASE
With Tyler and Hilary Jenkins
ISBN 978-1-50672-123-1
$19.99

CRIMSON FLOWER
With Matt Lesniewski and Bill Crabtree
ISBN 978-1-50672-197-2
$19.99

BLACK HAMMER '45: FROM THE WORLD OF BLACK HAMMER
With Jeff Lemire, Ray Fawkes, and Sharlene Kindt
ISBN 978-1-50670-850-8
$17.99

BLACK HAMMER: STREETS OF SPIRAL
With Jeff Lemire, Dean Ormston, Emi Lenox, and others
ISBN 978-1-50670-941-3
$19.99

THE WORLD OF BLACK HAMMER LIBRARY EDITION VOLUME 2
ISBN 978-1-50671-996-2
$49.99